Environmental Integration

Environmental Integration

Our Common Challenge

Ton Bührs

SUNY PRESS

Cover image by Ton Bührs

Published by
State University of New York Press, Albany

© 2009 State University of New York

All rights reserved

Printed in the United States of America

No part of this book may be used or reproduced in any manner whatsoever without written permission. No part of this book may be stored in a retrieval system or transmitted in any form or by any means including electronic, electrostatic, magnetic tape, mechanical, photocopying, recording, or otherwise without the prior permission in writing of the publisher.

For information, contact State University of New York Press, Albany, NY
www.sunypress.edu

Production by Diane Ganeles
Marketing by Anne M. Valentine

Library of Congress Cataloging-in-Publication Data

Bührs, Ton.
Environmental integration : our common challenge / Ton Bührs.
p. cm.
Includes bibliographical references and index.
ISBN 978-1-4384-2607-5 (hardcover : alk. paper)
ISBN 978-1-4384-2608-2 (pbk. : alk. paper)
1. Political ecology. 2. Environmental policy. 3. Environmental policy—Economic aspects. 4. Sustainable development. 5. Sustainable living. I. Title.

JA75.8.B82 2009
333.7—dc22 2008035107

10 9 8 7 6 5 4 3 2 1

To Planet Earth

Contents

Tables

Acknowledgments

The idea for this book dates back to 1998, when I spent my study leave researching "green planning" in Australia, the Netherlands, Germany, Denmark, Sweden, and Canada. Although belatedly, I still wish to express my thanks to the many people in these countries who generously shared their ideas and provided information: Graeme Aplin, Richard Cardew, Steve Dovers, Bob Fagan, Mark Diesendorf, Clive Hamilton, Stuart Harris, Peter Matthews, Bruce O'Meagher, David Throsby, and Andrew Ross in Australia; Kees Bastmeijer, Jan Bijlsma, Lieneke van Brederode, Maarten de Hoogh, Gerard Keijzers, Martin Lok, Felix Luitwieler, Klaas-Jan Moner, Maartje Nelemans, Theo Wams, Manfred Weisz, and Peter Winsemius in the Netherlands; Martin Jänicke, Helge Joergens, and Helmut Weidner in Germany; Stefan Brandstrup, Peer Frank, Lars Josephson, Marianne Rønnebaek, and Ule Steen in Denmark; Sune Eriksson and Ule Oskarson in Sweden; and Charles Caccia, Tom Conway, Brian Emmett, Beatrice Olivestri, David Runnals, Gene Nyburg, Rick Smith, and Glen Toner in Canada. In particular, I wish to thank Ross Taplin and Glen Toner, who were instrumental in providing me a basis for undertaking research in Australia and Canada, and to Christer Sanne for doing the same in Sweden. Since then, various events and factors on which I will not dwell contributed to making the process of writing this book slow and arduous, sometimes to the point that I wondered myself if it would ever come to a successful end. However, there was also a silver lining to this cloud as, with the passing of time, my thinking evolved and I became increasingly aware of the centrality of environmental integration as the underlying theme and collective challenge of which green planning is just one, albeit an important, part. For this change in my thinking I have many more people to thank than can be mentioned here, although a number are included in the list of references contained at the end of this book. If anything, although single-authored, this book illustrates how the works of many authors, addressing different and seemingly disparate topics, are part of a common enterprise. At the practical level, I also thank Lincoln University for providing the conditions for completing this project, notably by allowing me another stint of study leave in the second half of 2007, and Dr. Michael Rinella of SUNY Press for the patience shown in the long wait for the promised manuscript, and to Wyatt Benner for his meticulous editing. Most of all, I thank Nicole for her unwavering support, and Eric and Muriel for giving me even more reason to care about the future of this planet.

Abbreviations

CBA	Cost-Benefit Analysis
CRA	Comparative Risk Assessment
CSD	Commission on Sustainable Development
EAC	Environmental Audit Committee (UK)
EIA	Environmental Impact Assessment
EIP	Environmental Integration Principle
EM	Ecological Modernization
EMAS	Eco-Management and Audit Scheme (EU)
EMS	Environmental Management System
EPA	Environmental Protection Agency (US)
EPI	Environmental Policy Integration
ES	Environmental Space
ESD	Ecologically Sustainable Development
GDP	Gross Domestic Product
GNP	Gross National Product
GP	Green Planning
GPI	Genuine Progress Indicator
IDA	International Development Association
IEA	Integrated Environmental Assessment
IEM	Integrated Environmental Management
IPC	Integrated Pollution Control
ISO	International Standards Organization
NAFTA	North American Free Trade Agreement
NCSD	National Council for Sustainable Development
NEAP	National Environmental Action Plan
NEPP	National Environmental Policy Plan (Netherlands)
NEPA	National Environmental Protection Act (US)
NSESD	National Strategy for Ecologically Sustainable Development (Australia)
OECD	Organization for Economic Cooperation and Development
PCE	Parliamentary Commissioner for the Environment (NZ)
PP	Precautionary Principle

PPP	Polluter Pays Principle
RA	Risk Analysis or Risk Assessment
RIVM	Rijksinstituut voor Volksgezondheid and Milieuhygiene (Netherlands)
RMA	Resource Management Act (NZ)
SA	Sustainability Assessment
SD	Sustainable Development
SDS	Sustainable Development Strategy
SEA	Strategic Environmental Assessment
SEEA	System for Integrated Environmental and Economic Accounting (UN)
SEW	Sustainable Economic Welfare
SIA	Social Impact Assessment
SNA	System of National Accounts
TA	Technology Assessment
UNCED	United Nations Conference on Environment and Development
UNEP	United Nations Environment Programme
VA	Voluntary Agreements
WTA	Willingness to Accept Compensation
WTP	Willingness To Pay
WWF	World Wildlife Fund

Introduction

Although environmental integration lies at the heart of the environmental *problématique*, it is not a commonly used phrase, much less so than sustainable development, or even integrated environmental management. In this book, I will advance the notion of environmental integration as a means of making sense of the environmental challenge, discuss a variety of ways by which environmental integration is pursued (notably by governments), assess the merits and limitations of such efforts, and explore opportunities for improvement. Environmental integration, broadly stated, implies the integration of environmental considerations into all areas of human thinking, behaviour, and practices that (potentially) affect the environment. The main argument put forward is that the effectiveness of many approaches to environmental integration is limited by their skewed nature and because forms and tools are shaped and used to accommodate dominant, mostly nonenvironmental interests. To significantly improve environmental integration requires the development and adoption of more inclusive, comprehensive, and positive forms of integration, and a strengthening of the role and influence of environmental interests.

From the early 1970s, in many countries, environmental concerns have triggered considerable government attention and action. Most governments have created specific environmental agencies (departments, ministries, councils), appointed environment ministers, and passed new environmental legislation. For more than three decades, environmental issues have been the subject of much political debate, policy development, institutional reform, and action, not only at the national level but also, and increasingly so, at the international level. The environment, so it seems, has become a significant, perhaps even a core, area of government business.

But while governments may have done much to address environmental problems, questions about the effectiveness and adequacy of their environmental performance remain. While some analysts argue that things are getting better, many environmental problems persist and have become worse, in many countries as well as globally.[1] In particular, there has been a growing belief that a more integrated approach to environmental management is needed, for at least five reasons. First, to avoid that environmental problems are being shifted; for instance, stricter controls on air pollution have sometimes resulted in increased pollution on land. Second, as the array of environmental measures (legislation, regulations, agencies) has expanded over time, concerns have arisen about the inconsistency, overlap, inefficiency, and ineffectiveness of these arrangements. Third, there has been a growing recognition that, in order to address or resolve environmental issues, environmental concerns need to be (better) integrated into nonenvironmental policy sectors (such as agriculture, transport, and energy), as these often contain the causes or driving forces behind many environmental problems. Fourth, with the rise to international prominence of the notion of sustainable development, environmental issues have come to be perceived increasingly as being one strand of a broader ("development") *problématique* or challenge, which has economic, social and environmental dimensions that are, or can be made, complementary. Fifth, as economic concerns and economic globalization have become an important driving force behind environmental integration, fragmented environmental policy and regulation have increasingly been perceived as hindrances to development and economic growth.

As a result of these growing concerns, environmental integration has become an important theme in environmental management, at all levels of government (local, national, and international) as well as in the business sector. Since the late 1980s, especially following the publication of the Brundtland report, many governments have taken steps to advance environmental integration—by, among other, adopting more comprehensive environmental policies or sustainable development strategies ("green plans"), introducing integrated environmental legislation, and/or rationalizing responsibilities for environmental management. At the international level, environmental integration also has become an important focus of attention and action, such as reflected in the adoption, in 1992 at the Rio summit, of *Agenda 21*, a broad program of action for implementing sustainable development. UN agencies (such as the UNEP and the Commission on Sustainable Development/CSD), the Organization for Economic Cooperation and Development (OECD), and the European Union (EU) also have been promoting environmental integration.

Despite this growing recognition, however, environmental integration remains quite problematic, for several reasons. First, conceptually and theoretically, the idea remains poorly developed. Environmental integration, paradoxically, is not often discussed in terms of environmental integration. A wide range of approaches to environmental integration has developed, under many different labels. Much of the literature on environmental integration focuses on particular approaches, often from a partisan perspective. Very few efforts have been undertaken to make sense of a broad range of approaches, let alone to put forward frameworks that may assist in analyzing and explaining the relative merits, strengths, and weaknesses of different approaches. Second, it has already become apparent that, in practice, moves toward environmental integration encounter many obstacles and are often limited in their effectiveness. To a large degree, environmental integration is still more an idea or ideal than a reality. In many cases, environmental integration seems to have occurred mainly at a symbolic level, unmatched by changes or practices on the ground, in the public as well as the private and business spheres. If environmental integration is to be advanced, a better understanding of the obstacles and limitations associated with the various approaches, forms, and tools is required. Third, greater recognition needs to be given to the role and influence of politics. Environmental integration can serve different ends and interests, depending on the specific form it takes. In practice, much of the value or merit of environmental integration is determined by politics. Yet, the role and influence of politics in environmental integration is often ignored, in the literature as well as in practice.

The aim of this book is to contribute to filling these gaps on all three fronts. In chapter 1, I clarify what I mean by environmental integration, and put forward a framework that aims to make sense of different forms or approaches, and that can assist in identifying and analyzing their relative strengths and weaknesses, gaps and linkages. It may also serve as a basis for thinking about ways of approaching environmental integration from a more comprehensive and strategic point of view.

The following six chapters (2 to 7) describe and discuss a range of forms and tools that are often used to promote environmental integration. Many of these have emerged in Western countries but have since been adopted around the world. Each chapter focuses on one of the (six) categories of forms of environmental integration identified in chapter 1, and discusses the strengths and limitations of a variety of forms that have evolved within each category.[2]

Chapters 2 and 3 look at environmental integration efforts along the cognitive dimension of environmental integration, integration aimed at the "greening" of knowledge and views that guide human thinking, decisions, behavior and practices. Chapter 2 discusses some of the mechanisms or tools that are often used to integrate environmental considerations into the cognitive frameworks on which decision-making in areas not commonly regarded as environmental are based (referred to here as cognitive-external environmental integration), notably environmental impact assessment (EIA), cost-benefit analysis (CBA), and risk assessment (RA). Chapter 3 discusses several cognitive frameworks (some of which have been widely adopted by governments), used to provide substantive guidance or direction to environmental integration efforts (referred to as cognitive-internal environmental integration), including the ideas of sustainable development and ecological modernization.

Chapters 4 and 5 discuss and analyze forms of environmental integration on the policy dimension. Governments have adopted a range of mechanisms aimed at the integration of environmental concerns into policy sectors or areas not usually referred to as environmental, such as economic, energy, transport, and agriculture policy, but which harbor many of the most significant pressures on the environment. Forms of policy-external integration include strategic environmental assessment (SEA), sustainability assessment (SA), economic instruments, and voluntary agreements, discussed in Chapter 4. Chapter 5 discusses efforts directed at the development and implementation of more-or-less comprehensive and integrated policies that aim to guide and coordinate policies toward common environmental goals and objectives (here referred to as policy-internal environmental integration). The most common means in this category is "green planning," a label used for a variety of policies including sustainable development strategies (SDSs), national environmental action plans (NEAPs), and national environmental policy plans (NEPPs).

The integration of environmental values and interests into political, economic, and social institutions (to be distinguished from policies) is another important dimension of environmental integration, essential in particular for promoting or ensuring that environmental integration efforts have teeth and durability. However, the greening of nonenvironmental institutions, among others the "greening of government" programs, mechanisms aimed at the greening of the economy (for instance, through green accounting and the promotion of environmental management systems [EMSs]), referred to here as institutional-external environmental integration and discussed in Chapter 6, proves to be most problematic. In part, the weakness of these efforts is linked to, and matched by, the modest, and mostly symbolic, adoption by governments of overarching institutions that (can) provide a basis for guiding, pushing, and requiring the greening of institutions and policies based, for instance, on the cognitive-internal frameworks for integration discussed in chapter 2. Institutional-internal environmental integration, discussed in chapter 7, comprises moves toward the integration of environmental institutions, the adoption of environmental rights and duties, the institutionalization of environmental principles, and the creation of National Councils for Sustainable Development (NCSDs).

The final chapter addresses the question of how forms and approaches to environmental integration can be improved. Having established the strengths, weaknesses, and limitations of the various forms in earlier chapters, chapter 8 discusses how the effectiveness of approaches to environmental integration could be enhanced, notably by addressing gaps and weaknesses in the various dimensions or forms of environmental integration, the identification and strengthening of (strategic) linkages between forms, and/or the combination of means and mechanisms. Also, I offer some ideas for the further development of incipient frameworks for cognitive-internal environmental integration—notably, the notions of environmental space and environmental design. However, although ideas are important, the advancement of environmental integration depends to a large extent on politics, and on strategic thinking and actions on the part of advocates of environmental integration.

1

Making Sense of Environmental Integration

INTRODUCTION

Although the need for environmental integration has found growing recognition, the expression itself is neither clear nor common. Environmental integration is referred to under different labels, such as "integrated environmental management" (IEM), "integrated pollution control" (IPC), "holistic resource management," "ecosystem management," and "environmental policy integration" (EPI), just to name a few. In an otherwise comprehensive publication on environmental discourses, "environmental integration" is not mentioned as a distinct discourse.[1] The literature that explicitly uses the term "environmental integration" is rare, and even then the label "environmental policy integration" is often preferred.[2] Environmental integration, as it were, goes under many different guises, and is taken to mean different things. Yet, as I will argue in this chapter, the notion of environmental integration deserves a prominent place among the environmental discourses, as it lies at heart of the environmental *problématique*, and at the core of many different efforts directed at preventing, addressing, or resolving environmental problems, including those undertaken by governments.

This chapter has two main objectives. The first is to clarify what environmental integration is about. This involves a discussion of what I see as the main elements, dimensions, or challenges of environmental integration rather than providing a precise definition. Identifying the main elements is a first and important step toward making sense of environmental integration, in the light of the different interpretations, perspectives, approaches, and labels found in the literature. The second objective is to provide a framework for classifying and analyzing the array of more specific means of environmental integration that have been adopted by governments. From the 1970s onward, governments have introduced a growing range of tools or mechanisms to promote integration, many of which have been the subject of international diffusion. The framework can be used as a basis for comparing the integration efforts of governments or countries, and for assessing their comprehensiveness and orientation. In most countries, governments have adopted approaches to environmental integration that are skewed toward one or two management dimensions, and that favor particular forms of integration. As the forms adopted also vary in the degree to which they include different dimensions of the environment, the framework allows assessing the relative strengths and limitations of government approaches to environmental integration.

The first section elaborates on the meaning and importance of environmental integration, identifying the main tasks or challenges involved. The second section introduces the framework used to classify a range of forms of environmental integration adopted by governments; and describes succinctly the various specific means and the reasons for their selection.

WHAT IS ENVIRONMENTAL INTEGRATION?

Given the paucity of comprehensive and theory-based studies in this field, there is a need for reflecting on the essence of environmental integration and for establishing some benchmarks. Clarifying what environmental integration is about is not just a matter of providing definitions, although conceptual clarification is an important step in building knowledge and understanding. It is also about identifying the main tasks or challenges that are considered to be essential to the idea of environmental integration.

Perhaps it is superfluous to point out that environmental integration does not refer to the environment itself, but to a challenge that humans face. In broad terms, it refers to the need for humans to increase their environmental awareness and to act upon it with a view toward minimizing their environmental impact. The need stems from the ecologically unspecialized nature of human beings and the fact that, unlike other species, humans do not "naturally" adapt to their environment but intervene in and change their environment to suit their own needs and wants. Disregarding, and often unaware of, their connections with, and dependence on, ecosystems, they collectively act in ways that can bring about the collapse of the environmental basis on which their well-being, civilization, and even existence are based.[3] Consequently, to prevent and mitigate environmental damage, humans, individually and collectively, need to learn to find or identify their proper place in the environment, from the local to the global level.

To integrate, in common terms, means to "combine (parts) into a whole" or to "complete (an imperfect thing) by the addition of parts."[4] In the context of what has been described above, environmental integration means that humans need to add an environmental "part" or dimension to their knowledge and awareness, actions and behavior, and to the social institutions by which they are guided. Moreover, as they add this part, individually and collectively, in different contexts and ways, these parts do not necessarily combine into a whole. Individuals, groups, and societies develop different, often conflicting, views on the environment and how it should be taken into account in their actions and behavior. How people interact with and intervene in the environment differs widely, especially in modern, pluralist societies. Consequently, environmental integration involves two challenges: the integration of an environmental dimension ('part') into *all* spheres of human thinking and action that (potentially) impact on the environment, and bringing coherence and consistency between these efforts.

The challenges can be seen as two sides of the same coin or as two dimensions of environmental integration, which I will refer to as the external and the internal. Integrating environmental considerations assumes some idea about *what* needs to be considered and integrated (from the "outside," hence "external" integration). And to ensure consistency between integration efforts, there must be a common and coherent basis for integration (internal integration). In other words, environmental integration presumes the existence of a common framework for guiding integration efforts but is incomplete so long as there are areas of human activity (that impact on the environment) that have not been incorporated into that framework. In more graphic terms, external integration adds pieces to the environmental integration puzzle, while internal integration provides the picture used to guide putting the pieces together and to identify the pieces that are still missing.

This interpretation of environmental integration is quite broad. It depicts environmental integration as a challenge or process that involves all humans, individually and collectively. It affects (or should affect) all spheres of human action (behavior) and interaction that impact on the environment, even potentially, and all elements that provide a basis for such actions and interactions, including thinking, values, norms, goals, discourse, rules, and decision-making. Environmental integration can occur at the individual level, and in informal groups, as well as in formal organizations and in government agencies. Arguably, it is ultimately the integration of environmental concerns at the *individual* level that counts most. If *all* individuals were to integrate the environment in all of their thinking, decisions, and doing, in ways that are mutually consistent, environmental integration would be fully achieved.

It is hard to see how such a situation might occur on more than the smallest scale. To expect that all humans, on their own accord, are willing and able to integrate environmental considerations into all their thinking and actions in mutually consistent ways can be easily dismissed as utopianism. Although, in many societies, an increasing number of individuals do include environmental considerations into their thinking and behavior, many do not or do not consistently do so. Ensuring that most if not all people (including those in groups and organizations) take the environment into account, and in mutually consistent and supportive ways, is a collective challenge. Governments, still the most important agents of and for collective action in democratic societies, have a major role to play in advancing environmental integration. This does not imply advocating a totalitarian green government intent on brainwashing (or "greenwashing") all people. On the contrary, like many other environmental advocates I believe that enhancing democracy offers a preferred and better way towards the greening of states and societies.

Environmental integration, though, is more than just a process of balancing or weighing different and conflicting values, interests, and views, as is often implied in discussions of integration under the heading of "sustainable development." In line with the general definition referred to above ("combining parts into a whole"), it implies a process of *changing* values, interests, and views to bring them in line with one another, to make them compatible and mutually supportive. Moreover, as we speak of *environmental* integration, this implies change based on what is considered environmentally important or imperative (environmental parameters). Consequently, environmental integration implies adapting knowledge bases (cognitive frameworks), actions (policies), and human systems (institutions) on the basis of collectively decided environmental parameters, so that they become "environmentally rational." Where values and interests are only balanced or traded off against one another, this is not environmental integration but the common practice of bargaining and politics.

The crunch, of course, lies in determining what is environmentally rational and what the environmental parameters are. Obviously, people will also disagree on that point, based on different values, interests, and ideologies. What is environmentally rational is socially constructed, not an objective truth that is easily uncovered. This applies even more so to the notion of environmental rationality, which includes a "human well-being" dimension (as discussed below), than to the notion of ecological rationality.[5] This conundrum, one might argue, makes talking about environmental rationality and environmental parameters meaningless, as their definition, too, is subject to conflicting views, interests, and ideologies, and thus bargaining and politics. Groups and societies can and do end up with quite different definitions of environmental rationality and parameters.

The answer to this conundrum lies not in denying the reality (and value) of diversity and conflict, but in recognizing that, de facto, in collective decision-making (often through governments) groups and societies always do assign different priorities and weights to values, and interests, and that those who advocate more specifically environmental values and interests often do not have much of a say and tend to lose out, leading to aggravated environmental damage. In practice, then, environmental integration is about *enhancing* the incorporation of environmental knowledge, values, and interests in human thinking, decisions, actions, and institutions as well as about *promoting* the consistency between environmental management efforts by a variety of ways and means. Environmental integration depends on and requires the strengthening of environmental advocacy in the processes and institutions of collective decision-making with the ultimate aim that all policies and institutions are "greened" so that they no longer cause avoidable and unnecessary environmental harm and can thus be considered environmentally rational. Human actions will always have *some* environmental consequences, but there is enormous scope for reducing the tremendous (and growing) damage that is being caused now, and for bringing human practices more in line with collectively determined environmental parameters that now often are not even defined, let alone assigned priority. Although environmental integration is likely to be a long, arduous, and reiterative process by which humans improve their knowledge and capacity for minimizing their environmental impact (which implies also enhancing the environmental conditions for their well-being, as we will see below), much can and must be done in the short term and medium term to boost that capacity.

Advancing environmental integration at the collective (including government) level requires changing the way(s) the environment is managed. Management is used here in a broad sense, and relates to the ways humans interact with and intervene in the environment. It encompasses the ideas, assumptions, knowledge, and views on which environmental management is based (the *cognitive* dimension); the decisions, courses of action, and the choice of means and technologies (the *policy* dimension); and rules and organizations (the *institutional* dimension). The three areas or dimensions are intricately interwoven and interdependent: policies, decisions, and actions are based on cognitive (management) frameworks, and supported and implemented by (formal and informal) rules and organizations. Consequently, environmental integration efforts are incomplete and likely to suffer in their effectiveness if not undertaken consistently across all three dimensions. Yet, the environmental integration efforts of governments are often slanted toward one or two of these dimensions and are not backed up adequately by efforts in other areas. Here I will elaborate a bit further on each of the dimensions to clarify its importance to environmental integration.

How the environment is managed depends most fundamentally on the cognitive frameworks (belief systems, assumptions, knowledge, and information) that guide individuals, groups, and societies in their thinking, behaviour,

Table 1. Environmental Management Dimensions

Dimension	*Description*	*Examples*
Cognitive	The ideas, knowledge, interpretations, and frameworks that guide human interactions with the environment	Nature as a (mere) pool of resources; humans being above, at the center of, or part of nature; knowledge and views of ecosystems and of environmental problems, what causes them, and how they can, should, or must be addressed
Policy	Intentional courses of action affecting the environment (if by governments: public policy)	Aims, objectives, and practices, including choice of technology and other means, associated with agriculture, mining, energy use, transport, building, fishing, manufacturing
Institutional	Formal and nonformal rules and organizations that guide actions, behavior and practices affecting the environment	Taboos on (access to or use of) parts of nature; environmental laws and regulations; corporations, governments, environmental agencies and groups

and actions. Societies differ in the way(s) they interpret the environment and in the extent to which environmental views are integrated into dominant belief systems. Within modern, pluralist societies there is often a wide range of environmental views and considerable variation in the extent to which individuals and groups give consequence to these views in their behavior and actions. However, that does not mean that all views carry the same weight and are equally important in terms of their environmental impact. Moreover, in modern societies, implicitly or explicitly, some views will be much more prevalent and influential than others, with consequences for environmental impact. Environmental considerations may not figure much at all in the cognitive frameworks that dominate many of the decisions and practices of many governments, businesses, groups, and individuals.

Cognitive environmental integration, then, refers to the "greening" of knowledge and views that underlie human (including government) thinking, decisions, and actions. This involves two main aspects or challenges. The first is the integration of environmental knowledge into the cognitive basis for decision-making in areas where previously environmental knowledge has not, or has inadequately, been considered. In line with the distinction made above, this will be referred to as "cognitive-external integration." The second is the development and adoption of an overarching cognitive framework to guide or direct environmental integration efforts across all areas, which will be referred to as "cognitive-internal integration."

Governments have used a variety of mechanisms or tools, among which environmental impact assessment (EIA), cost-benefit analysis (CBA), and risk analysis (RA), to advance the integration of environmental knowledge into the cognitive bases of decision-making in different areas. The use of overarching cognitive (environmental management) frameworks to guide environmental integration efforts across the board has been of more recent date, but has become quite significant since the late 1980s. In particular, many governments have adopted the notion of "sustainable development" as a cognitive framework for their integration efforts.

Cognitive integration cannot avoid the complexity and uncertainty that is inherent to all human knowledge. As human knowledge of the environment and environmental problems, like all knowledge, will always be incomplete, tentative, and contested, there is always scope for improving understanding. Moreover, as new environmental problems keep on surfacing, to the extent that modern societies have become "risk societies,"[6] the need for enhancing knowledge is ongoing and keeps growing. Improving human understanding of environmental issues is often seen as holding to key toward more effective management.[7]

However, improving understanding is not a straightforward matter. The cognitive dimension lies within the domains of ontology, epistemology, and ideology. Individuals, groups, societies, and cultures have different conceptions of the world and of the place of humans in it, and they also have different ideas as to what is valid and important knowledge. Knowledge formation, including scientific knowledge, inevitably involves interpretation and making judgments, and is influenced by contextual values.[8] Consequently, environmental knowledge is subject not only to uncertainty, but also to different interpretations of what the environment is, of how it functions, and of the seriousness and causes of environmental problems. Cognitive environmental integration, most clearly in its internal forms, involves making value judgements about the place and rights of humans in the environment, about the place and rights of other species, and about the importance of environmental values relative to other concerns. Inevitably, it raises questions about the principles on which environmental management should be based. It thus is subject to contesting views and politics, as will be amply demonstrated later in this book.

As noted above, environmental management and integration efforts are always based, implicitly or explicitly, on a particular interpretation of the environment. Fundamentally, this begs the question of *what* needs to be integrated and taken into account. As there is no agreement on the interpretation of the environment, there is also no common yardstick for assessing the degree to which the environment has been incorporated into integration efforts. Fortunately, however, there is a characterization of environmental dimensions that has obtained considerable currency and that can provide a rough but useful measure for the degree of comprehensiveness or inclusiveness of cognitive integration efforts. These dimensions overlap to some extent with the three dimensions or aspects that are commonly associated with the notion of sustainability or sustainable development. I will label and define these three more narrowly as the ecological, resource, and human-environment dimensions.

The ecological dimension refers to ecosystems. Although, as I will discuss below, ecology and the notion of ecosystems do not provide the solid scientific basis for environmental management that some initially thought or hoped that they could or would, there are presently few people who would deny the importance of giving consideration to ecological or biophysical conditions, processes, and interconnections in the management of the environment. Early moves toward integrated management based on this recognition occurred when efforts toward the protection of animals were expanded to include their habitats. The protection of natural areas, such as parks and reserves, was a step toward more encompassing scales of integrated environmental management. More recently, the need for the protection of interconnected ecosystems, whether or not they have been set aside as parks or reserves, has been the subject of efforts toward integrated environmental management. In short, the ecological dimension of environmental integration refers to the extent to which ecosystem protection has been incorporated.

The resource dimension overlaps with the biophysical dimension inasmuch as animals, plants, and ecosystems also are resources. The term

Table 2. Environment Dimensions

Environment Dimensions	*Description*
Ecological	The biophysical environment encompassing all ecosystems, from local to global
Resource	Biophysical elements (potentially) of use to humans, including animals, land, water, forests, and minerals
Human environment	The biophysical environment shaped by humans, including the built environment, agricultural land, and human-made products

"resource" is defined here anthropocentrically as anything, living or nonliving, that is potentially of use to humans. In many parts of the world, the decline, depletion, or degradation of resources, such as land, forests, and water, has long been of concern. In 1972, concerns about resource depletion reached the global level with the publication of the Club of Rome's *Limits to Growth* report.[9] Although there have always been skeptics and optimists who deny (the seriousness of) problems of this nature, or who have unlimited faith in human ingenuity to overcome any such problems if they do arise, few people deny the desirability or importance of the judicious management of resources. Rational or science-based resource management became an important branch of environmental management in the nineteenth century. More recently, the need for managing resources (such as soil, water, plants, and animals) in a more integrated manner has become an important plank in resource management. In short, the resource dimension of environmental integration refers to the extent to which considerations regarding the long-term availability, and quality, of resources has been incorporated.

Economics is the discipline that focuses on the allocation of scarce resources, and this dimension of the environment is often referred to as the economic dimension. I prefer to use the term "resource dimension," since resources are substantive elements of the environment, whereas the "economic dimension," as used in the sustainable development discourse, has come to refer to nonenvironmental concerns, such as about economic growth, competitiveness, and profits. Therefore, talking about the integration of the *economic* dimension in environmental management is likely to shift attention away from a concern about the *physical* or *natural* resources and their long-term availability, in quantitative and qualitative respects.

The human environment dimension offers the greatest scope for confusion, as it could be interpreted to include all aspects of human life and societies, or to refer to the very elastic notion of "quality of life." Here, I use it to refer to those biophysical environmental conditions that have been shaped by humans. For many humans the environment is foremost about the "human environment," the environment shaped by humans, including cities and modified landscapes. Many, if not most, environmental problems have come to be recognized as problems because of the effects on humans of human-induced biophysical changes, such as pollution, urban sprawl, traffic congestion, noise, the decline of natural areas for recreation, and the physical conditions in which people work and live more generally. Efforts toward environmental integration that ignore such issues and aspects of the environment can be called integrated only in a limited sense.

More recently, "quality of life" has become an important topic in environmental and sustainable development discourse. Governments have incorporated quality of life as a concern in their environmental plans or sustainable development strategies, and quality-of-life indicators increasingly are adopted in environmental reporting systems. However, the notion of quality of life is commonly interpreted very broadly to include the extent to which people are affected by crime, unemployment, insufficient income, social breakdown, family abuse, and other socioeconomic conditions. Although such issues are important, it is debatable whether, or to what extent, such issues are, or should be called, *environmental* issues.

The approach advocated here is to delineate the human environment dimension by confining it to human-induced *biophysical* phenomena. Pollution, the built environment, the noise generated by human activity or machinery, the food manufactured by humans, sewage disposal practices, access to and quality of drinking water, housing conditions, and waste disposal practices are some of the most obvious biophysical conditions and processes that affect people's well-being, and many of these have been the subject of environmental management for quite some time. There is no doubt that transport, urban development, and housing are policy areas that have, or should have, a strong environmental component, as they create or affect biophysical conditions that impinge on human well-being, as well as on ecosystems and resources. While improving the biophysical conditions that affect people's well-being may contribute to reducing crime and other social problems, we should avoid interpreting all human conditions as environmental conditions, as this would make the "environment" concept all-encompassing. Crime, alienation, youth problems, care for the elderly, family breakdown, unemployment, and insufficient income are most of all social and economic issues that are, or should be, addressed by social and economic policies and institutions.

Ultimately, where to draw the line around these three environmental dimensions is a matter of judgment. For practical and political reasons, it makes sense to promote a notion of the environment that does not encompass everything. Promoting a virtually all-encompassing interpretation of the environment may further increase the risk that environmental issues like those described above are swamped by economic and social agendas and priorities. A totally comprehensive interpretation of the environment is likely to be less meaningful and helpful in identifying environmental priorities and the development of environmental policies. Given the broad nature of, and the connections and overlap between, the three dimensions described above, the integration of environmental concerns already is enough of a challenge.

The integration of environmental concerns into and across policies has been a second main area of environmental integration pursued by governments. Here (public) policy is understood as purposeful courses of action (including deliberate nonaction) undertaken by governments. Policy has an intentional component (which may take the form of official, nonofficial, or even hidden, goals, objectives, or targets), and also comprises what governments *do* to advance their intentions. At times, governments may not be clear or certain about their objectives, or do very little to advance officially stated goals. Nonetheless, even poorly targeted action and deliberate nonaction are part of policy as long as there is some intention behind such courses. Policy needs to be distinguished from single decisions and almost always comprises a series of decisions and actions stretched over a period of time, and commonly involves multiple decision-makers and actors. The intentional nature of policy should therefore not be equated with the notion of "rational-comprehensive" decision-making. More commonly, policies are the result of multiple and even conflicting goals and interests pursued by different actors rather than the product of rational design by a single policy maker. When constituting compromise, policies reflect (a mix of) intentions or purposes, even if these are not mutually consistent.

Policies need to be distinguished from institutions. Although some policies may receive institutional backing (in the form of legislation, or regulations), not all of them do. Moreover, as new governments inherit the legislative framework created by their predecessors, existing laws and regulations do not necessarily constitute or reflect the policies of the government of the day. In fact, governments usually adopt an agenda of legislative and/or regulatory change in the pursuit of their goals and objectives. In large part, institutions are the cumulative and sometimes enduring results of the policies introduced by governments of the past. Sometimes, the original intention or purpose behind institutions (traditions or rules) may have faded, or even have disappeared altogether. Nonetheless, such institutions may still be kept alive because of an inherent value or merit or because they have obtained some value or merit they did not have before. Depending on the political-ideological orientation of a government, the gap between the "frozen" intentions built into the institutional framework, on the one hand, and the policies pursued by that government, on the other, can be significant.

"Environmental policy integration" refers to the integration of environmental concerns into, and across, the array of policies pursued by governments. Given that many if not most government policies have (potentially) significant environmental implications, it is desirable or necessary that an environmental dimension is built into a broad range of policy areas, including economic (development), agriculture, urban and regional planning, and transport and energy policies.[10] Integration of this kind will be referred to here as *policy-external* environmental integration, or more colloquially as the greening of (nonenvironmental) policies or policy sectors. In the literature, environmental *policy* integration is often treated as synonymous to environmental integration, and interpreted to include the integration of environmental concerns into institutions.[11] However, as explained above, there is a significant distinction between policies and institutions. In fact, environmental policy integration and the integration of environmental concerns into institutions constitute two different paths or approaches that have received different degrees of emphasis across countries, as will become apparent in subsequent chapters.

The integration of environmental concerns *across* policy areas or sectors raises the question of consistency and coherence between integration efforts, and therefore of *internal* integration. What, and how, environmental concerns get integrated into policies or sectors can differ significantly, depending on the views, interests, and power held by actors within the respective policy communities. Weak integration within some areas or sectors may constitute significant brakes or obstacles to the success of environmental integration efforts in others areas or sectors, and may even negate achievements in the latter. The creation of some kind of overarching policy framework that guides or directs policy-external integration efforts, promoting their coherence and consistency, is therefore an important second element of environmental policy integration.

It should be noted that the terms "external" and "internal" integration are similar but not identical to the concepts of "vertical" and "horizontal" environmental policy integration put forward by Lafferty and Hovden. Although vertical environmental policy integration also refers to the integration of environmental concerns into sector policies (here referred to as external integration), this is seen by Lafferty and Hovden as largely a voluntary process controlled by the sectors themselves, even if guided by particular ministries or departments. This contrasts with horizontal integration, which is referred to as involving authoritative decision-making in the process of "balancing" conflicting interests while adopting a "strong supposition in favour of environmental concerns."[12] However, the terms "horizontal" and "vertical" in this context are potentially confusing, as vertical suggests hierarchy (mandatory integration stipulated from above), while horizontal could be interpreted as involving a process between "equal" parties. In practice, both types of integration may involve hierarchy (environmental integration into specific policy areas may be mandated by the government or a central agency, but based on a nonstatutory green plan). I therefore prefer to use the terms "internal integration" and "external integration," as these refer more clearly to the nature of the tasks or challenges involved rather than to whether they are imposed or voluntary.

Although environmental policy integration can overlap with policy coordination, the two concepts should not be seen as identical. Inasmuch as policy coordination is based on environmental parameters, goals, and objectives (substantive environmental policy coordination), it can be regarded as a form of policy-internal environmental integration. However, coordination can be based on nonenvironmental goals and objectives, and often involves more procedural mechanisms for consultation and/or a process or bargaining or "mutual adjustment" that do not necessarily assign any great importance to environmental interests or concerns. Procedural coordination is an essential and necessary mechanism for environmental policy integration but is not in itself a sufficient means for bringing about such integration.[13]

Governments have used a variety of ways or means to promote environmental policy integration of both kinds. Policy-external integration, or the greening of policies, has been advanced, among other, by strategic environmental assessment (SEA), the development of environmental sector plans, the introduction of departmental environmental strategies, and sustainability assessment and voluntary agreements. Policy-internal environmental integration has been pursued most notably through "green planning," a concept used to refer to the adoption of comprehensive and integrated environmental policies, plans, or strategies, including sustainable development strategies. Green planning has been heralded as a promising and significant new stage in the development of environmental policy, and arguably the capacity to undertake it effectively constitutes a pinnacle of environmental integration at the national level.[14] However, as we will see in chapter 5, the promise of green planning has been far from fully realized.

To the extent that efforts and tools directed at promoting cognitive integration and policy integration have been backed up by legislation or other rules, they overlap with institutional integration. The term "institutions" covers a wide range of things that guide or channel human behavior and actions, including collective decision-making and policy development. Institutions comprise formal and informal rules, including constitutions, traditions, and conventions, organizations, the allocation of responsibilities and powers, mandates, processes and procedures, and legislation and regulations. Institutions lie at the basis of relatively stable and entrenched structures and processes through which environmental management takes place. Interest in institutions, and in particular the state, and their role in directing societal development has seen a revival since the 1980s.[15]

As institutions guide or channel much of human behavior and action, in government as well as in the wider society, their importance to environmental integration is obvious. Many rules, including those that guide government and business organizations, traditionally did not require or even encourage people to take note of environmental concerns, let alone to assign significant importance to them. Over the last three to four decades, governments have introduced many institutional changes to promote or ensure that environmental interests receive greater attention, in the form of the establishment of environmental organizations (like environment departments or ministries), environmental legislation and regulation (for a whole raft of environmental issues), and even constitutional environmental rights. Also, many of the approaches, mechanisms, and tools directed at cognitive and policy integration, mentioned above, have been supported by the introduction of formal rules or legislation. For instance, in many countries, environmental impact assessment (EIA) has become a formal, legal requirement for particular categories of proposals, providing some teeth to cognitive-external integration efforts.

In fact, in many countries, the institutional environmental framework has become so elaborate and fragmented that it has become one of the driving forces behind moves toward internal integration. The introduction, over time, of laws and regulations for different environmental areas or media (such as for pollution of air, water, land, for waste management, and for hazardous substances) and the allocation of overlapping responsibilities to different agencies and levels of government, with their separate processes and procedures, have led to complaints about inefficiency and ineffectiveness, and the imposition of unnecessary costs and delays upon those who advocate development. The rationalization of environmental institutions, bringing them together into one, coherent whole, became an important plank of government policy in many countries the 1980s, but was perhaps most pronounced in New Zealand. New Zealand's bold reforms, and their limited effectiveness in promoting internal and external environmental integration, will be elaborated upon in chapter 7, alongside a discussion and assessment of a range of initiatives and developments in institutional reform in other countries.

As already noted above, how the environment is treated, and how environmental issues are dealt with, depends on what happens in all three areas or dimensions of management. Knowledge, policies (including their implementation), and institutions all shape or influence human action and behavior. To be effective, environmental integration efforts in each of these areas need to be consistent with and supported by efforts in the other two areas. Efforts directed at integrating environmental concerns in the cognitive realm, unsupported by policies and institutions, are likely to face considerable obstacles and to have limited effect. Environmental policy integration requires a knowledge basis, particularly with regard to the linkages between environmental problems, their causes, and proposed actions. Cognitive integration and policy integration are on firmer ground if backed up by institutions supportive of integration, especially when political support and commitment wanes. But institutional integration, even though it may give formal expression to integrative cognitive notions like sustainability, may not amount to much more than symbolism if not accompanied by environmental policy integration. The *scope* of environmental integration efforts refers to the extent to which they encompass the different dimensions of management. Environmental integration is likely to be most effective and enduring if it occurs in mutually supportive ways across all three dimensions of environmental management.

One further qualification needs to be added in this context. As noted above, the main focus in this book is on environmental integration efforts undertaken by governments at the national level. However, given the interconnected nature of the environment, from the local to the global level, many environmental issues can only be addressed effectively if tackled in concert at all levels. This implies that environmental integration efforts, on all three dimensions of management (cognitive, policy, and institutional), also need to consider the linkages between the local, national, and global levels. The scope of environmental integration, and its effectiveness, therefore also relates to the extent that environmental integration efforts at all levels of government are linked and made mutually consistent.

Environmental integration efforts may also vary in their focus or degree of emphasis with respect to the three environmental dimensions. Some integration efforts, like integrated pollution control (IPC), primarily address pollution (from a range of sources, or in different media), while others are directed at increasing resource efficiency as well as reducing pollution. Some forms of environmental integration, like green planning, may be aimed at formulating courses of action for environmental problems across all three dimensions. I will use the label "environmental inclusiveness" to refer to the degree to which these dimensions are included in integration efforts. Given the interconnections and interdependence between the three environmental dimensions, the assumption made here is that environmental integration efforts are more likely to be effective if they consider the linkages between environmental problems and processes between all three dimensions. Integration efforts that are confined to issues within one dimension, although they may be or seem effective in the short term, are likely to be less effective or totally ineffective in the long term.

In practice, forms of integration are often confined only to one area of management, and include only one or two of the dimensions of the environment. In other words, they differ in their *scope of management* and vary in *environmental inclusiveness*. In most cases, therefore, environmental integration initiatives only partially address the environmental integration challenge. This is not to say that this makes them worthless. The main point here is to identify and clarify differences between approaches to environmental integration, and to point out that most forms of integration are likely to focus on particular environmental and/or management aspects, possibly for good reasons. To some extent, the limitations of several forms might be addressed by linking or combining them with others. However, many of the limitations of the more specific forms adopted by governments are not the result of oversight but have been deliberately built in for political reasons, which makes overcoming them difficult. Nonetheless, there is a need for thinking about how approaches to and forms of integration can be improved, and I will set out to do so in chapter 8.

Having clarified what environmental integration is about, and having identified its main dimensions or aspects, I will now present a framework for classifying forms of environmental integration. The aim of doing so is, first, to make sense of the wide range of means, tools, and mechanisms that are frequently used to advance environmental integration; and second, to point out some of the strengths and limitations of these forms in terms of their degree of environmental inclusiveness and their scope of management. As most of these forms and means will be discussed more extensively in the following chapters, here they will be described only briefly, largely to explain why they have been selected for further discussion.

FORMS OF ENVIRONMENTAL INTEGRATION

As noted in the previous section, the growing recognition of the desirability, or even necessity, of environmental integration has led to the development of a variety of approaches to, and forms of, integration, in the literature as well as in practice. In this section, my aim is to make sense of this variety of approaches and forms, which has emerged under a confusing array of labels. Ironically, the rise of the notion or theme of environmental integration has added to the diversity of ideas and practices in environmental management. While this is not necessarily a bad thing, it has done little to address or overcome the fragmentation in thinking and action that characterizes much of the human endeavor to come to terms with the environmental *problématique*. Many forms of integration, so it seems, are associated with distinct schools of thought and/or practice, each pushing its own favorite wheelbarrow of ideas, models, tools, and techniques, without even acknowledging the existence, let alone merit, of other schools or forms, and their own limits in this common challenge.

Using the differences in foci of integration (cognitive aspects, policies, and institutions), and the distinction between external and internal integration as a basis, six categories of forms of integration can be distinguished: cognitive-external, cognitive-internal, policy-external, policy-internal, institutional-external, and institutional-internal. Within each category, a range of means, mechanisms, or tools can be identified.

Cognitive-External Integration

As described in the previous section, cognitive-external integration refers to the integration of environmental considerations into cognitive frameworks

Table 3. Forms of Environmental Integration

Management dimension / *External/internal*	*Cognitive*	*Policy*	*Institutional*
	Information, knowledge and interpretations of the environment	Policies, plans, programs, strategies	Institutions: rules and organizations
External forms	Environmental impact assessment, cost-benefit analysis, risk assessment, integrated environmental assessment, environmental assessment, environmental education	Strategic environmental assessment, sustainability assessment, economic instruments, voluntary agreements	Greening of government, green accounting, environmental management systems
Internal forms	Sustainable development, ecological modernization, environmental space, ecosystem management	Integrated pollution control, comparative risk assessment, green planning	Integration of environmental institutions, environmental rights, integrative principles, National Councils for Sustainable Development

that underlie human behavior and activities that affect the environment but that do not (yet) give consideration to environmental implications. In common terms, cognitive-external integration means the greening of nonenvironmental knowledge or knowledge frameworks—in particular, knowledge that guides human actions that impact on the environment.

Cognitive-external integration is more about processes, means, or mechanisms by which environmental knowledge is brought into cognitive frameworks than it is about the integration of *particular* knowledge. *What* knowledge (and associated values) is integrated depends, first and foremost, on the views of those who are involved in the integration processes used. Often, different views and interpretations will compete for integration, but the views held by those who are in *control* of the process, practically and/or politically, are likely to dominate or prevail. Although cognitive integration, especially of the external kind, is often portrayed as a matter of bringing in scientific and objective knowledge, it is in fact very much subject to the interplay between different worldviews, ideologies, values, judgments, and interests—in short, to politics. The scientific, technical, or professional nature of the tools or mechanisms used may actually disguise the politics that is associated with them, as will be shown in chapter 2.

Since the environment became a focus for public policy in the 1960s, the United States has been a leader in the development of processes directed at enriching the cognitive basis of decisions with environmental knowledge. EIA, first introduced in 1970 with the adoption of the National Environmental Protection Act (NEPA), provides for assessment of the (potential) environmental implications of proposals. In the United States and many other countries, assessments are required to be based on rigorous scientific methods. And although, to varying degrees, EIA may provide opportunities for public input, scientists and experts play a dominant role in the assessment process. In the 1980s, risk assessment (RA) and cost-benefit analysis (CBA) became increasingly popular as additional means for incorporating and weighing environmental values in decisions. Risk assessment, as a systematic method for assessing risks, originated from the need to come to terms with the (potential) hazards arising from human-made chemicals—in particular, pesticides. However, during the 1980s it was developed into a tool for assessing the risks associated with a broader array of (proposed) technologies, projects, and even policies. Like EIA, RA is science-intensive and is practiced mostly by experts and professionals. CBA is an economists' tool by which the (potential) costs and benefits of proposals are quantified in monetary terms, with the aim of identifying their relative attractiveness. Over time, the use of these tools, especially of EIA, has spread to many other countries.

More recently, there have been moves toward combining or even integrating these forms of integration. Increasingly, CBA is being undertaken alongside, or within the context of, EIA and RA. In some countries, like New Zealand, requirements for environmental assessment encompass elements of all three forms, and have been referred to as integrated impact assessment.[16] More recently, integrated environmental assessment (IEA), also referred to as integrated assessment, has emerged as a comprehensive form of external environmental integration. Developed initially to assess the effects and implications of climate change, it has been touted as a more generic tool for building a sound knowledge basis for decision-making, incorporating ecological, economic, and, to a lesser extent, social dimensions.[17] Like its predecessors, IEA is strongly science- and expert-based, and aimed at providing the "best" knowledge basis for decision-making.

Environmental education is a form of external integration that governments have adopted to instill environmental knowledge into individuals and groups in society. In many countries, environmental subjects have been introduced in school curricula, and many universities now offer courses in environmental science, studies, or management. Moreover, governments, especially at the local level, often use environmental education campaigns to enhance knowledge and awareness, and to promote particular behavior—for instance, with regard to waste disposal, recycling, and energy efficiency. Consequently, the environmental dimension that is sought to be integrated with environmental education can range from general knowledge about the biophysical environment to knowledge about more specific aspects or issues.

As environmental education programs offered vary in content and aims, and are not tied together by a coherent or particular set of environmental views, environmental education does not constitute a form of cognitive-internal integration. It is neither based on, nor necessarily brings about, common or shared interpretations of the environment and environmental problems. This does not detract from the importance and value of environmental education. Nor does it imply that environmental education *should* be based on a particular environmental view or ideology. Increasing environmental knowledge and awareness is a crucially important element for environmental integration, and *must* do justice to the diversity of views held in society. But this means that it cannot be relied upon, or expected to function, as a mechanism for bringing about coherence and consistency between actions and behavior affecting the environment.

Another limitation of environmental education is that its outcomes are difficult to assess. Although environmental knowledge and awareness in a society may change over time, it is problematic to attribute this primarily to formal environmental education efforts. News about environmental problems and campaigns by environmental groups, as well as changes in social, economic, and political conditions, also affect people's environmental views. Perhaps an even greater limitation is that environmental education can contribute to individualizing the environmental *problématique* if it is based on the assumption that every person is equally responsible for environmental problems, and that solving these depends primarily on changes at the level of individuals. It thus can divert attention from the structural, political, and economic causes behind environmental problems, and from the disproportionate contribution and responsibility of certain groups, organizations, and sectors in society. Such factors are unlikely to be affected by environmental education, unless it increases awareness and knowledge of such issues and leads to stronger demands for changes in policies and institutions. Given the difficulty of assessing the influence of environmental education as a form as a form of external integration adopted by governments, I will not elaborate further on it in this volume.

The main reason for grouping these forms of integration together in the category of cognitive-external integration is that they have in common a focus on greening knowledge, by a variety of means. By implication, they are *not focused* on changing policies and institutions, although they may contribute to such change. It is commonly argued that these forms are directed at improving the knowledge basis for decisions, but that it is up to the decision-makers to determine whether and how policies and institutions should be changed. They do not, at least not explicitly, advance normative or political-ideological views on the environment, and on whether and how societies should be changed to accommodate environmental concerns. They are often portrayed as neutral, objective, or scientific, and nonpolitical means for taking on board sound environmental knowledge in decision-making processes, actions, and behavior.

However, as I will discuss in chapter 2, the claims of objectivity and political neutrality of these forms is untenable. Moreover, although they may not be focused on, or directed at, changing policies and institutions in a particular way, their role and functioning is conditioned to a large extent by the political-institutional framework. What these forms bring about is largely conditioned by the specific way they have been shaped (including their institutional basis), and by the policies (environmental and other) pursued by governments.

Cognitive-Internal Integration

While forms of cognitive-external integration provide the means (tools, processes) by which the cognitive bases of human choices, actions, and behavior, individually and collectively, are greened, they do not, by themselves, advance a coherent view of the environment. The content of the knowledge infused depends in large part on the views of those who administer the means of integration, and is also circumscribed by the political context in which this occurs. In other words, the knowledge infused by external integration is diverse, fragmented, contested, and often the subject of disagreement and conflict. Consequently, cognitive-external integration efforts, by themselves, do not guarantee, or even provide a means for, creating coherence or integration between these processes.

Cognitive-internal environmental integration is directed at providing a degree of substantive coherence between external environmental-integration efforts. While external integration is mostly about creating or improving *processes* for integration, internal integration is about creating or improving some kind of overarching cognitive framework that can provide guidance about *what* should be integrated. Such overarching bases or frameworks can take a variety of forms, such as environmental principles, parameters, or environmental belief systems.

Given the diversity of interpretations and views of the environment, and the inherent and inevitable uncertainty and incompleteness of environmental knowledge, it is not surprising that there is also a broad range and variety of forms by which internal integration is advanced. More than is the case with external integration efforts, differences between worldviews, values, and interests play an explicit and important role in the debate about internal integration. Anthropocentric, ecocentric, "deep," and "shallow" green ideologies compete among each other and with many other views of the environment, shaped in different national, sociocultural, political, and economic contexts. Trying to force consensus on environmental ideology, even in a national context, let alone worldwide, can be dismissed as neither feasible nor desirable. In democratic political systems, it is often recognized (or at least claimed) that the diversity of environmental values, beliefs, and interpretations is to be respected and/or incorporated into environmental management. Public participation and open decision-making are often seen as important conditions for making better decisions, enhancing legitimacy, support, and feasibility.[18]

However, offering opportunities for public participation in decision-making does not imply that all views and interpretations enjoy the same level of support and influence on collective decisions, including government decisions. At any one time, some views will be more influential than others, perhaps even to the extent that they can be characterized as dominant. Inevitably, environmental management is based on some cognitive framework or other (including knowledge, ideas, values, and principles) that guides decisions, actions, and the creation and adaptation of institutions, including those of and by governments. Although there are many different cognitive frameworks that can provide a basis for internal integration, and environmental management in general, some forms obviously have been more successful than others in terms of gaining support. Fewer still have been adopted by governments as a basis for their environmental integration efforts.

Here I will shortly describe some of the frameworks that have been most prominent in the efforts of governments to promote cognitive-internal integration, and some that hold considerable promise and potential to become dominant cognitive frameworks in the future. These are: sustainable development, ecological modernization, environmental space, and (eco)systems theory. Since I will elaborate on these in chapter 3, in the following paragraphs I will mainly explain my reasons for selecting these forms of internal integration.

Since the publication of the *Our Common Future* (often referred to as the "Brundtland report") in 1987, sustainable development has become the dominant discourse for framing the environmental *problématique*, internationally and at all levels of government. Its rise to prominence has been nothing but remarkable, reflected in the appeal of this notion to almost the full spectrum of environmental advocates, from deep green to pragmatists, and in its ability to serve nonenvironmental (political, economic, and social) interests and agendas. As such, sustainable development provides a cognitive framework for a wide range of other frameworks and environmental ideologies, and is often identified as an element or cornerstone of other forms of integration. Yet, it is also used as a basis for formulating specific objectives and courses of action, perhaps more so than many other, less inclusive, frameworks.

Apart from the fact that sustainable development has become a basis for cognitive-internal environmental integration adopted in much of the world, a reason for selecting it for further discussion is that it takes the integration challenge beyond that of the integration of the environment into other spheres. The way sustainable development is often interpreted, especially by governments, lifts or shifts the debate on integration to many issues that are not usually labeled "environmental." While this is often perceived as a positive thing—moving the debate away from a narrow focus on environmental matters—it also carries significant risks, as already hinted at earlier in this chapter. Arguably, the challenge is to green the notion of sustainable development, given the tendency for this discourse to be hijacked by nonenvironmental interests.

Ecological modernization (EM), as a cognitive framework, can be classified as a form of external environmental integration, directed mainly at the greening of production and consumption systems, but also as a form of internal environmental integration. How EM is classified depends on one's interpretation, which can vary from narrow to broad, or from weak to strong.[19] In its weaker form, which emphasizes the potential for greening the economy notably by science and technology (policy), it can be classified also as a form of policy-external integration. It has been argued that by applying proper design principles, the rate of efficiency in the use of resources (and, associated with that, levels of pollution), can be improved by a factor 4, without too much trouble.[20] Others have called for a reduction of resource use (dematerialization) in the order of a factor 10 or higher.[21] That technological innovation offers both environmental as well as economic (competitive) benefits is a central theme of EM, particularly in its weaker version, which holds that environmental problems can be resolved without fundamental, systemic change.

But EM, especially in its stronger version, can also provide an overarching framework of ideas, principles, or objectives for environmental integration efforts, and thus function as a form of cognitive-internal integration.[22] EM embodies ideas that (potentially) provide guidance to environmental integration across policy areas and at the institutional level, traversing resource, human-environmental, and ecological dimensions of the environment.

The literature on EM has expanded rapidly during the past decade, reflecting a growing interest and support among environmental advocates and analysts. EM is often regarded as holding considerable attraction and promise, environmentally, economically, and politically, and as a means of advancing the sustainable development commitments of governments. It has received support from governments in some countries, be it mainly in the weaker version. However, as EM has the potential to provide a more encompassing framework, the stronger variety is more interesting for the purpose of cognitive-internal integration. Much of the EM literature focuses on the meaning and (potential) merits of EM, on manifestations of EM, and/or on the obstacles to, and conditions for, its viability. As such, EM appears to function foremost as a collection of ideas, principles, and prescriptions, including the expansion of democracy or public participation, directed at greening the cognitive basis for decisions and actions within the realms of government and business. To avoid overlap and repetition, I will discuss the merits of EM mainly in chapter 3.

The notion of "environmental space" (ES) is also complementary to the idea of sustainable development. ES has been advanced specifically as a means for "making sustainability concrete."[23] It involves calculating the amounts of resources available to a country, based on an assessment of biophysical limits (beyond which harm to the environment and humans would be unacceptable) and on a strong principle of equity. As the concept is broad but not all-encompassing, and can be used as a cognitive basis to provide clear guidance across policy areas and sectors, it is a form of cognitive-internal integration. Thus far, only a few governments have expressed an interest in the concept, and even fewer have sought to apply it. However, the allocation of CO_2 emissions quota in the context of the Kyoto Protocol can be seen as an application of the idea at the international level, arguably marking the beginning of a stage in which the distribution and allocation of environmental space at a global level will increasingly become an important, even dominant, concern. Although EM may be more popular in the environmental literature than ES, judging by the number of publications on each of these forms of integration, the notion of ES is likely to be more attractive to people in low-income countries—that is, to most people in the world. By contrast, EM appears to have the most to offer to high-income countries, and can even be seen as a strategy used by those countries to maintain their lead in the world economy while improving their domestic environmental performance.

Although several big obstacles will need to be overcome before environmental space is adopted as an integrative cognitive basis across the world, it deserves greater prominence in the discussion about environmental integration.[24] I will therefore elaborate further on this form of integration, and its prospects, in chapters 3 and 8.

Systems theory—and, in particular, one of its branches, ecosystems thinking—is also often seen as a promising, or even necessary, cognitive basis for environmental integration. Systems theory is based on the recognition of interdependence between phenomena, and thus makes eminent sense in the context of efforts directed at understanding the connections and complexities within the environment, and the interactions between humans and their environment. Ecosystems thinking, rooted in ecological science as well as in systems thinking, has developed a considerable following in the literature. Like EM, the ecosystems approach has been held up as attractive for ecological, social, economic, and political reasons, and as an emerging paradigm.[25] However, the uptake of ecosystems thinking, and its offshoot, adaptive management, as a basis for environmental integration has been quite modest. Applications have been mostly of an experimental nature, and confined to the local or regional level of environmental management. Applications of systems theory and ecosystems thinking at the national level have been very rare, especially in the form of cognitive frameworks that provide guidance to environmental integration across policy sectors and institutions.

Since (eco)systems thinking has been touted as a new paradigm in environmental management, and has gained considerable support among environmental advocates and analysts, it deserves further discussion and assessment of it integrative capacity or potential. In chapter 3, I will dwell upon its strengths and limitations, and suggest several reasons why the promise of systems theory, and ecosystems thinking, as a form of internal cognitive integration has not materialized on a larger scale, especially at the national level.

Many other frameworks or environmental ideologies have been put forward as bases for cognitive-internal integration. Ecocentrism, ecofeminism, bioregionalism, ecosocialism, ecological economics, and holistic resource management, just to name a few, offer overarching cognitive frameworks for internal integration. However, most of these schools of thought have, thus far, not been adopted, to a significant degree, by governments, especially at the national level. This does not necessarily diminish their merit or value. Ideas and ideologies can make sense of the environmental *problématique* without being embraced by governments (skeptics might argue all the more so!). Many of these frameworks do provide a basis for environmental integration for individuals and groups in society, without any government involvement. However, as the focus in this book is on the role of governments, especially at the national level, in advancing environmental integration, the discussion of cognitive-internal integration will be confined mainly to the frameworks mentioned above.

Policy-External Integration

A second approach to environmental integration that has been adopted by governments focuses on policy. As noted above, (public) policy is understood here as purposeful courses of action (or nonaction) adopted by governments. External forms of environmental policy integration (referred to here as policy-external integration) specifically aim at the integration of environmental knowledge, considerations, principles, and objectives into nonenvironmental policy areas. Policy-external integration is crucially important, as many non-environmental policies, such as economic, agriculture, transport, and energy policy, contain significant sources of environmental pressure.[26]

Whereas the integration of environmental knowledge into decisions on *projects* (development proposals) has been actively supported by national governments from the early 1970s (through a variety of means), the integration of environmental considerations into nonenvironmental *policies* has been of more recent date, and proves to be more problematic. The need for environmental policy integration started to receive greater recognition in some countries from around the mid-1980s, achieving a higher place on government agendas, especially in Europe. In 1987, the European Union made the integration of environmental considerations into nonenvironmental policy areas a formal commitment with the adoption of the Single European Act, and turned it into a legal requirement under the Treaty of Amsterdam in 1999.[27] The integration of environmental concerns and objectives into nonenvironmental policy sectors has also been an important plank in the work of the OECD.

One of the consequences of the late arrival of policy-external integration on government agendas has been that the means by which it is advanced and implemented are less well developed compared to those that are used to advance cognitive-external integration. Even to date, many governments appear to promote policy-external integration mainly in general terms, as a principle or objective, rather than through the systematic use of specific mechanisms. The principal means that have been used are strategic environmental assessment (SEA), the development of (environmental) sector plans or strategies, and the use of economic instruments and voluntary agreements.

Strategic environmental assessment is an offshoot of EIA, but explicitly directed at the consideration of the environmental effects of policies. Although, in principle, EIA systems can apply to policies as well as projects, in practice the former has occurred rarely. Political reluctance is likely to have been an important factor in this matter, but it has also been recognized that the methodologies that have been developed for undertaking EIA of projects are not easily applicable, or even appropriate, for the assessment of policies. In reaction to this acknowledgment, SEA has been developed as a means specifically suited for environmental assessment of policies.

Even SEA, however, has thus far not gained widespread following among governments. Less than a dozen countries have introduced formal provisions for SEA, and in only a handful has SEA received legislative backing.[28] In part, this can be attributed to the fact that SEA is still at an early stage of development. SEA thinking and designs have been heavily influenced by EIA thinking and methodology, which may have slowed its maturation as a form of policy-external integration. However, the adoption of SEA as a formal requirement by the European Union, in 2001, may be a sign that SEA is coming of age. It therefore deserves further discussion of its (potential) strengths and limitations as a form of policy-external integration in chapter 4.

Sustainability assessment (SA), basically an extension of the same ideas on which EIA and SEA are built, can be seen as the logical consequence of the shift in discourse from "narrow" environmental concerns to a concern about sustainability or sustainable development. Potentially, SA can be applied to any type of proposal (technology, project, plan, policy)—assessing it on its ecological, economic, and social consequences—related to the three dimensions commonly assigned to the notion of sustainable development. Thus far, applications of SA have been fairly rare, undertaken only in some countries, and confined mostly to free-trade agreements, but more recently it has been gaining ground, particularly in the European Union.

The discipline of environmental economics has generated a variety of ideas about how environmental objectives can be advanced or achieved by the use of economic instruments, such as environmental charges and taxes, and tradable property rights regimes. In many cases, the underlying rationale behind such ideas or suggestions is inspired more by economic concerns (about costs and efficiency) than by environmental objectives. As such, economic instruments can be seen and used as a means for integrating environmental concerns into economic decisions, or the reverse, for the integration of economic concerns in environmental policy. The weight assigned to each category of concern is, of course, largely a matter of politics, and influences the selection and design of such instruments.

For quite some time, governments have used economic instruments in a range of policy areas usually considered to fall within the realm of environmental policy, such as waste and water management. More recently, economic instruments have been introduced in nonenvironmental policy areas specifically to advance environmental objectives, although this often encounters considerable opposition. Whether, and to what extent, economic instruments contribute to the greening of nonenvironmental policy remains very much a matter of judgment and debate.

Voluntary agreements, notably between governments and particular industries or sectors, have also become an increasingly popular means for promoting environmental integration into economic management. Inasmuch as such agreements are used purposefully by governments as a means of "greening" economic objectives, activities, and practices, they constitute a form of policy-external environmental integration. While the increased use of voluntary agreements is sometimes interpreted positively as heralding a broader development from government to governance, and a shift from a reliance on "command and control" policy instruments toward "new environmental policy instruments,"[29] their effectiveness, including that with regard to the greening of economic policy and practices, remains the subject of debate and doubt. I will further pick up on this in chapter 4.

Policy-Internal Integration

While governments have been slow to warm to the idea of policy-external integration, they appear to have been flocking to policy-internal integration, especially in the form of green planning. As described above, policy-internal integration refers to integration across the range of policies that (potentially) impact on the environment. Nonenvironmental policies may be greened by policy-external forms of integration—although signs of this to date are modest—but to ensure consistency between these efforts, some kind of overarching policy framework is required. As policies adopted in one area frequently impact on other areas, or are interdependent with one another, moves toward environmental integration in one area may be hindered, blocked, or even negated by the lack of integration in others. For instance, the adoption of reduction targets for greenhouse gas emissions in the agricultural sector is unlikely to be looked upon as tenable if similar targets are not also introduced in other sectors, such as transport and energy generation.

That policies need to be coordinated or integrated to promote or ensure their coherence and consistency first became obvious within the realm of policies usually labeled as environmental. Policy development in this area, during the 1970s and much of the 1980s, had been ad hoc and fragmented, often with the result that problems were shifted rather than addressed, for instance, when the introduction of tougher water-pollution standards shifted pollution to air or land. Growing recognition of this problem led the introduction of integrated pollution control (IPC) as an early but limited form of policy-internal integration. Sweden was an early leader in adopting an integrated approach to pollution control, but many other countries have followed in its footsteps.

Comparative risk assessment (CRA) provides a broader framework for integration than traditional risk assessment, mentioned above. CRA involves the assessment of potentially all environmental problems and programs, based on the common denominator of "risk." It is classified here as a (rather limited) tool for policy-internal integration, as its main role and function is to assist in the setting of policy priorities. CRA was developed in the United States during the 1980s as a means of enhancing the cost-effectiveness of the federal government's environmental efforts, and for determining which environmental problems (defined in terms of risk) deserved to be given priority. As CRA incorporates elements of environmental assessment and CBA, and builds a cognitive basis for decision-making, one could argue that CRA is a mechanism for cognitive-external integration. However, as CRA is used primarily as a means of *ranking* environmental problems, and is not directed at the greening of nonenvironmental policies or institutions, it does not qualify as a form of policy-external or institutional-external environmental integration. And although it ranks environmental problems on the basis of a common denominator (risk), and implicitly advances a particular view or interpretation of environmental problems, CRA does not offer a substantive cognitive framework for improving or enhancing our *understanding* of the environmental *problématique*. Used primarily for setting priorities within the area of environmental policy, it is best understood as a rather limited form of policy-internal integration, as I will briefly discuss in chapter 5.

"Green planning" is a label used here to refer to a variety of efforts toward the development of (more) comprehensive and integrated environmental policies or plans. It includes policy efforts referred to under a range of different names, such as green plans, environmental policy plans, national environmental action plans, environmental strategies, and sustainable development strategies. Green planning arguably marks a new and promising stage in the development of environmental policy, by providing an integrated and long-term framework for environmental efforts across all or most sectors, and for translating the principle of sustainable development into more specific objectives and targets. However, green planning is not only a matter of finding or formulating common or complementary goals and objectives, although this is where attention is mostly focused on. It also raises issues about policy development *processes*, and in particular about the participation of the broad array of groups and interests in the development and implementation of green plans. The Netherlands and Canada are often perceived to have led the way in this area, but many low-income countries also have developed strategies as a prerequisite for obtaining development assistance. However, the reality of green planning is often not as good as the theory promises.[30]

Institutional-External Integration

The term "institutions" covers a wide range of things that guide or channel the process by which decisions and policies are developed, and includes formal and informal rules, constitutions, traditions and conventions, organizations, the allocation of responsibilities and powers, mandates, processes, and procedures. Institutions lie at the basis of the relatively stable and entrenched political, economic, and social structures and processes within which environmental management takes place. Interest in institutions, and in particular the state, and their role in directing societal development has seen a revival since the 1980s.[31]

Institutional-external integration is about the integration of environmental considerations into political, economic, and social systems, or, in popular terms, about the greening of nonenvironmental institutions such as the state, capitalism, corporations, schools, universities, research institutes, and the media. As human decisions, actions, and behavior in modern societies are strongly influenced, guided, or channeled through the formal and nonformal rules set forth and upheld by institutions such as these, institutional-external integration is crucial, especially where their (potential) negative environmental impacts are significant.

Government efforts toward greening nonenvironmental policies may be backed up by the introduction or change of rules, such as a requirement on government departments to consult with other departments when they develop policy that is likely to impinge on other departments' territories. Rules requiring policy coordination are common within public service systems, and sometimes consultation with environmental agencies (departments or advisory councils) has been made a specific requirement. Rules stipulating public access to official information, and opportunities for public consultation and input, can be also significant in terms of bringing in environmental considerations. The role, significance, and effectiveness of EIA, CBA, SEA, and other forms of external (cognitive and policy) integration depend largely on whether, and how, they have been formally institutionalized. Mandatory environmental reporting is an example of institutional-external integration affecting government departments or businesses.

As institutional integration, in external and internal forms, may overlap with the forms of cognitive and policy integration that have been referred to above, the focus here will be on some forms that have not been mentioned before, and on the efforts and developments in some countries where institutional reform directed at environmental integration has been relatively more significant. In particular, the efforts toward "greening government," of political and bureaucratic institutions, in the United Kingdom and Canada, which arguably have been leaders in this area, will be singled out for discussion. Governments have been even less forthcoming in efforts aimed at the greening of economic institutions. Some of the modest moves that have been undertaken in this direction—notably, green accounting and the promotion of environmental management systems—will also be assessed, given the considerable amount of support for these ideas in the literature and their potential for steering economic decisions into environmentally desirable directions.

Overall, however, governments appear to have been much more reluctant, unwilling, or unable to take bold steps toward the greening of nonenvironmental institutions. Much of the greening efforts of governments, have concentrated with varying emphasis on the development and adoption of cognitive and policy (external and internal) forms of environmental integration. Although an analysis of the underlying reasons for the weak(er) greening efforts of governments in the institutional sphere is beyond the scope of this book, some of the likely obstacles will be identified in the discussion of the institutional-external environmental integration initiatives and developments in chapter 6.

Institutional-Internal Integration

Institutional-internal integration refers to efforts toward creating (greater) coherence and consistency in environmental management by the (re)design, introduction, or reform of overarching institutions (rules as well as organizations). As noted before, external integration efforts are not necessarily consistent with each other, and their effectiveness may be adversely affected by the failure to pursue environmental integration across the full spectrum of management, including management in nonenvironmental areas. To the extent that institutional-external integration efforts are coordinated across a range of areas, they overlap with institutional-internal integration. However, institutional-internal integration also comprises the promotion of coherence between environmental integration efforts by more-or-less comprehensive institutional reform.

Bringing greater coherence to environmental institutions themselves is one means by which governments have promoted institutional-internal integration. Throughout the 1970s and 1980s, in most countries, environmental rules and organization were introduced and changed incrementally, often in reaction to specific problems. As a result, the institutional frameworks for managing the environment that evolved were, and often still are, fragmented, complex, and unwieldy, causing tensions, gaps, inefficiency, and ineffectiveness. These developments provoked demands and initiatives for rationalization and integration.[32] In many cases, such demands were supported by environmentalists and analysts who questioned the ability of existing political institutions to deal effectively with environmental problems, and advocated their strengthening and/or democratization.[33] The reforms in New Zealand during the 1980s and early 1990s, unprecedented in comprehensiveness and consistency, provide a good example of institutional-internal integration and will be assessed on their merits in chapter 7.

In many countries, environmental considerations have been integrated at the highest legal-institutional level, in constitutions—notably, in the form of environmental rights and duties. Given the fundamental nature of constitutional law, one would think that integration at this level has significant flow-on effects for decision-making at all levels of government, and across policy areas and sectors. By incorporating fundamental rules, rights, duties, and principles regarding the environment, constitutions are a form of institutional-internal integration of the highest order. How meaningful and effective this form of integration is depends, in large part, on other factors, in particular whether constitutional rights and duties can be enforced. However, the institutionalization of environmental rights and principles through normal legislation and other rules is not necessarily less effective in guiding policy development and decision-making across areas in the same direction—for instance, when sustainable development is integrated as a principle in legislation governing spatial planning, energy, and transport. The significance of the environmental rights and duties as a means for providing guidance to other environmental integration efforts also will be elaborated upon in chapter 7.

More recently, governments have also adopted and institutionalized principles that explicitly imply a need or requirement to integrate environmental considerations across a broad range of decisions, policies and institutions. Among these are the polluter pays principle (PPP), the precautionary principle (PP), and the environmental integration principle itself (institutionalized in the European Union). However, to what extent these principles can provide *substantive* guidance to other environmental integration efforts is open to debate, as well as their effectiveness in actually doing so, questions that will also be discussed in chapter 7.

The establishment of councils or other agencies with a mandate to advance environmental integration, often based on the notion of sustainable development, is another form of institutional-internal integration adopted in many countries. In most cases, such councils have been given only an advisory role, but their importance lies in their ability and/or responsibility to take a broad view of environmental integration issues and needs, within and outside government. Usually at arm's length from day-to-day requirements associated with environmental management, such bodies, at least in theory, have the capacity to bring a strategic approach to environmental integration, based on the consideration of cognitive, political, and institutional dimensions. To what extent such agencies have been, or could become, important catalysts for environmental integration also will be addressed in chapter 7.

CONCLUSION

Environmental integration, it has been argued in this chapter, constitutes the essence of the environmental challenge. It is about the integration of an environmental dimension into all spheres of human thinking, decision-making, interaction, action, and behavior. This interpretation implies two interrelated tasks: first, incorporating an environmental dimension into all areas of management that (potentially) impact on the environment; second, to ensure that integration efforts do not negate each other or, formulated more positively, to enhance the coherence and consistency between efforts. The first is referred to here as the external dimension of environmental integration and the second as the internal dimension. For environmental integration to work, both are essential. External integration efforts must be guided by internal integration to make sense, while internal integration without external integration is unlikely to change anything in practice.

Although environmental integration is a challenge that can and must be taken up by individuals, it inevitably requires deliberation, decisions, and actions at the collective level. Individuals and groups have different conceptions of the environment and environmental requirements, based on different interests, needs, and beliefs. For environmental integration to work at the collective level, these differences will need to be addressed to avoid or minimize the likelihood that integration efforts are inconsistent, incompatible, and even counterproductive. Notwithstanding globalization, national governments play a central role in the advancement as well as the obstruction of environmental integration. From the 1960s onward, environmental integration has been an item on the agenda of many governments, albeit with fluctuating fortunes. Across time and geographical space, governments have adopted a variety of approaches to, and forms of, integration.

The overview of forms of integration discussed in this chapter illustrates the multiple ways by which environmental integration has been sought and advanced, in particular by governments at the national level. Although by no means exhaustive, it illustrates that governments have adopted a wide range of (external and internal) forms, mechanisms, or tools to advance environmental integration in all areas or dimensions of management. However, this does not mean that all, or even some, governments have taken a concerted approach to environmental integration. Governments differ in the extent to which they have relied on cognitive, policy, and institutional forms of integration. Often, they have concentrated their efforts in the development and adoption of forms in one or two of the six categories identified, to the extent that some have become leaders in a particular area. Neither does it mean that all forms have been applied or implemented with great enthusiasm, or that they are all effective. How effectively these forms have been applied, especially in those countries that are often considered leaders in the field, will be discussed in chapters 2 to 7.

Given the diversity of approaches, forms, mechanisms, and tools, it is perhaps not surprising that the common element, aim, or challenge behind them is often not recognized. Originating in different sources and backgrounds, and operating with different frameworks in different countries and contexts, they are often seen and treated as unrelated to one another. The value of putting them together into one framework, like the one provided here, is that it makes apparent not only their differences and limitations, but also that they are all part of the broad, multifaceted challenge that I have called environmental integration. Each form contributes, in different ways, to this challenge, but none provides a complete answer. As noted earlier, there is scope for thinking about how environmental integration can be improved, for instance—by linking forms and approaches, and by developing and introducing new forms of integration.

However, improving environmental integration is unlikely to be brought about simply by calls for comparing notes and cooperation between the schools of thought and practice associated with the various forms. The approaches to environmental integration adopted by governments, and the specific forms that they have introduced, cannot be explained merely, or even mainly, on the basis of rational or professional initiative. Although advancing environmental integration is, in part, a matter of design, technique, and collective learning, it is also, and foremost, a matter of politics. Associated with these different approaches, or even inherent to them, are differences in interests, ideology, and power. Mechanisms or tools for advancing environmental integration are embedded within and shaped by different ideologies or worldviews, and have different sociocultural and political-economic support bases. Tools and mechanisms for environmental integration can serve aims, purposes, and interests that are not just environmental. Thus, they are not objective or apolitical, as will become apparent in the analysis and discussion in the following chapters.

2

Cognitive-External Integration

INTRODUCTION

In chapter 1, cognitive environmental integration was described as having two elements: first, the integration of environmental knowledge into human thinking, deliberations, decisions, actions, and behavior (cognitive-external integration); second, the development of some overarching framework to provide or advance a coherent knowledge/interpretative basis for integrated (or "holistic") environmental management (cognitive-internal integration). In this chapter, I will further discuss and assess some of the main forms of cognitive-external integration.

Much of the effort of governments in the area of cognitive environmental integration has been directed at the integration of environmental information, knowledge, and values into decision-making about specific (development) projects and issues. Most prominent among these cognitive-external integration efforts have been environmental impact assessment (EIA), cost-benefit analysis (CBA), and risk analysis (RA). Building upon these three forms, integrated environmental assessment (IEA) has been developed as a tool for more comprehensively integrating knowledge and information in decision-making. As noted in chapter 1, a common feature of these forms of integration is the use of methods that claim to be "neutral" or scientific in their treatment of environmental information and values. Scientists or experts play a dominant role in the design and implementation of these forms of integration. However, as will be shown in this chapter, these forms are not value-free or devoid of politics. Their design and implementation are influenced by assumptions, choices, and interpretations that are influenced by values, interests, and politics.

As noted in the previous chapter, the United States has been at the forefront in the development of forms of cognitive-external integration. Perhaps the most significant and influential among the forms that originated in the United States has been environmental impact assessment. Arguably, EIA has become the most commonly used mechanism for integrating environmental considerations into decisions, in the public and private sector, that impact *directly* on the environment, not only in the United States, but also in many other countries that have adopted EIA systems and processes. Risk assessment and cost-benefit analysis were also first developed and applied in the United States to integrate environmental values into decision-making, but have been used on a lesser scale, especially in other countries. I will, therefore, give more space to the discussion and assessment of EIA than of RA and CBA. Integrated environmental assessment is a more recently developed tool that builds upon, or integrates, these three other tools, with the aim of providing a more encompassing cognitive basis for decision-making. Although the application of IEA (by governments) is still limited, I have chosen to briefly discuss it here because of its potential to infuse decision-making with a more integrated and improved understanding of the environment and the impact of human actions, and because it shares many of its underlying assumptions with EIA, RA, and CBA. For each form, I will shortly discuss its origins, rationales and (possible) functions, designs, and implementation, and outcomes, strengths, and limitations with respect to environmental integration, highlighting the role and influence of politics.

ENVIRONMENTAL IMPACT ASSESSMENT

Origins, Rationales, and Functions

Environmental impact assessment originated in the United States, where it was first introduced with the National Environmental Protection Act (NEPA) in 1970. Since the early 1960s, Lynton K. Caldwell, who can be described as the father of EIA, and who was instrumental in the development of NEPA, had been searching for "some method or technique which would compel planners and implementers to consider the socioecological consequences of their actions."[1] Caldwell, building upon arguments for applied ecology, advocated the expansion of ecological science to a multidisciplinary enterprise, encompassing also the social and behavioral sciences, to overcome its previously peripheral status in policy development and decision-making.[2] According to Caldwell, one of the architects of the NEPA, EIA was an integral part of the act's framework for national environmental policy that was aimed at redirecting national priorities. EIA was required to force federal agencies "to take the Act seriously, and to consider the environmental policy directives of the Congress in the formulation of agency plans and procedures."[3] In other words, EIA was as much, if not more, directed at changing the dominant culture and values within organizations as it was to prevent or mitigate environmental damage.

Caldwell's views imply that EIA can, and should, serve two functions. First, EIA can be a mechanism for enhancing the rationality of decision- and policy-making. Second, it can be used as a means for institutional reform directed at instilling "ecological rationality." A third, and more sceptical, possibility that needs to be added to these two is that EIA can serve a legitimating function. The proposition put forward here is that the significance of EIA cannot be derived analytically from any or even all of the proclaimed goals that are commonly associated with it (such as the prevention of environmental problems), but that EIA means different things to different actors involved. The mode of its implementation is the resultant of an interaction between different views on EIA and of the relative strength of the interests and actors behind these views.

"EIA aims at logical and rational decision-making."[4] Often environmental impact assessment is looked at as an objective or neutral instrument designed to avoid environmental deterioration. At the core of the process lies the idea that before (development) action is undertaken, environmental implications need to be objectively assessed. The information generated is then communicated to the decision-makers, who can take it into account, weighing its importance against other aspects or interests. The task of the environmental assessor is thus the strictly neutral and objective one of information provider.[5] EIA, from this perspective, revolves around the question "how to improve the intelligence that goes into environmental policy making."[6] Associated with this is an emphasis on science, methodology, and professional development. For instance, Canter argues that "environmental impact studies must be conducted from a scientific perspective and basis" and that not doing so "represents a complete misunderstanding of the concept of environmental impact studies and their requirements and potential uses."[7] However, although EIA uses and relies on science, it is itself usually referred to as a (systematic) process or procedure rather than as a science.[8]

A second function that can be associated with EIA, and is emphasised by Caldwell, is the promotion of reform directed at institutionalizing environmental values within the decision-making framework of the administrative state. As environmental values have tended to be ignored or underrated in the decision-making process, the problem is how to achieve a change in attitudes and practices within the agencies that are responsible for initiating actions with environmental implications (particularly those involved in the development of resources). According to Bartlett, EIA institutionalizes both procedural and substantive ecological rationality: "By requiring and encouraging political actors, as individuals and as organizations, to think ecologically and to consider environmental values, EIA imbeds procedural ecological rationality in political institutions. By establishing, continuously reaffirming, and progressively legitimating environmental values and ecological criteria as standards by which individual actions are to be structured, chosen and evaluated, EIA institutionalizes substantive ecological rationality."[9]

EIA, as a mechanism designed to promote ecological rationality within the government bureaucracy, may be an alternative to organizational reform, which is often difficult to achieve and uncertain in its effects. EIA, by changing the process of decision-making, attempts to guide the attitudes and actions of those involved in the policy process in the direction of incorporating environmental considerations.

Within this EIA perspective two further approaches can be distinguished, one emphasizing the use of mechanisms to effect change from within organizations—by, for example, promoting education of existing staff, or by necessitating the hiring of new personnel with ecological qualifications to prepare impact reports (the internal reform model)—and one in which outside agencies and mechanisms (such as "control" departments, coordination, litigation, public participation, or making the organization dependent on other organizations) are used to induce a change in attitudes and practices (the external reform model).[10] These approaches are not mutually exclusive and may be combined. Taylor, in his analysis of the institutionalization of environmental values in the US Forest Service and Army Corps of Engineers, points out the interplay between external and internal factors. Institutionalization of "precarious" values requires not only the existence of a group within the agency committed to the value, but also outside support for the inside group's goals.[11]

Changing processes and introducing mechanisms should, however, not be seen as sufficient for causing change in policy, attitudes, and practices. It has been rightly pointed out that human agency is an important factor in the success or failure of EIA as a mechanism for reform. The impact assessment process is not self-sustaining and self-regulating, but evolves in an interplay with the broader political process. Individual political entrepreneurs, using a variety of strategies (such as building coalitions, making a case on merits, promoting values) make an essential contribution to the evolution and outcome of the EIA politics and process.[12]

Apart from institutionalizing environmental values, EIA can also be seen as contributing toward a more general process of reform of the administrative state. It has been argued that EIA, by providing new opportunities for public input and public participation, has provided an open door to the administrative state. It has helped to undermine the traditional belief that what the government does is automatically in the public interest and that decision-making by government departments (experts) is value-free. EIA legitimizes the public's right to know and can be seen as an important step toward greater democracy in the making of decisions affecting the welfare of society and the environment.[13]

With the introduction of EIA new opportunities were created for public input into development decisions. The specific nature and form of these opportunities varies from country to country, related to the particular EIA-scheme that has been adopted. They vary from public hearings, submission-systems, appeal procedures, panels, and telephone hotlines to seminars, workshops, surveys and "Delphi-exercises."[14] Indeed, the only common feature seems to be an agreement that public participation allows for the introduction of value judgments into the process before final decisions are being taken and that it is not just a mechanism for gathering more information (although the value of public participation in this respect is also often recognized). Potential benefits of public participation are seen in a reduction of opposition to proposals and consequently a facilitation of implementation, depolarization (a "safety-valve for pent-up feelings"), and an enhanced level of democracy and legitimacy of the decision-making process.[15]

Although EIA is not the only instrument used by environmental groups to express their concerns and promote their ideas, the new opportunities have been used more or less intensively, depending on how hot the issues are.[16] Overall, EIA has been supported by environmentalists as an important check on developers, and has been adopted as a provision that, if anything, needs to be strengthened and extended. On the other hand, however, it has been argued that EIA is too much a part of the "rational" tradition to allow for a more "ideological" approach, and that environmentalists run the risk of being trapped or captured by relying too heavily on EIA as an instrument.[17]

A third, more skeptical, perspective on EIA is that it serves to legitimize actions or developments that are socially or environmentally damaging. In this view, EIA is used by those committed to development in government, government departments and the private sector, for justifying development projects. EIA, on this basis, is a process for overcoming public opposition and for making projects acceptable by granting minor concessions, and particularly by subjecting proposals to a quasi-legal procedure providing them an official stamp of approval. This view has been associated with those theories of the state that emphasize its role in advancing "system imperatives." The state's function is to stabilize the system's performance by engaging in preventive crisis management and consensus-formation processes. These processes do not generally yield substantive solutions, but generate rules and procedures that appear to be optimally efficient and value-free. As such, they help to maintain the smooth functioning of the system and to legitimize the state's authority.[18] "For administrators . . . what is often politically useful about the EIS is not that it increases the rationality of their decisions—but that it enhances the *appearance* of rationality and thus serves to undermine environmental opposition to development projects."[19]

This perspective challenges the scientific nature of EIA as advocated in the first approach, and contradicts that EIA can be successfully used as a strategy for reform, as proposed in the second perspective. Instead, what it does is "provide legitimation to the State's environmental policies and procedures and to those groups that have the greatest stake in the continuance of those policies." Environmental assessments, in this view "are not designed to provide hard evidence that will be decisive in determining the direction of the State's concern with the environment. Rather, they tend to underwrite decisions that have already been made. Thus, social-impact assessments are more ideological than they are scientific."[20]

One does not have to agree with these theoretical interpretations, however, to observe that EIA may be used as a symbolic device. As Bartlett notes: "We know that EIA certainly can exist merely as symbolic window dressing, with little or no influence on choice processes."[21] In fact, much of the criticism on EIA provides support for the argument that it is a legitimating device. It has been argued that, if applied late in the decision-making process, it is little more than a paper exercise, "wasting money and ruffling tempers."[22] If only performed on a project level, leaving policies untouched, important sources of environmental degradation will persist. Clark states that "unless an environmental instinct is implanted at the policy determining level . . . EIA will tend to be a cosmetic exercise."[23] Dealing with development on a project-by-project basis, as EIA usually does, fails to address the cumulative effects of multiple developments, the combined strength of which may amount to a de facto policy change.[24]

In sum, EIA was advanced initially as a means for "greening" political and administrative institutions, processes, policies, and practices. However, the institutionalization of EIA sparked the growth of an industry of professionals and practitioners that gave it an aura of objectivity and rigor, confirmed by the way courts, notably in the United States, weigh "evidence" about potential environmental effects. At face value, then, EIA has become a "rational" tool for cognitive environmental integration that is scientific, multidisciplinary, objective, and geared toward enhancing knowledge of the (potential) environmental implications of proposals, as an input into the decision-making process. However, EIA can also serve to legitimate development under the cover of science and objectivity. Which function EIA performs (most) depends on the way it has been institutionalized, and on the relative power and influence exerted by the parties involved in the process.

Designs and Implementation

The (mix of) functions EIA serves may differ from country to country, or system to system, and depends on its specific form (whether and how it has been institutionalized), and on the relative power of those involved in shaping and implementing it. The rational, science-based view of the EIA trend has been particularly strong in the United States, where the Council of Environmental Quality enunciated in the 1979 regulations for federal EIAs that every attempt should be made to use scientific and quantitative techniques.[25] And as environmental impact statements can be legally challenged, the production of environmental impact statements that would stand up in the courts became the main concern. As a result, many impact statements entered into considerable detail and made use of sophisticated modeling and techniques to demonstrate the (limited) effects of proposed actions, or how they can be mitigated. At the same time, agencies tried to meet this legislative requirement (regulation) in a way that caused the least disruption to their traditional roles and practices. However, many other countries have avoided introducing EIA systems of such a litigious nature.[26]

Nonetheless, EIA has been the subject of widespread emulation around the world. Australia, Canada, and New Zealand were early adopters, but many other countries followed.[27] The spread of EIA has been facilitated by international organizations, such as the OECD, the United Nations Environment Programme, and the World Bank. Although no international agreement requires low-income countries to introduce EIA legislation, many may have done so believing that this would enhance their chances of getting foreign aid. In 1989, the World Bank made it compulsory for all projects sponsored by the bank that could have a significant negative impact on the environment to be subjected to EIA, a practice that was subsequently followed by other development banks.[28] International organizations are said to have been effective in diffusing EIA; especially so because of "their appearance of being objective, impartial, and consultative," and as EIA methodology has been imparted with science's aura of impartiality and claims of objectivity and universality.[29] In the European Union, EIA became mandatory for member countries with the adoption of the European Council directive on EIA in 1985.[30]

Despite the differences between EIA systems, it appears that there have been common themes in their development. In part, this can be attributed to the development of EIA as a discipline. Among the sizeable literature on the topic, one can find many (hand)books on how to undertake EIA, presenting and discussing a range of guidelines, tools, and techniques, based on "best practice" and principles and criteria that are considered essential.[31] Much of the literature provides a positive perspective on EIA, regarding it as an important tool in the anticipation and prevention of environmental problems, and for seeking "a harmonious relationship between development and the environment" and advancing sustainability.[32] Among the experts, considerable agreement appears to have emerged about the important steps or elements of EIA, such as screening, scoping, the consideration of alternatives, public consultation or participation, review of the impact statement, and monitoring.[33] Such elements are often used to evaluate EIA performance or the quality of EIA systems across countries.[34]

Although EIA advocates and professionals commonly interpret "environment" in broad terms, encompassing biophysical (ecological), social, and economic dimensions or aspects, in practice institutionalized EIA systems are often based on less-comprehensive definitions of what is environmental. In some systems, like that adopted in the United Kingdom, the biophysical effects of activities, and notably the impacts of pollution on the natural and built environment as well as on humans, tend to be the focus of concern, whereas in other jurisdictions the environment, for the purpose of EIA, is defined more broadly to include cultural, social, and economic factors.[35] In Ontario, Canada, the environment is defined to include social, economic, and cultural conditions, whereas the federal Canadian system is more restrictive, focusing on biophysical aspects, and considering the social, economic, and cultural effects only where these result from biophysical effects.[36] A similar situation exists in New Zealand, where the term "environment" is defined in legislation as comprising social, cultural, and economic elements, but where, in practice, these are interpreted mostly in a biophysical context. As noted in chapter 1, restricting the social dimension of the environment concept to biophysical conditions that have a (potential) impact on human well-being makes sense, as it prevents the concept from becoming all-encompassing and thereby meaningless.

EIA systems also differ with regard to the rules that govern what proposals should be subjected to environmental assessment, and what should be included in environmental impact assessments, often referred to as "coverage" in the EIA literature. Coverage relates to both the range of activities or proposals for which an EIA is formally required, and to the range of (environmental) aspects or issues that need to be covered by an EIA, also referred to as "scoping."[37] Often, EIA is only formally required for proposed developments of a minimum size or that meet certain criteria, specified in lists, as in the Netherlands and the system adopted by the European Union.[38] By contrast, the New Zealand system is almost infinitely flexible, leaving it to proponents and consent authorities to determine the kind of environmental assessment that needs to be undertaken, and what to include.[39] In general, the rules or guidelines for EIA are directed at identifying "significant" environmental effects of development proposals rather than at ensuring the assessment of *all* proposals or *all* possible effects. Scoping was first introduced in the United States in 1979 as a formal requirement to prevent the environmental assessment process from getting bogged down in debate about detail, as appeared to occur increasingly during the 1970s; it has been adopted in several other countries since.[40]

What "significant" environmental effects are is open to interpretation, and influenced by knowledge, values, and environmental ideology. It is not unusual for concerns to focus on the effects on "glamor species" rather than on the effects on "lower" species, or ecosystems as a whole. Where the effects on ecosystems are considered, it is often assumed that the effects are acceptable as long as "environmental bottom lines" are not crossed; they are not measured against existing or desirable levels of environmental quality. However, given the complexity of ecological systems and interactions, the notion of ecological bottom lines is highly problematic. In practice, the tendency in environmental assessments is to focus on effects that can, by some measure, be quantified, and to assign less weight to effects of a qualitative nature. For instance, when EIA includes an assessment of effects on social impacts or human well-being, quantifiable effects like noise and the value of properties tend to carry some weight, whereas less-tangible aspects such as people's dislike of a proposed development will not usually be regarded as an important or legitimate ground for withholding approval. However—to some extent, at least—the scope of an EIA is influenced by public pressure and politics.[41] The stronger the public opposition to a proposed development, the more likely it is that the concerns expressed will be incorporated in the assessment.

So, although EIA has the potential to consider the environmental effects of proposals comprehensively and in an integrated manner, the extent to which it does so is contingent on the particular system and context. In practice, the tendency is to narrow the scope of EIA to the more immediate ecological or biophysical effects on the environment. Resource considerations (such as the impact on global resource availability, or whether developments imply a desirable or wise use of resources), broader social issues (such as impacts on community perceptions of a desirable environment), and the effects on the environment and people of other countries are often considered to be beyond the scope of EIA. But the biggest limitation of EIA is that it is mostly confined to the assessment of projects on a case-by-case basis. Although EIA systems often require the consideration of cumulative effects, this is not only difficult because of the complexity of assessing these, but simply impossible in the absence of a policy or planning framework that takes account of local, national, and global environmental limits and competing demands in a global and long-term context. Arguably, this could be remedied by linking EIA with sustainable development policy, possibly by expanding environmental impact assessment to sustainability assessment, which will be discussed in chapter 4.

As noted above, EIA is often touted as a scientific and objective mechanism for establishing the environmental implications of proposals. Although most advocates and analysts of EIA acknowledge that values and judgements inevitably influence environmental assessment, science and experts are commonly assigned a central role in the process. This is often confirmed by the institutional arrangements for EIA in terms of requirements, responsibilities, and decision rules. However, science, despite its mantle of objectivity, is not value-free,[42] and increasingly scientists play a partisan role in development, as employees of companies, as (research) consultants, or because they have a direct financial stake in the development of new technologies.[43] Although most EIA systems provide for public input in the process, the influence of citizens and environmental groups is usually constrained by limitations of time and other resources, more so than is the case for proponents and public officials. This also limits their ability to mobilize scientists and experts as their advocates in the EIA process. Science and experts play a crucial role in the politics of EIA. As in all politics, the EIA playing field is far from level.

Outcomes, Strengths, and Limitations

That decision-making techniques like environmental impact assessment, cost-benefit analysis, and environmental dispute resolution play a political role has been pointed out cogently by Douglas Amy.[44] Amy notes how, in the United States, "the adoption of particular methods is often more a response to powerful political interests than the product of an intellectual search for the most rational technique" and that "we must understand how these techniques have served the interests of powerful groups both inside and outside the state and how the distribution of power among those groups has changed over time."[45] EIA, according to Amy, has been introduced primarily as a means for rationalizing and legitimating decisions made on nonenvironmental grounds. It serves not only development interests, but also the interests of administrators by enhancing "the *appearance* of rationality" (original emphasis) of decisions.[46] It also helps to undermine or silence the more radical environmental critics of development, as their opposition can be dismissed as irrational. This rather cynical view of EIA has received support also in other countries. Weston, for instance, argues that in the United Kingdom EIA is part of a political decision-making process that has not been fundamentally altered with its introduction, and that in a legal-adversarial decision-making system like that of the United Kingdom, there is no incentive for developers and authorities (both of whom regard the public as "the enemy") to promote public participation or to produce more than minimal impact statements, as the process is likely to increase the demands on them regardless of the statements they produce.[47] In Canada, EIA has remained discretionary and under the control of the provinces, which can be attributed to the constellation of politics and power associated with the importance of, and dependence on, resource industries.[48] The way EIA has been applied in some low-income countries leads Briffet to note that it often serves "as a means to show how environmentally friendly a development can be, using mitigating measures which are invariably too late, too insignificant, too ineffective or too difficult to implement."[49]

That political interests and bias (can) influence EIA is often borne out by its outcomes. Given the way EIA is institutionalized in many countries, and that the playing field is often tilted in favor of economic and pro-development interests because of their greater resources, command of or access to expertise, and legal constraints on public input and scrutiny, it is not surprising that economic interests prevail in most cases, and that EIAs seldom stop development proposals altogether. In the United States, examples of the manipulation of science, including via the environmental impact assessment process, have been provided in two recent reports of the Union of Concerned Scientists. In one case, the Bush administration created a review team made up of predominantly nonscientists who proceeded to overrule a plan for managing old-growth forest habitat and reducing the risk of fire. In another case, an environmental impact statement on the practice of mountaintop strip mining was manipulated in an effort to play down its environmental effects.[50] Moreover, in some countries, such as the United Kingdom and New Zealand, legislation or official policies establish formally a presumption in favor of development.[51] Despite the costs and delays that may be associated with EIA, therefore, it can be seen as serving development interests as it legitimizes proposals, providing them a "green gloss" by tagging on environmental mitigation measures. It has also been argued, however, that political bias can also influence EIA methodology in such a way that negative effects of development proposals are exaggerated.[52] Where EIA allows for public input, environmental groups and citizens who are opposed to particular development on social or philosophical grounds can try to use EIA to stop such development by exaggerating the potential effects on the biophysical environment. Businesses sometimes use it to try to stop competitors from establishing themselves or expanding in "their" area.

One way or the other, EIA is not the objective or scientific tool that some advocates make it out to be. These observations demonstrate that EIA is not simply a process of informing decision-making, of "feeding" decision-makers with the "best-quality information" about the likely impact of proposals. Rather, the process of gathering, selecting, and presenting information is shaped in large measure by the interplay of political-ideological and social and economic interests operating within in a particular institutional context, at a particular time. As EIA is influenced, or even shaped, by politics, the outcomes tend to reflect the relative power and interests of groups and individuals in society. That does not mean that EIA cannot deliver environmental benefits, especially in the form of avoiding or mitigating (more) environmental harm. But the extent to which it does so depends on the power and influence of the various parties involved, largely assisted or obstructed by the way it has been institutionalized. Rather than being a neutral, knowledge-based decision-making support tool, it is really just another battleground where conflicting interests and views compete with knowledge and science as the main weapons.

How effective EIA has been in terms of integrating environmental values and interests into policies, decisions, designs, and actions, and in preventing or mitigating environmental harm, is difficult to determine, methodologically as well as empirically. Assessing the effect of EIA in a context where many other factors (such as the influence of public opinion, countervailing interests and powers, and other developments) impact on the environment is problematic. In many countries, systems for monitoring the "uptake" of recommendations or decisions from EIA statements are weak or nonexistent. The European Union's EIA directive does not prescribe the audit of the implementation of EIA, or the monitoring of outcomes, and no such provisions have been adopted in the United Kingdom.[53]

Some research has been undertaken on the effects that were foreseen in environmental impact statements. Studies in the United States and the United Kingdom indicate that about half of the predictions about effects that could be tested proved to be accurate, and that, in general, there were no significant unanticipated effects.[54] But most evaluations of EIA rely on criteria related to the principles, processes, and conditions (including institutional arrangements) for undertaking "good" assessments, such as the stage at which EIA has been initiated, scoping requirements and practices, provisions for public input or participation, independent auditing, and the institutional-legal basis of EIA.[55] Such evaluations are based on the assumption that environmental considerations are more likely to be integrated into decision-making if these criteria are met. However, whether the quality of EIA systems can be assessed objectively on the basis of one model or ideal system, or general criteria for "best practice," is questionable. EIA systems have been introduced and adapted to the specific needs and institutional arrangements of countries. For instance, countries that already have elements of EIA in their planning and decision-making systems may not choose to introduce totally independent EIA decision-making systems, such as in the United States.[56] However, this does not mean that there is no scope for improving EIA performance in all countries.

Based on the normative criteria used by Wood, the EIA system adopted in the Netherlands can been considered as one of the better ones. The Dutch system almost fully meets the full range of Wood's fourteen criteria, whereas that in the United States meets eleven, the UK system only meets four; the systems adopted in Canada, Australia, and New Zealand are somewhere in between.[57] However, given the difficulties associated with such assessments, such findings should be treated with caution. They do not measure actual outcomes, and are best seen as indications of the level of development of EIA in a country. Even in countries with well-developed EIA systems, the extent to which EIA has been effective in terms of providing environmental protection and mitigating or preventing environmental damage remains largely unknown. Weston argues that the overall impact of EIA in the United Kingdom has been marginal, as less than 0.07 percent of the total number of planning applications in each year is subjected to EIA.[58] In New Zealand, where nominally all development proposals are subjected to some form of environmental assessment, the extent to which EIA prevents environmental deterioration is an open question, because of a weakness of monitoring capacity and practices. The ability of implementing agencies to undertake their EIA responsibilities may be constrained by inadequate funding and expertise. This is often the case in low-income countries,[59] but can also be an issue in richer countries.[60]

Arguably, in line with Caldwell's original vision, the main significance of EIA lies in the extent to which it forces agencies to green their policies, decisions, and actions and, more fundamentally, contributes to the internalization of environmental awareness within organizations, the business sector, among decision-makers, or in society at large. Several analysts argue that, in the United States, EIA has indeed effected changes in organizational behavior.[61] However, given the issues associated with the implementation and the politics of EIA discussed above and its limitations with regard to influencing policy development, the extent of change that EIA has brought about, and is able to bring about, in organizational, policy, and business cultures is debatable. Moreover, the extent of this influence is also hard to establish, because the level of environmental awareness in organizations and society at large is also affected by other factors, including exposure to environmental problems and disasters, the activities of citizens' and environmental groups, the amount of attention given to environmental issues in education and the media, and government support for environmental issues.

More fundamental, however, are the inherent limitations to the notion of EIA itself. One limitation already mentioned is that it deals mostly with projects (or even plans and policies) on a case-by-case basis, and cannot cope with the cumulative effects of numerous developments in an anticipatory way. EIA methodology is based on the assumption that the basic elements of a proposal have been determined within a particular organizational and geographical context (at most extended to a few alternative sites) within which the effects of proposals can be predicted with a reasonable degree of accuracy or probability. EIA does not, and cannot, provide a framework for determining and steering development based on environmental criteria, such as resource considerations, the ecological capacity of regions, and social desiderata, across sectors and organizations. It is not a mechanism for *designing* (types of) developments based on such criteria. EIA only kicks in after the desirability of proposals has been determined on economic and/or political grounds. Even if undertaken at an early stage, EIA is reactive and tagged on. In practice, it can only mitigate (or perhaps avoid) the *additional* environmental effects of (a proportion of) the continuous stream of development initiatives driven by economic and political "imperatives." And even where EIA is applied in a system that has adopted sustainability as an overarching principle or goal for resource management, as in New Zealand, it is implemented in a way that focuses attention mainly on the biophysical *effects* of proposals.[62] EIA has not *reduced*, and cannot reduce, the *overall* impacts of human activities.

To achieve the latter, environmental rationality will need to be integrated into the decisions, policies, and institutions that drive and guide economic growth and development within and across countries. Arguably, this is what is implied in the notion of sustainable development. It also underlies the idea of strategic environmental assessment (SEA), as well as other mechanisms aimed at the greening of policies, which are discussed in chapter 4.

COST-BENEFIT ANALYSIS

Origins, Rationales and Functions

CBA finds its roots in the notion of "marginal analysis" developed by Jules Dupuit in the mid-nineteenth century, but it was first applied in the 1930s in the United States, especially in the assessment of the costs and benefits of public works.[63] Increasingly, following a growing recognition of the economic importance of environmental values, it is also being used to integrate such values into decision-making.[64] In the United States, its application received a boost in 1981 under President Reagan, who introduced a requirement for all new major regulation to be subjected to CBA (Executive Order 12291). A similar requirement was also introduced in the United Kingdom in 1993 and in the European Union for directives.[65]

Like EIA, CBA is generally regarded as a decision-support tool, used to inform decision-makers, not a substitute for decision-making. However, whereas (environmental) scientists play a central role in the design and implementation of EIA, CBA is practiced mostly by economists. The main rationale underlying CBA is to provide a monetary assessment of the likely effects (positive and negative) of proposals, or to identify the most cost-effective means, measures, or solutions that have been put forward to achieve certain objectives. As governments and most other decision-makers have limited amounts of money available to them, and are unable to meet all (competing) objectives and demands upon them, CBA is seen as a useful or valuable tool for deciding what gives the biggest bang for a buck. Proposals that generate more costs than benefits are unlikely to be regarded as attractive or acceptable. When different proposals or solutions are able to meet certain needs, demands, or objectives, it makes sense to assess their relative merits in monetary terms. Not surprisingly, as the costs of addressing environmental problems and meeting environmental objectives rise and governments are confronted with budget constraints, CBA comes to be seen and adopted as an attractive tool in helping to decide on priorities.

The main function of CBA, therefore, lies in enhancing the cost-effectiveness of decisions, not in creating a better understanding of the (potential) environmental effects of proposals, or in preventing or mitigating environmental harm. CBA relies on information from science and experts (and often EIA) for identifying (potential) effects, measures, or solutions. Practiced by economists, the function of CBA is not to identify or understand better the nature or causes of environmental issues, or to identify or design the means, solutions, or courses of action that may be desirable or essential from an environmental point of view. Problems, interpretations, and possible solutions are taken as givens, provided by other experts, decision-makers, or the public at large. In other words, CBA practitioners do not impose their own views, interpretations, or solutions on their assessments, but incorporate those put forward by others. This, combined with the quantitative and apparently neutral methodology used by CBA, gives it the appearance of objectivity and rigor.

However, as with EIA, CBA can serve other functions than those that are commonly put forward as its main rationale, in this case enhancing cost-effectiveness. CBA can serve, and has served, political purposes, and can be used as a basis for legitimating decisions that affect the environment, and environmental action, detrimentally. It can also justify decisions not to adopt environmental measures or proposals, as their monetary costs are considered to outweigh their benefits. CBA, as we will explain in the next section, can serve almost any purpose, depending on the way it is designed and implemented.

Designs and Implementation

The variability of CBA-applications begins with the many different ways by which CBA is defined. There is not one generally agreed definition of CBA. Lumley notes that "almost every facet of CBA is subject to some level of disagreement" and that "there are almost as many definitions of CBA as there are books about it."[66] Despite this diversity, however, the following elements appear to be common in many interpretations: the costs and benefits of a proposal are assessed in monetary terms; it is based on the "expressed" or "revealed" preferences of individuals; where no markets and prices exist, CBA uses methods for generating prices; and future values (of costs and benefits) are discounted (discount rate). Although CBA has been applied mostly at the project level, it can be applied also to plans, programs, or policies.

Many environmental values (such as clean air, biodiversity, and ecosystems) are not traded, and therefore have no market price. CBA practitioners use a range of tools to determine the monetary value of such goods, including the Contingent Valuation Method, which measures individuals' willingness to pay (WTP) or willingness to accept compensation (WTA), the travel-cost method, and the hedonic pricing technique.[67] The "monetized" preferences, potential costs and benefits, as assessed by selected individuals are added up to determine whether the potential gains of the proposal outweigh the costs. Future costs and benefits are recalculated to reflect their value at the present time, using a discount rate based on a variety of considerations.

As an economists' tool, CBA is grounded in economic ideas, theory, and underlying assumptions associated with economic theory. Most important among these are the assumptions that environmental values can be quantified and expressed in monetary terms, and that the value of environmental goods consists of the sum of individual preferences. Moreover, while modern welfare economics has rejected the possibility of cardinally measuring utility, CBA assumes cardinality by adding up the money measures of utility to show how far a project is preferred to its alternatives, rather than merely ranking alternatives.[68] CBA also assumes that consumers are well informed, and are knowledgeable about environmental consequences. And it recommends that options be selected on the basis of the *assumption* that losers can be compensated by winners (while still leaving the latter better-off), whereas in practice no actual compensation need take place (the Kaldor-Hicks criterion).[69]

All these assumptions can be contested, however. The "monetization" of environmental values has been the subject of considerable debate, in part because of the reductionist and anthropocentric views of the environment on which it is based, and because of its social-psychological consequences,[70] reasons for many environmentalists to oppose CBA. Although some economists dismiss much of this opposition as "emotive and irrational,"[71] others agree that in many cases this is problematic, in particular since calculations based on the utility of such values for individuals cannot be equated to the ecological values (functions) of ecosystems, or to the value of collective goods to society. Given the assumptions underlying CBA, there is a lack of clarity and agreement as to what it is actually measuring. Even among economists there is an ongoing discussion about the merits and shortcomings of CBA, leading one author to state that "as more and more research on both theoretical and empirical grounds is being accumulated, the more distant seems the convergence over an agreement on the validity and usefulness of the relevant technique for decision-making purposes concerning the environment."[72]

Much of the controversy about CBA relates to its (potential) use for political ends. It has been argued that CBA has been promoted in particular by proponents of the "free market" and the New Right, who wish to minimize the role of the state and reduce regulation, often promulgated under the guise of concern about the inefficiency of government.[73] As noted above, CBA got a considerable boost in the United States when its application to all proposals for major new regulations was made mandatory, arguably to forestall new regulatory policies and to assist in the deregulation of the market economy.[74] The rise in the popularity and spread of CBA among governments appears to have followed the ascendance and spread of neoliberal ideology around the world.[75] Where CBA is based on the Kaldor-Hicks criterion, referred to above, and transfers indeed do not take place, CBA may benefit the haves at the expense of the have-nots, and may well lead to "adverse distributional consequences."[76]

In part, the political nature of CBA derives from its underlying assumptions and methodology that are in line with neoclassical economic theory, and that advance a conception of society as the simple sum of self-interested individuals whose main aim in life is to maximize their own interests. Whereas CBA, in theory, claims to include *all* costs and benefits, in fact it is concerned with only one core value: money. CBA "has no moral context beyond that of utility maximization,"[77] and ignores values that are of a collective and less tangible nature such as justice and equity, the intrinsic value of nature, community cohesion, and a sense of security, solidarity, and ethical considerations in general. The amount that people are willing to pay, or to accept as compensation, is undeniably affected by their level of income and wealth. Yet, CBA takes for granted existing inequalities in income and wealth, and thus its outcomes are biased in favor of those with a greater purchasing power.[78]

In part, also, the political nature of CBA flows from its malleability in the hands of its practitioners. To a large extent, the outcomes of CBA are affected by the choice of techniques, the discount rate, the selection of respondents, and how questions are formulated. The selection of WTP or WTA as a basis for measuring preferences consistently produces different results, as people systematically value gains less than equivalent losses, and reflects different political-ideological positions regarding property rights.[79] The choice of discount rate affects the outcome of CBA, and raises complex issues about the intergenerational equity and the substitutability between natural and human-made capital. Higher rates make resource exploitation projects less attractive because they yield lower benefit/cost ratios,[80] but whether a high or a low discount rate is environmentally preferable depends also on the type of project. CBA can also be manipulated to achieve certain results by the exclusion of long-term future costs, and the selection of the population over which the benefits are aggregated.[81] Lekakis notes that "alternative descriptions of the ecological good yield different images of the good to respondents" and that, when additional information on the ecological good is provided to respondents, this results in significantly different WTP values.[82]

All in all, it seems that CBA can be manipulated to the degree that one gets what one is looking for. Despite its inherent ideological bias referred to above, therefore, it is not impossible that it *can* be used to advance environmental interests, especially in cases where projects make little economic sense. Arguably, this is a reason why, in the United Kingdom, the Environment Department now is an advocate of CBA, whereas the Department of Transport opposes CBA; taking account of the environmental costs of building roads possibly makes expanding the road network look less rational, even from an economic point of view.[83]

This makes the questions *who* undertakes CBA and *by what process* it is undertaken all the more important. Several authors note that there is a risk of "institutional capture," and refer to instances where CBA has been applied by agencies to serve their own interests or those of powerful interest groups.[84] Undertaken by pro-development agencies, public and private alike, it is most likely to deliver different results than if it is done by economists of a pro-environmental bent. Where CBA is undertaken on conditions that allow for wider public and environmental input and review, it is may generate outcomes that are less biased in favor of development. In Australia, a CBA of a mining proposal in the vicinity of a national park, undertaken independently from the proponent, became "highly controversial," as the methodology used was strongly contested by the mining companies involved. Ironically, however, a permit for the mine was refused not because of the outcome of the quantitatively based cost-benefit analysis, but on sociocultural grounds—namely, the value of the area to the indigenous people.[85]

Outcomes, Strengths, and Limitations

The example referred to above illustrates a discrepancy between the outcome of a CBA and a government decision that is not uncommon. Pearce notes that, in the United Kingdom, there is an "apparent gap between the widespread practice of CBA and the fact that decisions appear not heavily influenced by CBA."[86] In many situations, governments will (need to) consider a broader range of demands and factors than those related to economic efficiency, including other economic considerations such as competitiveness and employment. CBA, therefore, is indeed just one of the tools or inputs of government decision-making, and most advocates of CBA would agree that it has to be that way. Pearce notes that part of the opposition to CBA may have been fueled by some of the advocates of CBA who "overstated their case, making it sound as if CBA substitutes for decision-making."[87] But increasingly, noneconomists take part in the debate about CBA, often from a critical stance, making it harder for economists to stake their claim on such a position.[88]

Given that CBA can be, and often is, used as a political tool, one should heed the advice offered by Hanley and Splash that "analysts should proceed with great caution in conducting and appraising CBA studies."[89] Never should it be allowed to become a substitute for decision-making under the guise of claims that it is an objective, science-based tool for weighing up the costs and benefits of proposals, including their environmental costs and benefits. The fact that CBA and its outcomes are inevitably molded by decisions regarding methodology and techniques makes reference to it as an evolving science, a "science of benefit estimation,"[90] both inappropriate and misleading. As the methodology and techniques of CBA are *inherently* political, as explained above, serving and affecting interests differently, CBA does not simply feed information or knowledge into the decision-making process.

In some respects, CBA provides for a more comprehensive approach toward environmental integration than EIA. Although EIA systems may provide for the assessment of social effects of (proposed) developments, in practice the scope for doing so is often narrowly circumscribed; for instance, it may confine the assessment mainly to effects on human health and amenity values. In EIA, the emphasis is usually on the assessment of biophysical environmental effects. Social impact assessment (SIA) has been developed as a separate ("side") branch of impact assessment, and economic issues and aspects are commonly excluded from EIA. CBA, however, offers scope for including an analysis and assessment of economic and social effects, as well as biophysical ones, or even *all* effects, as is sometimes claimed.

However, although CBA may appear to be a more integrative tool than EIA, it is in some respects more *reductionist* than EIA. Whereas EIA sets out to capture the complexity of ecological systems and environmental effects, complemented by an assessment of the implications for the quality and availability of resources, CBA reduces the environment and environmental effects to one common denominator, money. Apart from the methodological issues that this raises, already referred to above, such an approach reduces the debate about the merits and demerits of proposed developments or actions to their monetary consequences. The focus on (potential) monetary gains and losses for affected parties is likely to deflect the attention away from the reality of biophysical and social consequences and implications, and their importance in nonmonetary respects. If one accepts the assumptions underlying CBA, such as the assumption that CBA is based on *perfect* knowledge, that humans are *solely* driven by money, and that the *only* value of the environment lies in its potential for humans to gain financially from it, this might not matter. But for those who see more in the environment than monetary value, this approach to cognitive environmental integration offers a bleak outlook on the world.

RISK ASSESSMENT

Origins, Rationales, and Functions

Risk assessment (RA), which also goes under the labels "risk analysis" and "risk management," like EIA and cost-benefit analysis, also originated in the United States. Although humans have assessed and managed risks throughout history, RA as a means of systematically and quantitatively assessing risks started to play an important role in the policy process in the 1960s, and became a distinct discipline in the early 1970s.[91]

Originally, RA was applied mostly to the assessment of the hazards associated with chemicals, which became an important responsibility of the Environmental Protection Agency (EPA) after its establishment in 1970. In the course of the 1960s, the potential effects of chemicals on human health—in particular, by causing cancer—had become a major public health issue. RA methodology was developed specifically for assessing the risks associated with this issue. Central concepts in this methodology are the notions of hazard, magnitude, exposure, dose-response assessment, and probability. Initially, the main use and aim of RA was to determine the levels at which human exposure to hazardous substances become a threat to human health, as a basis for the regulation of those substances.

Over time, however, RA came to consider also risks to the environment, not only for humans, and to include an assessment of economic costs and benefits. Faced with the need to regulate numerous substances that potentially posed a threat to humans and the environment, RA assisted the EPA to: (1) set priorities, (2) adjust national regulations to the degree and distribution of the risk to be controlled, and (3) make site-specific decisions by considering the nature of the pollutant, the sensitivity of the environmental setting, and the availability of control techniques.[92] Thus, RA provided the basis for the comparative risk assessment (CRA), the systematic comparison of a range of risks, as an information/knowledge basis for making decisions about priorities. It will be discussed in chapter 5.

Designs and Implementation

As a decision support tool, RA shares similarities with EIA in that it is directed at improving decision-making by identifying the potential effects of decisions. Both tools rely heavily on science and rational-analytical methods for the identification and interpretation of the potential consequences of decisions. The main difference between the two lies in the characterization of effects and methodology. Where EIA characterizes effects as "environmental" (interpreted-more-or less broadly, as discussed above), RA interprets effects as "risks." Although the term "risk" also can be (and has been) interpreted differently, as we will discuss below, it bears or emphasizes an element of threat, especially threat to humans. Whereas EIA suggests less of an anthropocentric focus, and can center on the potential consequences for nonhuman species (implying a higher degree of environmental inclusiveness), RA focuses on the implications of effects (including ecological effects, if considered) to humans. Moreover, RA "translates" and reduces risks in quantitative, and often monetary, terms (assessing the costs and benefits of options), to identify optimal or best solutions, or to determine priorities, whereas EIA methodology usually does not involve reducing effects to a single common denominator (as CBA and RA do) as a basis for arriving at conclusions. With this specific focus and methodology, RA has evolved as a particular discipline with its own professional bodies and journals. However, in practice, both CBA and RA are often used in combination with EIA, informing EIA findings and recommendations and vice versa.

The emergence of risk assessment as a discipline brought with it a notion of risk that could be objectively and scientifically analyzed and assessed. Risk analysts, according to this line of thinking, are able to understand and measure quantitatively the "real" risks that humans (and/or the environment) face. In traditional RA, the chances of death, injury and illness (in particular, cancer) were used as the main measures for the risk to health, as these can be quantified and objectively determined. Consequently, risk analysts took (and often still take) the view that they can develop a true picture of the risks facing people in society. They often contrast this with the wrong perception that most people have of risks. To educate the public (by one-way communication) about the real levels of risks, "risk communication" developed as a specialist branch within RA. Although two-way communication (listening to the public) is now seen as important to understanding people's attitudes to risk, the literature in this field continues to be concerned mainly with efforts to explain the "irrational" cultural and value aspects of risk perception.[93]

From very early on, risk analysts have admitted that determining what levels of risk are acceptable is beyond their capacity to answer, and belongs to the realm of policy and politics. Proponents of a scientific approach to RA commonly distinguish between risk analysis or assessment, which is seen as a largely scientific enterprise (assessing what the risks are), and risk management (determining what level of risk is acceptable, what should be done about them), which is regarded as a value-based or political assessment. This distinction, first advocated by William Lowrance, received endorsement from the EPA and "remains a basic tenet in the literature on risk assessment."[94]

Many have challenged the view that values and politics can and should be kept out of risk analysis. Russell and Gruber note that the separation between risk analysis and risk management is not easy to sustain, as the former inevitably involves making (policy) assumptions.[95] What is a risk depends in large measure on who does the analysis. As Armour points out, the notions of risk and risky are products of sociopolitical processes, and how these terms are defined and explained "necessarily reflects the value judgments of those doing the defining and explaining."[96]

Andrews argues that "[g]iven these many unavoidable judgements, the conclusions of health risk assessments are inevitably shaped far more by their assumptions than by objective 'facts.' "[97] O'Brien comments that uncertainty and a lack of complete knowledge and understanding make it inevitable that risk assessment involves making numerous guesses or assumptions.[98] Risk assessments are based on many estimations. Swaney states that "risk analysis is inherently value laden, and comparative risk analysis even more so."[99] Often, however, the values underlying the choices made remain hidden, as implicit underlying assumptions.

Even those who take a sympathetic view toward RA as a science note that its methodology is rather crude. RA offers scope for making different decisions at a number of decision points, which may lead to disagreement among scientists. Davies argues that, depending on which methodological assumptions are used, "its results may vary a hundredfold or more."[100] To provide for "consistency and orderly decision-making" (and avoid idiosyncratic decisions or judgments), guidelines or "rules of thumb" are used.[101] Some authors refer to RA as the "illusion of technique."[102]

With the emphasis in "hard" RA on science and facts, and on the separation between facts and values in decision-making, the role of the public tends to be limited to participation in the debate on values. However, as several commentators have pointed out, the dichotomy between scientists and the public—whereby scientists are concerned about knowledge and the public about values—does not hold. Citizens take their clues primarily from groups that they trust, including experts and scientists. They rely also on such groups to act on their behalf. As Tesh argues: "[C]itizens have to organize into groups to have much influence. The strange thing about the risk literature is that it misses this point."[103] Where there are different perceptions of risk, and conflicts about proposals, these commonly go back to disagreement between scientists, not to conflicts between facts and values.[104]

That hard or science-based risk assessment actually may be pursued to advance particular values and interests is noted by Hornstein, who argues that hard versions of RA based decision-making "tend to exclude viewpoints on risk aversion, equity, and cost-benefit trade-offs," and that RA can also become "a device for politically powerful groups to effectuate their interests—now clothed as merely the "objective" determination of science—at the expense of less powerful but equally legitimate viewpoints and groups."[105] Because of the strong emphasis on facts and science in RA, citizens and environmental groups also rely on scientists and experts to influence the outcomes of risk assessment. However, as Clayton and Krier point out: "The logic of collective action predicts that the technical process of making risk-based decisions is more accessible to those special interests that can consistently afford to deploy technically competent scientists, economists, attorneys, and public relations firms to represent their interests at all important decision and predecision points—a theoretically based prediction for which there is ample empirical support."[106]

This is confirmed by O'Brien, who notes that risk assessors are generally hired by private industries or by the government. She provides examples of where unpublished information provided by corporations is fed into risk assessments to come up with findings that are favorable to those companies.[107] "*Risk assessments can be created so as to benefit not the exposed victims but the industry or government agency involved*" (emphasis in the original).[108] Holland and Kellow also argue that "most of the research available to regulators is either provided by or funded by the proponents of the technology," and thereby creates a bias in their favour.[109] This leads Hornstein to argue that "the danger is that risk-based reforms will *exacerbate* the unequal power that special interests may already have over general (public) interests" (emphasis in the original).[110]

Not surprisingly, given that the game of RA (and, in particular, "hard" RA), is not played on a level playing field, environmentalists have been less charmed with risk-based decision-making than advocates of economic interests. In the United States, Republicans have generally been more supportive of risk legislation than the Democrats, and quantitative risk assessment was boosted in the 1980s by Reagan's Executive Order 12291, which required "regulatory impact assessments," while environmentalists have generally opposed efforts to promote risk analysis.[111] Hard or scientific forms of (comparative) risk assessment are often advocated to enhance the rationality of decision-making, and to keep ("dirty") politics away from it.[112] However, such efforts toward depoliticization hide the political nature of risk assessment in all its stages, and de facto disenfranchise citizens from participating in the assessment of risks. Under the guise of science and experts, risk assessment legitimates the framing of problems, and the determination of priorities for decision-making, by dominant political-economic interests. Not without reason, citizens and environmentalists have been cautious, and even distrustful, of risk-based decision-making.

In the United States, this distrust, and the controversy generated by the application of (comparative) risk assessment, has led decision makers to the introduction of "softer" forms of risk assessment, especially at the state level. With the broadening of risk assessment to CRA came also a change in methodology. Whereas traditional RA relied on quantitative methods, CRA, as practiced by the EPA from the 1980s, is not a formal *quantitative* risk assessment, but based on the consensus of perceptions of relative risk by managers or experts, and on comparisons of these perceptions with those of the general public.[113]

With this evolution, the idea of risk assessment as science is even more difficult to uphold. As the notion of risk employed in CRA is much broader than that in traditional risk analysis, and as the complexities and uncertainties in determining environmental effects are even more formidable than those associated with calculating the chances of human death and cancer from single substances, the conception of CRA as a (hard) science is even more difficult to uphold. As Swaney notes, hard CRA is a misconception. Implicit in any form of risk analysis is always an interpretation of what poses a risk and why. Inherently, the concept of risk is value-based.[114] Lash argues that rather than defining risk in terms of hazard and exposure, it can be better described along the lines of "the possibility of change that negatively affects something we value."[115]

Many American states have introduced a form a CRA that allows for public participation at all stages of the process, and as a means for publicly debating issues rather than as a science-based approach for ranking risks. In those states, CRA is used "as a vehicle for informed public discussion in order to integrate expert knowledge and judgment with public values."[116] Swaney argues that, used in this way, the value of CRA lies in its institutionalization of opportunities for citizen discussion on possible solutions to social problems, and even refers to it as "an experiment in participatory democracy."[117]

However, such applications of risk assessment are seen by those who emphasize the need to ground decisions on science and rationality instead of "irrational" public perceptions and attitudes, as compromising the scientific nature of RA.[118] Much risk analysis, such as that related to the assessment of chemicals, continues to be based on a narrow conception of risk, and to be undertaken by scientists and risk-analysis experts. Many risk-assessment professionals hold on to the notion of (C)RA as a science, and resist its opening up to discussions about values out of fear that the scientific nature of risk assessment may be compromised. They insist on maintaining the distinction between risk assessment and risk management, also in the context of CRA. Notwithstanding the fact that many people have pointed out that risk analysis involves making judgments and assumptions that are not based in science, the view of risk analysis as a science still holds considerable currency.[119] Perhac, discussing the case for public participation in CRA, takes the view that public involvement should be confined to value-related issues, to avoid compromising the "integrity" of CRA.[120]

In the United States, RA and CRA, with a built-in cost-benefit analysis component, became important decision-support mechanisms, in particular for the EPA. Although risk assessment has been introduced also in other countries, CRA has been much less adopted by environmental agencies as a means for setting priorities. There are also differences in the way how risks are being evaluated, in part because of differences in the role and interpretation of the "precautionary principle," which plays a significant role in decision-making about risks in Europe—in particular, in Germany. As Holland and Kellow[121] note, the United States and the European Union have adopted fundamentally different approaches to risk analysis and management. This greatly complicates international discussion and negotiations on free trade, an area where RA has also been introduced for determining when countries can legitimately impose restrictions on trade based on environmental and human health concerns. Nonetheless, despite these differences, the concepts of risk, risk analysis, and risk management have come to play a major role in the interpretation and management of environmental issues in many countries as well as internationally.

Outcomes, Strengths, and Limitations

Risk assessment has led to the regulation of hazardous chemicals that pose a (potential) threat to human health. The United States, in that respect, played a leading role in the 1970s and 1980s, as the EPA imposed what were often perceived to be stringent standards on the use of hundreds of chemicals, and in some cases banned chemicals altogether. Christoforou notes that "[u]ntil the 1990s the US system was probably more rigorous in its risk analysis requirements and aimed to achieve a level of health protection, both broadly and in concrete cases, higher than that sought by the European

Community and its member states."[122] Although it is enormously difficult to assess how much damage has been avoided because of the application of RA, to humans as well as to other life and the environment in general, these benefits should be appreciated.

Inasmuch as the adoption and application of RA has strengthened the capacity and influence of regulatory agencies whose mandates aim at environmental protection, it also can be judged positively. The adoption of risk assessment by regulatory agencies can enhance their power vis-à-vis regulated interests. Andrews describes how RA became a powerful political tool for the EPA, as it provided a lever for controlling the agenda of regulatory debate, and as risk (not only the dollar) could be used as a powerful currency in the policy debate. RA "allowed the EPA to wrap its decisions in the legitimacy and apparent objectivity of science, and in the language of health effects rather than merely economic benefits."[123] However, it is also a tool that can be used by regulated interests to challenge a regulator's decisions, especially on the ground that these are not based on hard, scientific evidence. In the United States, the chances of this happening were increased after a Supreme Court decision in 1980 that implied that standards for chemicals could be invalidated if the EPA could not justify them by quantitative risk assessments.[124] The result has been that RA became "yet another weapon in the battles between regulators and their opponents, each side with its bevy of experts laying claim to the "real facts" of the matter. . . ."[125]

Moreover, RA has several serious limitations. First, given the time and costs associated with assessing risks, the capacity for RA is limited by practical, financial-economic, and political conditions. Only a small fraction of potentially risky substances have been assessed, and many new ones are introduced every year. Unless the resources of RA agencies would be enormously increased, it is impossible to have all suspicious substances assessed. This is unlikely to happen for political-economic reasons. Second, as this continuous backlog indicates, RA is a *reactive* mechanism, applied after substances have been invented and developed, and in many cases years after they have been introduced and when problems have become apparent. Third, given the uncertainties and methodological issues and weaknesses inherent to RA, it is far from fail-safe, and no guarantee that significant risks are identified and prevented. Fourth, although RA has been broadened to include environmental risks, analyses tend to focus on threats that are more directly relevant to humans, and that can be measured in monetary terms. Ecological phenomena that have no apparent (monetary) value to humans tend to be ignored. Fifth, RA offers or produces a narrow and very limited understanding of environmental values and concerns. Environmental values come into the picture (and are integrated into decisions) only to the extent that (potential) *damage* is demonstrable and considered *serious* enough to warrant attention (often because of the implications for humans). RA does not offer any *positive* guidance to decisions to ensure that technologies and products do not harm the environment (for instance, in their design, production process, use, and disposal), and does not put forward principles or ideas for environmental management.

In conclusion, while risk-based decision-making can be used to integrate environmental concerns, the terms on which it does so depend to a large extent on who is in control of defining (and ranking) risks. Risks can be defined as ranging from very narrow (for instance, as risks to human life) to very broad (to anything or everything that people value). What risks are perceived, and how they are defined, depends very much on sociocultural values, and on one's social position and political-economic ideology. But although risk assessment is fundamentally a value-based and political activity, it can be, and has been, practiced under the guise of science, as a tool for depoliticizing decision-making and legitimating decisions about (potentially) controversial issues. At worst, as Beck argues, risk management and science assist in the process of denial in the name of rationality, and in legitimizing global contamination.[126] In many cases, the environmental, social, ethical, and political-economic aspects of issues are underexposed or not considered at all. Moreover, as the starting point of risk assessment usually lies in existing conditions (that are defined as problems/risks) and/or with newly developed technologies, it is quite limited in its capacity to take a broader or deeper view of issues. As various authors have pointed out, risk assessment does not inspire to lateral thinking, and to thinking about alternatives. It may be a tool for assessing (cost-effective) measures for managing pollution and other problems, but has little or nothing to offer in terms of preventing pollution and problems, and for developing ideas and strategies for promoting more positive and sustainable practices and societies.[127]

INTEGRATED ENVIRONMENTAL ASSESSMENT

In the 1990s, the need for developing a more comprehensive framework for the integration of environmental information, bringing together many if not all of the previously mentioned approaches, was recognized, especially in scientific circles, with the growing concern about climate change. This led to the emergence of integrated environmental assessment (IEA, not to be confused with EIA).

Integrated environmental assessment (IEA) is loosely defined as policy-relevant, multidisciplinary research on environmental issues.[128] In various forms, IEA, especially in the form of integrated environmental assessment models, has been around for decades, but it was only in the 1990s that the term started to get used more widely and that IEA became the subject of theoretical discussion and development in the literature. Instrumental in that development has been the rise of the climate change issue on the policy agenda, as this issue made the need for the development of more integrative and consistent frameworks apparent.[129]

Although IEA is concerned with the integration of knowledge and understanding across all disciplines (including science, economics, and the social sciences), and potentially could be applied to all kinds of environmental issues, it has de facto been dominated by scientific and economic modeling, and been applied to a limited range of environmental issues—in particular, acid rain and climate change. There has been much less involvement from the social sciences (other than economics). And although the aim of IEA is to inform policy, the literature on IEA hardly refers to, let alone links with, the policy and political science literature, albeit some authors link it with risk management and offer a crude outline of policy stages under the label "risk management functions."[130] Although some advocates of IEA refer to the need for participatory approaches and assessments,[131] and for involving decision-makers and stakeholders in the development of models, from their conception to their use,[132] much of the IEA literature is preoccupied with models and modeling (also referred to as "integrated analysis").

IEA is sometimes presented as the most advanced stage in the development and use of policy-oriented knowledge integration, building upon environmental impact assessment, cost-benefit analysis, and other tools that have been used for cognitive environmental integration. IEA is referred to as "an umbrella concept that covers many present and earlier efforts in various problem areas that satisfy the definition of IEA but have not called themselves such."[133] However, although the distinctions and boundaries between IEA and these preceding approaches are not sharp and clear, it is also recognized that, as yet, IEA is more a multidisciplinary than an interdisciplinary undertaking.[134] Sometimes, preceding approaches, like environmental impact assessment, are referred to as earlier forms of IEA (although not by name), and some refer to technology assessment (TA) and social impact assessment (SIA) as its "close cousins."[135] In other places, IEA is referred to as an umbrella concept or as an overarching framework within which all previous and existing efforts (frameworks and tools) toward knowledge integration are brought together, including EIA, decision support systems, adaptive assessment and management, policy exercises, and focus groups.[136]

There are also differences in interpretation about the centrality of science and knowledge in IEA. Some authors emphasize the integration of knowledge/information from diverse scientific disciplines with the aim of developing a "synoptic perspective," if not a "truth machine,"[137] while others emphasize the importance of integrating a diversity of values and of making explicit value-laden assumptions. Schneider, for instance, argues that integrated assessment models "can help describe quantitatively the logical consequences of an explicit set of assumptions—including those of different values and beliefs. Beyond that, values and beliefs take over."[138] It is the responsibility of integrated assessment model builders to make explicit the assumptions, values, and beliefs underlying their models.

Although IEA advocates like to present it as an overarching framework for many other approaches toward the integration of knowledge and interpretations of environmental issues, its development thus far suggests several limitations. First, as already mentioned, there appears to be little input into IEA from social scientists (other than from economists). Possibly, one of the reasons for this is that many social scientists (other than economists) are lukewarm about modeling as a tool for analyzing social and political processes and developments. In part, this reluctance is based on the fact that, despite Schneider's call for making explicit the value-laden assumptions underlying models, modeling is often presented as an objective and scientific way of interpreting phenomena and informing decision-making. Such a view may appeal to many scientists—in particular, those who conceive of science as a "truth machine"—but it is a view much less held and appreciated in the social sciences, where the influence of values at all stages of research, including the selection or design of analytical frameworks, is more commonly recognized.

Other limitations of IEA relate to the fact that it is still at an early stage, and that there is a lack of agreement about a range of issues. The European Forum of Integrated Environmental Assessment offers a platform for discussing theoretical and methodological issues as well as the role of knowledge integration, including that undertaken by scientists, in the policy process.[139] Several authors refer to IEA as a means for improving communication between scientists and policy-makers, and for enhancing the role and influence of scientists in the policy process. On this point, it is acknowledged that personal interactions, inspiration, and personal qualities are important, especially with regard to the development of the participatory element.[140] But these efforts are hampered by the fact that many models lack transparency, are not user-friendly, and do not link well (if at all) with the worldviews, values, and priorities of decision-makers, or with those of the wider population. As Tol and Vellinga note: "A few models are secret, most are not fully documented, some are enormously large, some are badly programmed, some are written in an unfamiliar programming language, some are documented in an unfamiliar tongue."[141] This seems hardly a promising basis for advancing more inclusive interpretations of environmental issues, especially from nonscientists, and for acknowledging the underlying values, interests, and ideologies of scientific models. Without this, IEA is unlikely to find much favor in broader circles and to (be able to) serve as an overarching cognitive framework for guiding environmental integration within the policy and institutional realm. At most, like its forebears, EIA, CBA, and RA, it may *influence* decision-making on particular issues (such as climate change), but it will be unable to provide guidance for environmental integration across policies and at the institutional level.

CONCLUSION

Cognitive-external integration refers to processes that aim to promote the integration of environmental considerations into the cognitive frameworks that guide human decisions and actions. In other terms, it involves the "greening" of interpretations, knowledge systems, and ideologies. The integration of an environmental dimension into human cognitive frameworks is fundamental in bringing human actions and behavior in line with what is considered to be necessary or desirable from an environmental point of view. Cognitive frameworks are not value-free but weave together information, knowledge, interpretations, and values. Given the diversity of views on the environment, the inevitability of uncertainty and imperfect knowledge, and the mingling of facts and values in all human interpretations, the integration of an environmental dimension into cognitive frameworks poses a big challenge, even at the level of individuals. This applies all the more so to the collective level, and especially in pluralistic societies, as different interpretations and views, supported by a diversity of belief systems and interests, compete in decision-making processes. Although it is unlikely that full agreement on the integration of the substance, or even nature, of the environmental dimension can be achieved in many, if any, decisions, governments cannot escape having to make choices, on some cognitive basis or other.

Governments have adopted a variety of mechanisms for promoting cognitive-external integration, in particular EIA, CBA, and RA. The United States has led the way in the development and use of these forms of integration, which increasingly have been adopted also in many other countries. A common characteristic of these forms, and IEA, is the dominant role of science and experts in the construction of the cognitive frameworks that inform decision-making. The environmental dimension that they put forward for integration is created predominantly by the use of scientific or discipline-based methodologies and methods that imbue an objective and authoritative nature to the information and knowledge that is presented. However, as the discussion of these mechanisms has shown, they are far from value-free, and often hide the underlying assumptions and values on which they are based. Largely, what comes out of these processes depends on the views, values, and interests of those who administer or control them. Although scientists and experts may play a dominant role in the practice of these forms of integration, practice is influenced by contextual factors, not in the least by the affiliations and interests of the scientists and experts involved.

Being far from objective, these mechanisms may politicize scientists and experts by pitting them against each other in decision-making processes about controversial proposals. However, in another way they can serve to depoliticize decision-making and hide the value and interest basis underlying decisions. The main focus of the debates associated with these mechanisms is on facts, not on values or interests. Battles are won on the basis of claims to superior knowledge and demonstrable (mostly quantitative) data, not on the political, sociocultural, or ethical merits of proposals. Although assessments of economic costs and benefits may identify winners and losers, conclusions are based on "net" benefits, not set against the existing distribution of income, wealth, and access to social and collective goods. Moreover, who wins often depends on the relative access of parties to (authoritative) scientists, experts, and resources. Thus, although processes associated with these forms of integration can involve conflict, they also create the impression that they are about generating the best available knowledge, and hide the political-economic and ideological basis that influences that knowledge.

Furthermore, the effectiveness of EIA, CBA, and (C)RA, as well as IEA, as mechanisms for integrating environmental knowledge and values into decision-making, while variable depending on their institutionalization and implementation, is fundamentally constrained by the narrow way they conceive of the environmental *problématique*. Taking for granted the driving forces behind "development" and the values and interests on which it is based, they focus on avoiding or mitigating *effects*. They aim at minimizing harm, but do not question the rationale or nature of development itself, and do not provide a cognitive framework for steering development based on ecological, social, and resource management principles. They may assist in identifying the "least bad" options once the "need" for development has been determined (mainly on economic and political grounds), but they have nothing to offer as beacons for development and (integrated) environmental management. This confirms the status of these mechanisms as *external* rather than *internal* forms of environmental integration. They may *influence* decisions, but they do not initiate and shape them. To do the latter, more overarching cognitive frameworks, providing guidance to efforts at external integration, are required. In the following chapter, I will discuss some of the frameworks that have been put forward, and to some extent used by governments, to advance internal integration.

3

Cognitive-Internal Integration

INTRODUCTION

As explained in chapter 1, integrating environmental knowledge assumes and requires the existence of a *substantive* cognitive environmental framework, an *interpretation* of the environment (including values and principles) that can provide coherence and consistency to cognitive-external integration. However, given the diversity of environmental interpretations, belief systems, and ideologies in the world, disagreement and conflict about *what* knowledge or interpretations should provide a basis for decisions and actions is a normal feature of life and collective choice. Although collective decision-making may involve searching for common ground (for instance, in the form of principles or goals), almost inevitably some views will be more influential than, or dominate over, others.

A variety of overarching cognitive frameworks for environmental management have been put forward and, to greater or lesser extent, adopted by governments. Among these are sustainable development (SD), ecological modernization, environmental space (ES), and ecosystem management. These frameworks are usually not presented as objective or scientific, but as involving (different) values and interests that require "balancing" or integration. The ideological and political nature of such frameworks is commonly recognized. Not surprisingly, the interpretation of these cognitive frameworks, and the ways they are being used, has been the subject of much debate. Analysts and commentators often disagree on the meaningfulness of these ideas—in particular, as used by governments and in the business sector—and on their (potential) usefulness for advancing environmental integration. Given the considerable debate and disagreement about what these frameworks mean, they are perhaps better referred to as discourses rather than as concepts that can or should be clearly defined.[1]

Nonetheless, governments that use or rely on these ideas to provide guidance to their environmental (integration) efforts cannot escape making choices with regard to their interpretation and implementation. Governments are important actors, rather than passive recipients of views, in the interpretation or definition of these ideas, favoring some views over others. Governments themselves play a central role in the politics of sustainable development and the politics associated with the adoption, framing, and implementation of other cognitive frameworks. In this chapter, I will discuss the political nature of these frameworks and their strengths and weaknesses as means for cognitive-internal integration.

SUSTAINABLE DEVELOPMENT

Since the publication of the Brundtland report by the World Commission on Environment and Development in 1987, the concept of "sustainable development" has become common currency around the world. Many governments have adopted it as a cornerstone for (policy) development and as a general aim or principle underlying green planning and legislation. This has led also to a raft of other initiatives and institutional changes.[2] It has also been adopted by a growing number of businesses to demonstrate their commitment to social and environmental as well as economic goals. Sustainable development appears to have become the dominant discourse in the environmental debate, encompassing that on environmental integration.[3]

Sustainable development, as interpreted in the Brundtland report and in many other writings, has three dimensions: environmental (or ecological), social, and economic.[4] The environmental dimension relates to the concern about ecosystems and other problems commonly referred to as "environmental" (mostly pollution and its effects on the natural environment and humans). The social dimension relates to concerns about living conditions and quality-of-life issues, including access to food, water, adequate housing, health care, and education. In the Brundtland report, this dimension received most emphasis, as the achievement of decent living standards, especially in low-income countries, was seen as a human and political priority, and as a precondition for environmental care. The economic dimension, according to the report, relates to the need for economic growth to be able to address the concerns associated with the social and environmental dimensions.

Economic growth, according to the Brundtland report, is a necessary requirement for lifting the living conditions and quality of life, especially in low-income countries, although it is also acknowledged that poverty in these countries has been "exacerbated by the unequal distribution of land and other assets."[5] But "as developing countries are part of an interdependent world economy" and "their prospects also depend on the levels and patterns of growth in industrialized nations," an economic growth rate of 3-4 percent in industrialized countries is a "minimum that international financial institutions consider necessary if these countries are going to play a part in expanding the world economy." The commission argues that such growth rates could be environmentally sustainable if industrialized nations can uphold the trend toward relying on less material- and energy-intensive activities, and on improved resource efficiency.[6]

Thus, the notion of sustainable development as promulgated by the Brundtland Commission, and adopted by most governments and many businesses, combines environmental, social, and economic concerns and objectives. A key to the strong support that this interpretation of sustainable development generated lies in the claim that the concerns and objectives in all three areas can be met concurrently, and that they are compatible, even mutually reinforcing, rather than in conflict with one another. Social concerns appear to lie at the core of the notion of sustainable development advanced by the report, but economic growth is required to address these concerns, and economic growth can be of a kind that that is not detrimental to the environment. The argument neatly integrates social, economic, and environmental concerns. However, it is based on a range of assumptions that are open to debate.

Some of these assumptions, hinted at in the report, are that economic growth leads to higher living standards of the poor and to a higher quality of life for all. As Daly and others have pointed out, gross national product (GNP) measures "positives" as well as "negatives."[7] Whether economic growth enhances total social welfare depends on whether the positives outweigh the negatives, and on how the positives and negatives are distributed. However, the distribution of the material benefits of economic growth is highly dependent on political-economic factors, and the experience in many countries shows that the poorest in society often do not benefit (greatly, if at all) from economic growth, whereas the rich benefit most. Moreover, even if economic growth leads to a higher material standard of living for most or all, this does not necessarily imply that people's quality of life increases as well. As quality of life is a relative and subjective thing, associated closely with social factors and conditions that may actually be negatively affected by economic growth, this is a problematic assumption.[8] Underlying these assumptions are other assumptions about what constitutes "the good life" and "the good society," about the relative importance of individual and collective goods to people's well-being, about the value patterns associated with, and affected by, economic growth and the prevailing economic system, about acceptable or desirable levels of equity and distributional justice, and about the desirability and feasibility of (often rapid) technological and social change.

Interpretations of the economic dimension of sustainability also differ on whether infinite economic growth is possible. Central to the debate on this point is the question whether natural resources are limited, and/or whether natural capital can be substituted by human-made capital. Optimists often deny or downplay the existence of absolute limits, and/or believe in the ability to overcome these with human ingenuity and substitution. The "weak" interpretation of sustainability is based on the assumption that human capital can substitute for natural capital, whereas the "strong" interpretation takes the view that the natural capital basis needs to be kept at the same level and that nonrenewable resources should be used at a rate not higher than that by which substitutes are developed.[9] As Daly points out, even the adoption of a weak notion of sustainability would be an improvement on prevailing accounting practices, which do not take account of reductions in natural capital associated with economic growth.[10]

The assumption that infinite economic growth is possible because human ingenuity enables an infinite increase in resource-use efficiency, and can *and will* be of a nature that does not have any further detrimental effects on the environment, is highly debatable. On this point, the Brundtland Commission appears to express strong faith in the notion of "ecological modernization," discussed in the next section. Here it suffices to say that the concept of sustainable development, as promoted by the commission and adopted by many governments, considers that the limits to economic growth, if any do exist, are flexible rather than absolute, and that they can be pushed back indefinitely.

Although the notion of sustainable development as promulgated by the Brundtland report provides, at face value, a cognitive framework for the integration between social, economic and environmental values and interests, it offers no clear guidance for external and internal environmental integration. It simply assumes that technological and economic development can be "greened," and that improved standards of living and quality of life will not bring about environmental deterioration (based on the ecological modernization thesis). It does not provide specific guidance on the question of *how* environmental interests can or should be integrated into economic theory and practices, or *how* environmental imperatives and the notion of quality of life, with its individual and social aspects, can or should be accommodated, although it has generated some debate about (sustainable) *consumption*, especially in rich countries. It is often argued that sustainable development *integrates* social, economic, and environmental concerns, but it does so only at the highest level of generality. What sustainable development means in terms of specific and compatible goals or objectives, and how such goals and objectives can be achieved, is left wide open to interpretation.

This may be one of the reasons for the attractiveness of the Brundtland message. The notion of sustainable development leaves enormous scope for defining goals and objectives in all three areas (with varying degrees of specificity and emphasis), and for determining *how* these can or should be met. This enables almost everyone, including governments and businesses, to express a commitment toward sustainable development, expressed in three separate sets of goals, without considering the possible need for significant change—for instance, change in economic systems or policies and practices that may be required to ensure integration and achievement of environmental objectives.

In practice, governments and businesses that adopt the principle of sustainable development often treat it as the *combination* rather than the *integration* of environmental, social, and economic goals. Programs adopted by governments and businesses usually put forward goals, objectives, and practices separately for each dimension. Thus, sustainable development tends to simply become the *sum total* of social, economic, and environmental objectives, based on different and separate (social, economic, and environmental) rationalities, interests, or system requirements ("imperatives"). Based on these separate agendas, measuring progress toward sustainability becomes a matter of "triple bottom line" reporting instead of assessing progress toward (common) objectives that are the result of the *integration* of "imperatives."

A consequence of this interpretation of sustainable development is that where goals and objectives are in conflict with each other (as they have not been integrated), they need to be *balanced* or *weighed* against each other. As, a priori, environmental interests are not seen as more important than social and economic interests, it means that the former can, or even must, be compromised to accommodate social and economic needs. In practice, this means that the debate and decisions about integration under the umbrella of sustainability and sustainable development mostly centers on how different interests can or should be weighed or balanced, based on different and often conflicting bottom lines. Given the relative power of economic, social, and environmental interests and advocates in society and politics, sustainable development may do little if anything for the position of environmental values and interests, and may even be used as a means for legitimizing economic and social priorities, and for keeping the lid on environmental demands. Instead of using ecological limits or imperatives as a basis or framework for integrating (and adapting) economic and social interests, sustainable development can be used to justify the expansion of the role of "the market" (in practice, corporate interests) in the provision of environmental and social goods and services, like drinking water and waste management, as demonstrated by the emphasis on "private-public partnerships" at the environmental summit in Johannesburg in 2002.[11]

However, despite the growing popularity of the notion of sustainable development among governments and businesses, it remains a widely contested concept, and debate continues about its meaning and significance. Many have become skeptical or even cynical about the discourse, as it has become a cover for "business as usual" and continued social and environmental exploitation. Some people, therefore, draw the conclusion that the concept should be abandoned.[12] Others, although sharing a degree of skepticism, think that the concept can be redeemed; they say it should not be given up, both because of its moral appeal and because it can be used as a basis for demanding and legitimating stronger policies and institutional reform.[13] As Torgerson argues, at the least the concept of sustainability has enabled "public discourse for reflection on the purpose and direction of development in the modern world" and has contributed to the fact that the notion of "progress" is no longer taken for granted. The ambiguity of the concept does not *exclude* the possibility of significant cumulative change, as is apparent from the fear sometimes expressed by business that incremental change based on the concept is the "thin end of the wedge."[14]

The issue, perhaps, is whether the concepts of sustainability and sustainable development can be rescued from inappropriate usage. It can be argued that using the adjective "sustainable" in the broader social (rather than "human environment") and economic (rather than "resource") context is inappropriate. In a social context, whether conditions or practices are sustainable is not the most important or even relevant question. More important criteria for judging social conditions and practices are long-standing values and criteria like justice, equity, and freedom from oppression and exploitation. People may live in conditions that are severely lacking in these respects but that are sustained by power, force, and manipulation. Undemocratic and socially oppressive and exploitative systems can be sustained over long periods of time, as history has shown time and again. It seems more appropriate to use values and criteria like those referred to above as a basis for judging and changing social conditions and practices rather than the criterion of sustainability, even as an indirect or proxy measure.

The same argument applies to the use of sustainability as a criterion for assessing economic conditions and practices other or broader than those related to the sustainability of the use of resources (referred to in chapter 1 as the resource dimension of environmental management). Whether the existing economic system is good or bad, and worth sustaining, depends on one's views on what purpose it serves and should serve, how well it satisfies human or society's needs, and what it brings about in terms of inequality in incomes and wealth, social cohesion, and environmental consequences. Whether or not economic growth can or should be sustained is a question better answered on the basis of such questions, assuming the economic system serves human purposes rather than its own.

By contrast, sustainability is an eminently relevant and crucial criterion for judging and guiding human and societal behavior and practices with regard to the environment, with the three dimensions defined in chapter

1. Sustaining ecosystems and the resource basis on which all life, including human life, depends is a fundamental imperative, regardless of the choices people make in the social, economic, and political sphere. And inasmuch as human health and well-being are affected by the way humans modify their biophysical environment (including the built environment), sustaining conditions that affect their health and well-being positively also can be considered important. Trying to create or maintain such conditions while maintaining ecological and resource sustainability can be regarded as the true challenge of sustainable development.

The broader challenge is to change or create social, economic, and political systems that are not only conducive to maintaining environmental sustainability, but that *also* can be considered desirable on the basis of other social-political values that societies deem important. Environmental sustainability does not guarantee just and equitable societies, but neither do just and equitable societies (even if they were to exist) guarantee environmental sustainability.

Continuing the sustainable development discourse, then, assumes that it can and will be used to develop a coherent cognitive framework for meaningful environmental integration and management, across policies and at the institutional level. A variety of moves in this direction can indeed be discerned. Ecological modernization can be seen as an effort toward integrating environmental concerns into economic and technological decision-making and institutions, and often makes reference to sustainable development as a guiding principle. The notion of environmental space has been developed specifically with the aim to make sustainability concrete, and has been put forward as a basis for policy development across areas and sectors. Ecosystems thinking, also taking its clue from the sustainability discourse, has emerged as potentially a new and integrated paradigm for environmental management. In the following sections, I will discuss the merits of these ideas as overarching cognitive frameworks and to what extent they (can) provide more specific guidance for environmental integration in a political context.

ECOLOGICAL MODERNIZATION

The notion of ecological modernization (EM) is based on a belief in the innovative/adaptive capacity of technology and economics to resolve environmental problems. Technological innovation and changes in economic management based on environmental principles are seen as being capable of reducing environmental impacts to sustainable levels, in particular by enhancing material and energy efficiency, even with continued economic growth (referred to as "decoupling"). As noted above, it is an idea on which the Brundtland report's interpretation of sustainable development relies heavily. The notion of EM was developed and coined before the Brundtland report was published.

Apart from the belief in technological innovation and economic management, however, advocates of EM differ on many points. Huber, who is commonly referred to as the father of EM, believes that market forces (competition between producers and consumer demand for green products) would more or less automatically bring about EM.[15] By contrast, Martin Jänicke conceives of ecological modernization as a process involving political and administrative systems. Governments have an important role to play in enhancing the capacity for technological modernization and overcoming institutional and other obstacles to it.[16] Still others interpret EM as a broader societal process that also involves more fundamental political-economic and value change.[17] Like sustainable development, EM has been referred to as a discourse rather than as a concept that can be sharply defined.[18] Interpretations of EM that focus mostly on technological, managerial, and economic means have been labeled as "weak" EM, and the more encompassing form, requiring more fundamental political-economic and societal change, as "strong" EM.[19] The various strands of EM are not necessarily incompatible with each other, however, as many of the broader interpretations can be seen to focus on the conditions for EM defined as "the implementation of preventative innovation in production systems (processes and products) that simultaneously produces environmental and economic benefits."[20]

Given the crucial importance of integrating environmental concerns into the economic realm, even weak forms of EM are potentially significant. Weak versions of EM, focusing on technological innovation and more-efficient economic (resource) management, provide a potential basis for the greening of technology and economic decision-making. Most advocates of weak EM, including those who take the view that governments have an important role to play in that process, assume that environmental concerns and demands can be accommodated by, and within, the existing economic and political systems. In this respect they disagree with more radical analysts and environmentalists who argue that capitalism and liberal democracy are unable to deal effectively with the environmental challenge, and that fundamental changes are required to address the environmental *problematique*.[21] Even if such views are not explicitly expressed, weaker versions of EM contribute to the depoliticization of environmental issues by mainly focusing on the technological aspects of environmental and economic management.

At face value, EM should be attractive to governments and industries that are committed to economic growth and environmental protection. EM is said to enhance the competitive position of industries and economies as a whole, as resource use (especially of energy and imported materials) is reduced and the demand for green products (even if more expensive than regular products) grows with rising environmental awareness. However, although EM has found considerable support from (some) industries and governments in some countries—in particular, Germany, Japan, and the Netherlands—it has not become as popular as one might expect.

Several reasons for the relatively slow and limited uptake of the idea of EM can be advanced. One is that taking the lead in technological innovation may require significant capital investment, and carries considerable risks and uncertainty, especially if the returns are not immediate. Another reason is that the knowledge and expertise required are not (sufficiently) available within or to industries, but are "locked up" in research institutes and universities, or are inadequately disseminated. A third factor is that the attractiveness, and even feasibility, of EM varies with the structure of an economy, and the degree of dependency on imports (of energy and raw materials). It has less to offer to countries where the industrial sector is relatively small and whose economies are based primarily on resource exports, such as Australia, Canada, New Zealand, oil-producing countries, and many low-income countries. Finally, even in highly industrialized countries, existing institutions and vested interests pose significant obstacles to EM. While EM produces winners, others may bear the costs or lose out (such as the coal, oil, and gas industries). For all these reasons, it is not surprising that thus far EM has found only modest support among industries and governments.

But even in countries where EM has found support, EM has provided little in the way of an overarching framework for environmental integration and management. In these countries, the focus has been foremost on technological development and increasing resource efficiency in some industrial sectors (weak EM). It has done little if anything with regard to the integration of environmental imperatives into the overall framework of economic policies and institutions, and in the transport, energy, and agricultural sectors. In the German context, Weidner concludes that "it is doubtful that the concept of ecological modernization is sufficient to pave the way for sustainable development" and notes that the integration of environmental concerns into some policy sectors, such as land use and transport, still needs to occur.[22] As an idea, EM may have a sharper focus than sustainable development, especially in its weaker versions, but at a cost. Focused mainly on increasing resource efficiency, and inasmuch as it produces economic spin-offs, EM has nothing to say on the ecological limits within which the economy (production, transport, energy use, and consumption) needs to stay to remain or become ecologically sustainable at all levels, including the global level. EM also provides no guidance with regard to the social or human dimension of the environmental *problématique*. Potentially or ideally, especially in its stronger form, EM triggers public debate about desirable and undesirable future developments in science and technology ("reflexive modernization").[23] In practice, government support for EM comes down mostly to the promotion of resource efficiency and some technologies like wind power that are considered to be environmentally friendly. Government-initiated or government-sponsored public debate about the sociopolitical aspects of modernization is rare, and carefully managed if it occurs, given the potentially radical political-economic implications. If such debates occur, they do so on terms that virtually guarantee that economic- and science-based interests and views have the upper hand.[24]

Although, mainly in rich countries, there has been some "decoupling" between economic growth and *some* indicators of pollution, this has been brought about, to a large extent, not by EM (which implies *innovation*), but by other means such as fuel switching. Although there is likely to be great *potential* for developing production systems and products that are not detrimental to the environment, this is not easily realized. Ecological modernization, it has become apparent, requires a considerable commitment on the part of governments, and overcoming political, economic, and social institutional barriers. Thus far, only a handful of high-income countries can be said to have started on that path, and ecological modernization in other countries appears to be even more of a challenge.[25]

Arguably, EM is even more important to low- and middle-income countries than to high-income countries. If it is accepted that the gap between rich and poor countries needs to be reduced, and if EM simultaneously produces economic and environmental benefits, boosting economic competitiveness while reducing pollution, then it should be particularly relevant and attractive to (notably, middle-income) countries that are in the process of building their industrial and technological capacity. However, for a variety of reasons, the introduction of EM in such countries appears to be even more difficult than in high-income countries; it comes about mainly when and where external/international actors are involved. Such "internationally led" EM poses certain risks to middle-income countries, notably in terms of promoting inappropriate development and increasing external (financial and technological) dependence.[26]

Unless EM is interpreted or developed as a program for (re)designing and implementing economic systems (for production, consumption, transport, and energy) as a whole, encompassing the global, national, and local levels, and is based on ecological principles and social-environmental considerations, it does not offer a comprehensive framework for environmental integration between the ecological, social, and resource dimensions of the environmental *problématique*. The weak form of EM that has been adopted by some governments, at most, offers benefits to some industries in some countries. Such forms may buy time in the sense of postponing the need to address the more fundamental drivers of ecological degradation, but does not eliminate it. Over time, economic growth will cancel out efficiency gains and initial reductions in pollution.[27] At worst, EM increases the gap between the haves and have-nots, as some of the richest countries expand their (technological and financial) lead in the global economy and as resource intensive industries, and pollution, are exported to poorer countries.

Given the reality of increased global economic competition, it is possible, and perhaps even likely, that EM, in its weaker form, will find growing support in some countries where industries stand to gain the most. With government support, many of the national-level obstacles to EM mentioned above can be overcome. For political-economic and strategic reasons, it is therefore understandable that the approach has found much favor as a "realistic" course of action with the more pragmatic environmental advocates in those countries. However, we should not be led to believe that such forms of EM provide an adequate basis or overarching framework for environmental integration. EM is not very environmentally inclusive, as it does not even aim to integrate the truly ecological and human-environmental dimensions of the environmental *problématique*, and looks at the resource dimension exclusively from a national (competitive) perspective, ignoring the need to ensure their sustainable and equitable use at a global as well as national level. In that respect, the notion of environmental space has more to offer.

ENVIRONMENTAL SPACE

The concept of "environmental space" has been put forward as a tool for the operationalization of the principle of sustainability, it is supposed to "make sustainability concrete."[28] According to Davidson, the notion of "environmental utilization space" was first introduced by Horst Siebert in 1982, and can be defined as "[t]he total space provided by the earth for our use without diminishing the possibilities for the future."[29]

In contrast to the earlier concerns about the limits to growth associated with the quantities of resources available for human use, the proponents of the concept of environmental space are concerned primarily about the ecological impacts of resource use: "[E]ven if resources are not limited, the environmental impacts of resource exploitation set limits to the sustainable extent of that exploitation."[30] Although it is not possible to define environmental limits with precision, it is not hard to find examples where (human) resource overuse has brought about the collapse of resources and ecosystems, with severe consequences for those who depended on them.

Proponents of the notion of environmental space advocate a conservative (precautionary) approach to the use of resources based on the best available knowledge of these limits.

The limits on the use of a range of resources are calculated on the basis of their estimated continuous availability (renewability), their ability to be reused (recycled), and their effect on the environment (such as CO_2 emissions). In the case of particularly harmful substances, the limit is set at zero (implying the banning or phasing out of such substances). Although it is admitted that these calculations of available space are "rough,"[31] and that they involve making (value) judgments and entail debate, they are considered to provide a good and robust-enough basis for policy guidance, better than well-meaning but vague commitments to sustainable development.[32]

Almost inevitably, the reliance on environmental space as a means for operationalizing the principle of sustainability draws attention to issues of environmental equity and justice. Based on the acknowledgment of limits, the calculation of environmental space (available and used) highlights the question of distribution of, and access to, resources. Therefore, it is not surprising that the environmental-space approach to the operationalization of sustainability is accompanied by the strong egalitarian principle that all people have the right to the same amount of resources.[33]

Based on the calculation of the total (global or regional) amount of space available, per capita space (resource) availability can be calculated by dividing the total amounts by world (or regional) population. This then can be used as a basis for calculating the entitlements of each country to a particular resource (assuming an equal distribution of resources over all people in the world), and compared to existing levels of resource use of countries. The difference between these figures indicates the amount of over- or underconsumption per country, which, in the case of overconsumption, can be labeled the "sustainability gap" (the gap between what a country presently uses and what it should use to remain within sustainable levels of use). According to these calculations, most high-income countries consume resources well beyond sustainable levels. In general, Europe, the United States, and other rich areas use and consume resources way above the environmental space that they are entitled to on a per capita basis.[34]

In various respects, the concept of environmental space is similar, and complementary, to the notion of "ecological footprint." The idea of calculating ecological footprints is also based on the view that sustainability needs to be made more concrete. The difficulty of the term "sustainability," according to Wackernagel and Rees, lies in the lack of agreement over its policy implications, associated with ideological differences, not its essential meaning.[35]

Ecological footprints also quantify people's use of resources, whether they are within or outside their own country or region. Footprints can be calculated for countries, for individuals, and for all kinds of groups, organizations (such as companies), products, and activities. The actual footprint per capita can be compared with the amount of productive land that is available to each person on earth (assessed in 2003 at about 1.8 hectares). Like the advocates of the environmental space approach, the proponents of the ecological footprint take the view that all people on earth have the right to an equal share of its resources, and thus reveal the inequality in resource use and levels of over- and underconsumption. For instance, North Americans, with an ecological footprint of 9.4 ha per capita, claim about five times their fair share of the earth's resources, Japan and the Netherlands use about two and a half times, and China (with 1.6 ha per capita) and India (with 0.8 ha per capita) use less than the world average.[36]

Closely related to the notions of environmental space and ecological footprint is the concept of "carrying capacity," which can be defined as the maximum population of a given species that can be supported indefinitely in a particular area.[37] At a global level, the carrying capacity of the earth can be seen as equivalent to the total amount of environmental space globally available. But as the concept of carrying capacity has mostly been applied to particular areas or countries to identify the level of population that can be sustained in that area or country (which may lead to the suggestion that an area is over- or underpopulated), its application to humans can be seen as less appropriate, given the ability of humans to use environmental space (and thus leave ecological footprints) outside the area in which they live. As trade enhances or diminishes local carrying capacity, and as the ability to sustain populations depends very much on their standard of living, it is problematic to speak of over- and underpopulated areas or countries. And as the concept of carrying capacity has been used to advocate "ecofascist" positions based on perceived overpopulation, it has become also a politically suspect and controversial concept.[38]

Rather than trying to assess how many people a particular area or country can support (which is variable for reasons mentioned above), the concepts of ecological footprint and environmental space focus attention on the resources used by a particular population, wherever these resources are located or come from. Thus, by "turning carrying capacity on its head," the proportion of global resources effectively appropriated by a population is revealed, and the global dimension of the sustainability question is made more apparent.[39] Although there may still be uncertainty with regard to how much global environmental space (or carrying capacity) there is, the question how space is apportioned across the world is much harder to ignore when using the concepts of ecological footprint or environmental space than when the concept of (local or regional) carrying capacity is taken as a basis.

The notions of environmental space and ecological footprint, although relying on different methodologies, are very similar in what they demonstrate (the imprint of a population on the global ecology) and raise the same kind of questions (regarding equity, reallocation). In some respects, however, the concepts offer different perspectives on these questions, and have been put forward with different purposes. The concept of ecological footprint, by aggregating resource use with the help of a single denominator (productive land) is particularly helpful for educational purposes directed at calculating and comparing a population's overall environmental demands. Its most significant contribution lies perhaps in its potential to raise awareness regarding the (often hidden and/or distant) pressure exerted by (groups of) people on the environment. The concept of environmental space focuses on differences in resource use between countries, and has been put forward more explicitly as the basis for objectives and action regarding specific resources. The environmental space concept, therefore, seems to offer greater potential as a basis for policy development than the concept of ecological footprint.

As the notion of environmental space is based on the recognition of ecological limits, a strong equity principle, and is directed at sustainable resource use, it has, just like the concept of sustainability, environmental, social, and resource (economic) dimensions. The main difference between the two concepts is that the concept of environmental space provides a more specific environmental management framework, especially with regard to the limits of resource use (often in quantitative terms), on the global as well as the national level. If it were to be instituted, the prescriptions of environmental space would provide the basis for a considerable redistribution of (the right to or benefits derived from) resources, and would impose clear limits and obligations on governments with regard to the exploitation of resources. Not surprisingly, the concept does not arouse much enthusiasm among governments and in the business sector. Its adoption faces a range of big hurdles, both practical and political.[40]

Although, as noted above, the notion of environmental space includes a social dimension (notably with regard to equity), it does not provide goals, objectives, or means for guiding collective choices with regard to the human-environment dimension more broadly. The discourse of environmental space is largely focused on determining the *limits* of resource use, based on the recognition of ecological and equity considerations. It does not, by itself, provide substantive guidance for *how* resources should be used, and on how the biophysical (including urban) environment can or should be shaped within the ecological and equity parameters adopted. Thus, although the notion of environmental space can be seen as useful or even essential with regard to clarifying the ecological and resource dimensions of sustainable development or environmental management, it has little to offer in terms of guiding environmental integration on the human-environment dimension. In this respect, another concept, that of "environmental design," which will be discussed in chapter 8, is more useful. However, the concepts of environmental space and environmental design can be used in complementary ways to rescue the notion of sustainable development from the conceptual fog and political abuse from which it suffers.

Thus far, the support basis for the application of the idea of environmental space has been confined mainly to some environmental groups and academic circles. Only a handful of governments have expressed an interest in the concept and adopted it as a basis for their environmental integration efforts. In Denmark, it was introduced in the national Environmental Plan in 1995, and links can also be seen with the Dutch National Environmental Policy Plan.[41] However, the greatest effort toward its application has come from nongovernmental actors, especially from Friends of the Earth, the main promulgator of the approach, which has produced a significant number of reports for individual European countries to which the concept has been (often tentatively) applied.[42]

However, notwithstanding these obstacles and scant formal adoption at the national level, in some areas the idea of environmental space has been de facto introduced (albeit not explicitly), at the international level. The international agreements on the phasing out of ozone depleting substances can be seen as a case of identifying ecological limits that provide a basis for quantitative reductions in the use of environmentally harmful substances over specified periods. Similarly, the Kyoto Protocol sets quantitative limits for emissions of greenhouse gasses, globally and for specific countries, within a time-frame. Although both agreements are not based on the strong (per capita) equity principle associated with the environment-space approach, equity considerations have played a role in the allocation of rights and obligations among countries. Thus, where environmental limits can be identified and quantified at the international or global level, and where the need for action has found sufficient worldwide support, there appears to be scope for adoption of the environmental space approach, even if it is only in a modest and inadequate form (especially in the case of greenhouse gas emissions).

Given the "free rider" problem and that, fundamentally, the pursuit of sustainability cannot be successful only on a local or national basis, but requires also agreement and action at the global level, it is likely that the concept of environmental space will gain significant ground at the national level only if and when support for applying it at the global level has become stronger.

(ECO)SYSTEMS THINKING AND THEORY

Systems theory is often regarded as holding much promise with regard to producing more integrated and superior understanding of the environment and environmental problems. In *The Turning Point*, Capra points out the shortcomings of approaches to social, economic, and environmental problems based on narrow and fragmented knowledge produced by modern (Cartesian-Newtonian) science, which takes a mechanistic worldview (looking at the world and people as machines) and fails to recognize the systemic and interconnected nature of problems. He also notes developments toward a new worldview in physics that is "organic, holistic and ecological," and that can be described as a "systems view, in the sense of general systems theory."[43] Based on a "systems view of life," which recognizes the "essential interrelatedness and interdependence of all phenomena . . . profound transformations of our social institutions, values, and ideas" will be required to resolve these problems.[44] In the *Web of Life*, Capra puts forward general "principles of ecology" as a basis for behavior change (interdependence, the need to understand relationships, feedback loops, and flexibility).[45]

The linkages between ecological and sociopolitical factors were also recognized by another early advocate of a systems approach, Karl Deutsch, who used the term "ecosocial system" to refer to the combination of ecological and social systems, the latter including the subsystems of economics and politics. Deutsch explored the emerging field of ecosocial science and ecopolitics—"that is, about the growing interplay of mankind's social and economic activities and its natural environment, and about the political challenges and decisions which this growing interplay produces or requires."[46] Given the size of the task, however, Deutsch foresaw that the development of a general systems theory of these interactions was going to take a long time, and that a plurality of methods would be used in the meantime.[47] Yet, he seemed optimistic, and believed that a systems approach held the promise of delivering powerful methods and insights. This reflected a more widespread faith in systems theory in the 1960s and 1970s, including in social and political science and policy analysis.[48]

However, it seems that, as yet, general systems theory offers little in terms of more specific guidance for environmental integration. The general themes of interconnectedness, feedback loops, and flexibility (or adaptation) that underlie systems approaches do not, by themselves, provide claims or insights about the specific connections between ecological, sociocultural, and political-economic factors and developments. Connections are commonly depicted at a very general level, such as between belief systems; political, social, and economic systems; human values; interests and actions; and environmental effects. Where general systems theorists move toward offering more specific ideas for advancing environmental integration, these are commonly based on findings or ideas developed in more delineated (middle-range) areas of study and theories that are not based on general systems theory. For instance, the more specific suggestions that Capra offers (such as ecological tax reform, greater cooperation, "partnership," and democracy)[49] do not have their roots in systems theory, but in environmental economics, environmental policy, and ecopolitical thinking. Similarly, the recommendations put forward by advocates of a systems approach to sustainability also depend largely on ideas developed independently from systems theory, such as recycling, increased efficiency, and impact assessment.[50]

As yet, the cases where general systems theory has been adopted by governments as a basis for environmental integration are rare. The first Dutch National Environmental Policy Plan, adopted in 1989, allegedly was based on systems thinking, and systems theory has been explicitly applied in the analysis of particular policy sectors, such as transport, energy, and agriculture.[51] However, general systems theory appears still far away from being adopted as a cognitive framework for integrating political, social, economic, and environmental institutions and systems along the line advocated by Deutsch. Thus far, the (political) support basis for using general systems theory as an overarching framework for environmental integration appears to be confined to relatively few philosophers and academics. However, one of the "derivatives" of systems theory, the idea that ecosystems (knowledge) can and should provide a basis for integrated environmental management, has received more support, especially at the subnational level of government.

Ecology or ecological science arguably provides a cornerstone for the development of a more specific cognitive framework for guiding environmental integration. Ecological science is often referred to as the basis for ecosystem management.[52] Without knowledge and recognition of the complex and dynamic relationships between organisms and their environment, environmental integration, it can be argued, does not make much sense. Scientific interest in, and efforts toward, increasing our understanding of ecosystems, has led to a growing involvement of scientists in initiatives toward integrated environmental management.[53] The idea that ecological science has much to offer, especially by creating a broad and sound knowledge basis for environmental management, has been an important reason for its appeal.

Although Sir Arthur Tansley has been credited for coining the concept "ecosystem" in 1935,[54] it has been argued that much of the groundwork for modern ecological science was laid in the late nineteenth century by Norwegian, Danish, German, and British scientists who sought to understand changes in fisheries populations by studying their habitats and physical environment.[55] Shortly after World War II, research into the dynamics and variety of influences on fisheries within the oceanic environment was given a major push in California following the collapse of the sardine fishery, in a project that "stands as an exemplary model of "large marine ecosystem research" fully four decades before the concept moved to the center of ecologists' and policymakers' attention."[56]

But it was only in the 1970s that ecosystem thinking started to be applied in environmental management more broadly. Lynton Caldwell was a pioneer in this respect, advocating the application of the concept as a principle for public land policy in 1970.[57] Like Capra, Caldwell saw an ecosystems approach as "essentially a total systems approach,"[58] involving a "wholistic emphasis."[59] Ecosystem management, Caldwell argued, should be rooted in scientific knowledge, providing an "objectively rational basis for land policy" and "an objective basis for mediating otherwise irreconcilable disputes."[60] Although an ecosystems-based policy, grounded on objective, rational, scientific knowledge, might be difficult to formulate, given complexities and uncertainties, he noted, it can provide a better basis for management than existing land policies, which "are often consequent to decisions made in banks, bars, and bedrooms"[61] and than the present system in the United States, which is based on multiple and conflicting laws, organizations, and regulations.

However, the idea that environmental management can be based on knowledge acquired by ecological science has proved to be problematic. It has been noted that ecological knowledge is limited and subject to much uncertainty. Because of "third order interactions, cascading trophic effects, and nonlinear relationships,"[62] ecosystems prove to be "far more complex and difficult to manage than was thought."[63] It has been argued that, in practice, we do not (yet) really know how to manage ecosystems.[64] Some critics take the view that because of the lack of precision that is inherent to the ecosystem concept, it is an unsuitable basis for guiding environmental policies in general.[65] But while some of the advocates for taking an ecosystems approach may have been too optimistic about its potential to provide the main or only glue for integrated environmental management, based on ecological knowledge, this is no reason for abandoning the notion of ecosystem management. Uncertainty is a common feature of all knowledge underlying environmental policy—or all policy, for that matter. Even if not complete or total, knowledge about ecosystems can and should provide a significant input into the decision-making process. But it cannot, and should not, be the only basis.

The limitations of ecological science in providing guidance to environmental integration and management now appear to be widely acknowledged. However, this does not seem to have brought about a loss in appeal of the idea of ecosystem management. Paradoxically, the popularity of the notion of ecosystem management seems to have grown, despite the fact that it failed to live up to the promise of providing such a basis, and despite growing doubt that it will ever be possible to develop such a basis.[66] Increasingly, ecosystem management has been interpreted as something else than ecological-science-based environmental management. In part, the move toward broadening the concept of ecosystem management can be attributed to growing support for the belief that ecosystem science—like all science, for that matter—is and cannot be value-free. Ecosystem management is seen as invoking normative questions, and consequently, the role of the ecologist has moved away from one of providing a solid knowledge basis for ecosystem management ("ecological engineering"), or even that of expert, to that of "contributor to a societal consensus on our comportment toward the environment"[67] or "educator, public relations specialist, technical advisor, or some combination of these."[68] Although ecosystem knowledge and research continues to provide a degree of scientific status to environmental protection efforts, the normative significance of the concept has become increasingly important, and coincides with a growing involvement of social scientists in discussions.[69]

The broadening of the notion of ecosystem management can be attributed at least in part to the growing involvement of social scientists in the debate. Although Caldwell and Deutsch both recognized the need for bringing social, economic, and political variables or factors into a systems approach to environmental management, many advocates of ecosystem management left humans and societies outside the picture. Only in the mid-1990s, when more social scientists started to get interested in this field, was the "human dimension" made an integral part of the study of ecosystems.[70] This development has not only widened the attention to sociocultural and political-economic aspects of ecosystem management,[71] but has also brought about a redefinition of the concept. Some authors take the view that ecosystem management is a new social or environmental movement, which takes a decentralized, participative, and holistic approach to management, seeking to integrate environment, economy, and community.[72] Focused on changing practices, it is seen to prepare the ground for political-institutional changes at higher levels of government.

But this development has also created considerable confusion, as the concept appears to mean "something quite different" to different advocates.[73] The ecosystem literature encompasses a diversity of philosophical, political, and theoretical positions, from anthropocentric, conservative, technocratic ("top-down"), and science-based approaches, to ecocentric, radical, democratic ("bottom-up"), and values-based ones,[74] with a variety of positions, such as "symbiotic," pragmatic, "consultative," and "science fused with politics" ones, in between.[75] Many authors take a prescriptive rather than an empirical or analytical approach to the topic, and are often "somewhat uncritical of the value of ecosystem management."[76]

Despite its broadened perspective, the ecosystems approach appears to focus mostly on the local, rural, or regional level of environmental management (catchments, river basins), and largely ignores the urban environment, in which many people (most people in industrialized countries) live.[77] Much of the literature has little, if anything, to say about the environmental integration needs or efforts at the national and international level, integration into or across policy sectors, or about obstacles and issues related to the dominant political-economic system. Some advocates of ecosystem management who place it explicitly in a broader political context conclude that fundamental political, economic, and social changes are likely to be required for it to become a new paradigm.[78] However, they offer few specific ideas or suggestions about the kind of changes that may be required to ensure that environmental concerns are integrated into and across policies and institutions, nationally as well as internationally, apart from creating "better linkages between the economic marketplace and the political marketplace."[79]

The notion of ecosystem management, especially in its broader interpretations, overlaps with various other cognitive frameworks that have been put forward as a basis for more integrated environmental management, especially at the local or regional level. Integrated environmental management (IEM), adaptive management, and holistic resource management also advance the idea of integrating (ecological) knowledge and social and economic needs and interests, and take sustainable development as a guiding principle. These frameworks appear to offer more specific prescriptions or guidelines for environmental integration than ecosystem management, and have found some application, mostly in the form of experiments, at the local or regional level.[80]

While these approaches may have considerable merit and potential in addressing, in an integrated way, difficult environmental issues "on the ground," they also have their limitations and risks.[81] First, they are highly demanding in time, organizational requirements, resources, and willingness to cooperate, conditions that are often in short supply. Second, they may shift the burden ("pass the buck") for resolving environmental issues to groups and communities that are not in a position or inclined to address the sources or driving forces that underlie many of these issues—for instance, in the realms of economics, technology, and politics. Third, and related to the second point, these approaches have little to offer in terms of insights or guidance about environmental integration challenges with regard to policies and institutions at the national and international level.

CONCLUSION

This chapter has discussed and reviewed some of the cognitive frameworks for cognitive-internal environmental integration, frameworks that offer broad or "holistic" interpretations of the environmental *problématique* that (can) provide overarching cognitive frameworks for other forms of integration. This is important, as separate and disjoint integration efforts are not necessarily mutually supportive or compatible, and may conflict with each other and even cancel each other out. However, given the diversity of interpretations of the environmental *problématique*, shaped by different and conflicting worldviews, ideologies, and interests, reaching agreement on such a framework at the national level, and even more so at the international, level, seems utopian. Yet, ideas and frameworks do not enjoy the same level of (political) support. In practice, some ideas are, or may become, dominant, while others are relegated into the background. The question, therefore, is to explain why some ideas or frameworks receive the upper hand, what the merits of these frameworks are, and whether they should and can be substituted or complemented by other frameworks.

The cognitive framework that by far has become the most popular among governments, and perhaps the world at large, is that of sustainable development. Although more a discourse than a clearly defined concept, sustainable development proclaims the possibility of a pattern of development in which environmental, social, and economic concerns and needs are heeded and made compatible. Extensively debated and critiqued, the shortcomings and risks associated with the notion of sustainable development are well known, especially its potential to be used for symbolic purposes. The dominant interpretation of sustainable development, although providing a possible basis for environmental integration, encompasses more than environmental concerns, and can also be used to subordinate these to other (economic and social) interests. It is this ability to serve many and different interests, including dominant political and economic interests, combined with its moral appeal, that explains much of its political support. Because of the popularity of sustainable development as a framework, it probably provides the strongest platform for legitimating and advancing meaningful environmental integration at all levels of government, across policies, and into institutional frameworks. However, given its shortcomings and use for promoting nonenvironmental interests, it is crucial not to lose sight of the "environmental core" of the notion and to rescue the concept from inappropriate usage. The notion of environmental integration, as advanced here, may assist in keeping a focus on the place of the environment within the wider sustainable-development debate, and as a basis for greening the social and economic dimensions of that discourse.

The notion of ecological modernization, on which faith in the compatibility of economic growth and environmental protection expressed in the Brundtland report is largely based, focuses, in practice, on the large potential for using resources more efficiently, through existing and new technology and changes in management. However, for various reasons, the promise of EM does not appear to be taken up by many governments, and the prospects for this to change significantly seem slim. EM may offer substantial benefits to some industries in some countries but has much less potential for, and poses risks to, many others. Taken up in mostly rich countries, it may actually aggravate, at a global level, the gap between rich and poor, and shift environmental pressures toward the latter.

The notion of environmental space, directed at making sustainability concrete, combines ecological, social, and resource concerns, and thus offers an environmentally inclusive framework for environmental integration and management, from the local level to the global one. However, apart from promoting equity and defining limits beyond which harm to the environment and humans is likely to arise, it does not provide more *positive* guidance with regard to the human-environmental dimension. Despite this limitation, and the fact that its adoption faces a range of issues and obstacles, it has much to offer to those who take the notion of sustainability seriously, and to advocates of environmental integration and social justice in particular. Thus far, political support for the idea among national governments has been very low, but in a modest form the environmental space approach has already been applied at the international level.

General systems theory arguably offers the most encompassing cognitive framework for understanding the linkages between environmental, social, economic, and political phenomena and developments. However, its support basis is very small and mostly confined to "thinkers" rather than "doers," and as yet offers little in the way of specific guidance to environmental integration efforts across the spectrum of policies and institutions. Most of the more specific and practical ideas and suggestions offered by systems theorists are based on middle-range theories developed in different disciplines. Arguably, the level of abstraction inherent to general systems theory, as in all efforts to design general, all-encompassing theories and explanations, makes it unsuitable as a guide for specific efforts and actions directed at environmental integration.

Yet, one offshoot of systems theory, ecosystems theory, has been put forward as an integrated cognitive framework for environmental management. The notion of ecosystem management, initially founded on the idea that ecological science can define the parameters for environmental management, has attracted considerable support, especially at the subnational level. However, as ecosystem management evolved from a science-based framework for environmental management to a (much) broader one, open to many different interpretations, its capacity to provide guidance to more specific efforts and actions directed at environmental integration has become even more problematic than in its initial form. Although it is possible, or even likely, that support for ecosystem management and related approaches will continue to grow at the subnational level, its ability to function as an overarching framework for environmental integration at the national and global levels appears quite limited.

The assessment of cognitive frameworks in this chapter indicates that the notion of sustainability appears to hold most sway as an overarching framework for environmental integration. Nationally and internationally, it enjoys a level of support unmatched by the other frameworks discussed in this chapter. It also offers a comprehensive basis for environmental integration in and across the five other categories of forms of integration identified in chapter 1. Its main weakness (and strength) lies in its capacity to serve a broad range of interests, given the dominant (inappropriate) interpretation. As the discourse of sustainable development is unlikely to fade away in the near future, the main challenge facing advocates of environmental integration is to advance environmentally meaningful interpretations of the concept, and not to be overwhelmed by uses that seek to diminish or even marginalize environmental concerns. As discussed above, the notion of environmental space, which can be used as a supplementary framework to make sustainability concrete at all levels of governance while incorporating the ecological, social, and resource dimensions of the environmental *problématique*, appears to be most capable of advancing environmentally meaningful interpretations of sustainable development. Although its existing political support basis is quite limited, it is quite possible that it will grow, especially at the international level.

In the meantime, the notion of sustainable development has already been used also as a guiding principle for policy and institutional integration. In the following chapters, I will discuss the various ways by which the integration of environmental concerns into and across policies and institutions has been advanced by governments.

4

Policy-External Integration

INTRODUCTION

This chapter will focus on how, and to what extent, governments have sought to internalize an environmental dimension into policies that are usually not considered to be core environmental policy, such as economic, energy, transport, and agricultural policy. The importance of environmental integration (or greening) of such policy areas lies in the fact that many of the immediate sources or causes of environmental pressure are located in the spheres of economics, energy, transport, and agriculture. Government policies in those policy areas contribute, directly or indirectly, to the degree of environmental pressure emanating from those spheres. I will use the label "environmental policy integration" (EPI) to refer to efforts directed at the greening of nonenvironmental policies, as distinct from "green planning," which is used as a generic label for the development of comprehensive and integrated policies that guide environmental integration across a broad spectrum of policy areas (policy-internal integration).

That government policies do or may contribute to environmental problems, directly or indirectly, has been recognized for quite some time. In many countries, governments have been, and still are, involved in a broad range and variety of activities that have a direct impact on the environment, most notably to provide the infrastructure for further development, such as roads, canals, airports, dams and power stations, the power (electricity) grid, telecommunications, land clearance for agriculture, mining, and heavy industry. Moreover, it was not unexceptional for governments to also own and run industries that have little or nothing to do with providing infrastructure, such as car factories, shipping industries, textile and other manufacturing industries, and tourism, and other service industries. This made or makes governments directly responsible for the considerable environmental damage often caused by such activities. With the rise and spread of neoliberal ideology in the 1980s, the governments in many countries have reduced their direct involvement in such activities (by privatizing state-owned assets or setting up commercial enterprises operating at arm's length from the government). However, promoting development and economic growth remains one of the core imperatives of governments, whether by direct or indirect means. Increasingly, this role has created tension with the growing responsibility of governments as environmental stewards and protectors of the environment. Although the notion of sustainable development has been adopted by many governments as a formal commitment, and may seem to have eased that tension, it has far from disappeared.

In this context, I need to reiterate that the notion of public policy is interpreted here as what governments do or do not do, intentionally, not just what they proclaim to be doing (formal goals and objectives). This implies that policy integration may involve the integration of environmental interests into the *processes* associated with policy formation and implementation, and in the selection of *policy instruments*, not only into formal goals, objectives, or targets (referred to here as the *substantive* aspect of policy). Although governments can and do use legislation to advance goals and objectives, it should be noted that much legislation is more in the nature of providing institutional frameworks (rules and regulations) that guide or channel human or organizational activities rather than an indicator of what governments deliberately *do* (or do not do) and aim to achieve. Governments come and go, and the legislative framework that they inherit may not necessarily reflect or match their actual goals and actions. Therefore, legislation (including environmental legislation) should not be conflated with government policy, but is better seen as part of the institutional framework. However, government efforts directed at *changing* legislation or at passing *new* legislation can be seen as a more reliable indicator of government policy.

It is important to keep in mind the political nature of environmental policy integration. Although policy development, and therefore policy integration, is a more overtly political phenomenon than cognitive integration, there is also a tendency for EPI to be approached from a technocentric and bureaucratic angle, moving it out of the limelight of politics. While this may seem to offer certain advantages, such as creating a "nonpolitical" and common ground for the development and implementation of long-term goals and objectives, and overcoming or bypassing the constraints associated with political decision-making, it also hides the political nature of the choices and decisions that are inherent to EPI. EPI involves not just the assessment of the (potential) environmental impacts of policies, but also the opening up of formal and nonformal processes of policy development to environmental advocates. The extent of environmental integration into nonenvironmental policy areas depends in large measure on the relative power and influence that environmental advocates, within and outside government, are able to exert in the processes of policy formation and implementation. This, in turn, is conditioned by the institutional framework within which the policy process is embedded. Successful environmental policy integration, therefore, requires institutional frameworks conducive to integrating environmental concerns and interests, an issue that will be addressed in chapters 6 and 7.

This chapter discusses some of the more generic means by which governments have sought to promote the integration of environmental concerns into nonenvironmental policy areas or sectors. One of the mechanisms that governments have used to advance policy-external integration is strategic environmental assessment (SEA). Although, in the United States, initially EIA was considered to be applicable also to policy proposals, in fact it has, for several reasons, been applied mostly to (development) projects. SEA has been advanced as a means for filling that gap. However, SEA is still a fairly new tool and has been adopted by a relatively small number of governments. Sustainability assessment (SA) is an even more recent mechanism. SA also builds upon the EIA tradition, but explicitly uses the notion of sustainability as a basis for assessment. In the policy realm, SA has been adopted by some countries, such as Canada and the United States, for the assessment of proposed free trade agreements. Arguably more important in terms of receiving widespread support and application is the use of economic instruments (in particular environmental taxes and charges). Economic instruments have been used to a smaller or greater degree by many governments as a means of internalizing environmental costs into the price of goods and services. Their use is also strongly supported by international organizations, in particular the OECD. However, their value and merit as a means for policy-external integration is not uncontested, and their adoption and performance has been quite variable across governments and policy areas, influenced in large part by political-economic factors and obstacles. In recent years, voluntary agreements and "partnerships" have become relatively popular means by which governments seek to integrate environmental concerns into nonenvironmental policy areas. But also these are not uncontroversial, and their effectiveness remains to be proven.

STRATEGIC ENVIRONMENTAL ASSESSMENT

Much of the thinking behind strategic environmental assessment (SEA) can be traced to the ideas associated with environmental impact assessment (EIA). As noted in chapter 2, Lynton Caldwell, one of the main architects of EIA in the United States, had in mind that EIA would apply to all government actions, projects, and programs, as well as to policies aimed at changing the dominant culture and values within organizations as well as preventing or mitigating environmental damage.[1] Thus, EIA was intended, at least from the point of view of some of its main advocates, to contribute to the greening of policies, including nonenvironmental policies, as well as institutions (rules and organizations). And indeed, formally, the EIA provisions in the US National Environmental Policy Act, which entered into force in 1970, apply to policies and programs as well as to projects.

In practice, however, EIA has been mostly applied to projects and, to a lesser extent, to plans and programs with relatively clear (geographical and/or sectoral) boundaries. With the exception of a few countries, EIA has been applied relatively rarely to national-level policy proposals.[2] Some of the reasons for that relate to methodological issues. EIA methodology has been developed for, and commonly assumes, proposals of which the environmental impacts are mostly of a biophysical nature and can be identified within a particular geographical area or at least on a geographical scale. EIA works best where and when the proposed activity is specific and geographically centered. It is much harder to apply to proposals that are based on broad, vague, and perhaps even conflicting goals and objectives, that are pursued by a range of means and instruments of which the effectiveness cannot be precisely determined, and of which the effects are likely to be scattered across large geographical areas and different groups of people.

SEA has been developed in recognition of the limitations of EIA and the issues associated with its application to policies, plans, and programs. Although project-based EIA can be valuable as a means of identifying, mitigating, or preventing undesirable environmental effects, it deals unsatisfactorily, if at all, with the cumulative and synergistic effects of developments. Moreover, projects seldom stand on their own, but find their source, and are embedded in, policies that provide them with their rationale, objectives, and often the specific terms for their design. That it is therefore important to rise above the ad hoc approach associated with project-based EIA, and to look "upstream" and address the environmental merits of policies, plans, and programs has long been recognized by critics as well as by advocates of EIA.

Despite the growing recognition of the need for strategic environmental assessment, until recently only some twenty-five countries and jurisdictions had adopted a form of SEA.[3] In the United States, SEA has been applied to programs and plans in the context of legislative requirements and arrangements for EIA (NEPA) from the 1970s, though on a far smaller scale than to projects.[4] Systems and arrangements for SEA started to be introduced in various countries in the 1990s, including Canada, Denmark, Australia, Finland, New Zealand, and the Netherlands. With the adoption of a SEA directive by the European Union in June 2001, which entered into force in July 2004, its introduction in member states has become compulsory. This has given a considerable boost to SEA, although its implementation is likely to be slow and diverse, largely because the EU directive only provides a framework. It is recognized that considerable time may lapse before SEA systems in all member countries will be fully operational.[5]

One of the reasons why, until recently, the uptake of SEA among governments was slow is that there is a wide range of views on what SEA is, and what it should entail. Dalal-Clayton and Sadler, who provide the most comprehensive overview of SEA systems that have been introduced until 2004, refer to SEA as a an umbrella concept that comprises a "family of tools and processes" for assessing the environmental or sustainability effects of policies, plans, and programs.[6] The diversity of interpretations and practices makes it difficult to explain to policy-makers what SEA is and what purpose it serves: "At present there is anything but clarity. Instead, there is an expanding plethora of different acronyms, descriptions and interpretations of SEA and SEA-type approaches in use internationally. . . . This reflects the fact that SEA is seen as a means to an end, a multi-lane route to addressing the environment and promoting sustainable development."[7]

Systems, approaches, and labels vary from country to country. Although some principles for SEA have been put forward,[8] significant differences continue to exist in approaches and methodology. As Brown and Therivel note, "there are considerable difficulties moving from a useful concept to widespread and enduring practice."[9]

Much of the lack of clarity and agreement about SEA can be attributed to its parenthood, EIA, and to different views about the appropriateness of EIA methodology for the assessment of policy. The assessment of policies raises a whole raft of issues that are usually disregarded in EIA thinking and practice, such as the fact that policies are often broad and vague, not usually the outcome of "rational" decision-making but of multiple and conflicting demands and interests, and that often the effects and implications cannot easily be geographically and physically delineated.

Nonetheless, there is a tendency among some advocates of SEA to treat it as an extended form of EIA, involving the application of the same principles at a higher tier of decision-making.[10] Others, however, take the view that SEA requires different approaches and methodologies, depending on the way policies are developed,[11] and that SEA should be based on principles that emphasize the qualitative and value dimensions of decision-making, in particular the importance of public participation and transparency,[12] and that recognize the role of interest groups, power, and politics.[13] As apparently there is no consensus among advocates of SEA regarding its design, or even principles, it is not surprising that a range of different SEA approaches and systems has evolved.

Theorists and analysts of SEA have tried to make sense of this diversity by identifying several broad categories of approaches. Sheate et al., based on more than 100 case studies drawn from twenty-five countries, identify four broad models of SEA: EIA-inspired SEA, appraisal-inspired SEA, integrationary SEA, and ad hoc SEA.

EIA-inspired SEA originates from ecological/resource management disciplines, emphasizes technical methodologies and baseline data, and is often used at the program level. Policy analysis/appraisal-inspired SEA originates from political science and policy analysis, and uses objectives as a preferred basis; it is often used within regional and spatial land-use planning. Integrationary SEA is focused on an objectives-led process, and is a combination of the first two models, with public participation usually being an important component of the process. It is "more likely to be found where there is a strong national environmental legislation and policy framework."[14] SEA as an ad hoc mechanism of environmental integration refers to the use of mechanisms such as roundtables, audit committees, and state-of-the-environment reports.[15]

Dalal-Clayton and Sadler use a slightly different classification, distinguishing between formal SEA procedures, other near-equivalent processes, integrated systems, and para-SEA systems.[16] The first category comprises EIA and EIA-based systems like those of the United States and the European Union, EIA-modified systems as adopted in Canada and Denmark, and the "dual track" systems introduced in the Netherlands and Finland. Examples of near-equivalent processes are environmental appraisal, regional assessment, and sustainability appraisal. These involve separate processes of environmental assessment aimed at integrating environmental concerns into policies, plans, or strategies, though not under a formal SEA label. In integrated systems SEA does not occur as a separate process, but takes place under broader processes or arrangements, for instance, under New Zealand's Resource Management Act (RMA), and in the context of integrated assessment and planning and substantive integration as practiced, respectively, in the United Kingdom and Australia. Para-SEA comprises approaches or procedures that have some but not all of the features or characteristics of SEA but have the same overall purpose.[17]

Although the lack of clarity and agreement on what SEA is and/or how it should be undertaken probably has been a factor in its relatively lukewarm reception among governments, the slow uptake of SEA, as well as the form that it is given when adopted, can be attributed also to political factors. As Sheate et al. note, the particular form of SEA adopted is sometimes constrained "for fear of constraining political choice."[18] Governments and government departments are reluctant to give up discretionary powers. Moreover, as policy assessment may expose interests, biases, and weaknesses, it is inherently a political activity. More generally, in a competitive democratic system, governments do not like to have their policies and policy proposals scrutinized and evaluated in a way that that can be easily exploited by political opponents.

The inherently political nature of environmental assessment, also at the level of plans and programs, may help explain why EIA-based systems of SEA appear to be more popular, and stand out as "the main cornerstone on which SEA is founded."[19] Grounding SEA on the same principles and methodology that have become widely accepted for EIA, with an emphasis on objectivity, science, and experts, can assist in depoliticizing assessments. It may also help explain why SEA has been less applied to broader policies. Broader policy principles and parameters (fundamental policy choices), including those associated with economic policy, remain out of bounds in SEA of programs and plans. This is also the case with the SEA directive of the European Union, which only prescribes SEA for certain plans and programs, and does not apply to legislation and national-level policies.[20]

How effective SEA has been in integrating environmental concerns into policy areas, and in particular nonenvironmental policy areas, depends on the form that it has been given and the way it is implemented. SEA in the form of program and plan evaluation may, in practice, not amount to much more than the application of EIA to multiple rather than single projects. Buckley notes that the application of SEA to programs in the United States has been more in the nature of giant project-type assessments, looking at a number of projects in a particular geographical area together rather than on a case-by-case basis.[21] Such an approach is still likely to leave beyond discussion and assessment broader and/or fundamental policy choices and issues, such as those related to global ecological implications, the socioenvironmental implications at the national level and in other countries, and the implications for the availability of resources (in quantitative and qualitative terms) in the long(er) term. To an even lesser extent, such approaches are likely to address underlying issues like the perceived need for the projects, the driving forces and interests behind them, the root causes of environmental problems, and the linkages with policies and policy priorities, even though such factors shape the choices made at the level of plans and programs.

Canada, Denmark, and the Netherlands are among the few countries where SEA has been applied to national-level policy proposals. In 1990, Canada was the first country to introduce a "new generation" SEA system separate from EIA legislation. The process provided for a flexible approach to the assessment of policies, programs, and policies initiated at the federal level. However, the implementation of the system during the 1990s has been judged to be ad hoc, uneven, inconsistent, inadequate, and unsatisfactory.[22] A revised Cabinet directive for SEA was issued in 1999, followed by the publication of updated guidelines in 2000. Flexibility remains a core feature of the approach. The guidelines emphasize that there is not one best method for undertaking an SEA, and agencies and departments are encouraged to "apply appropriate frameworks or techniques, and to develop approaches tailored to their particular needs and circumstances."[23]

How effective the Canadian system has been in terms of integrating environmental concerns into nonenvironmental policy areas remains unclear and is difficult to determine, in part, because no central register is kept of SEAs. An interesting feature of Canadian SEA practice is the application to trade agreements. Based on some sources, Dalal-Clayton and Sadler conclude that SEA practice has improved and become more visible,[24] but no evidence of a substantive nature is provided. However, like most evaluations of SEA (and, for that matter, EIA) systems, this assessment is based on the perceived merits of procedural and institutional aspects, not on actual outcomes.

In Denmark, SEA was introduced in 1993. In the 1993/94 parliamentary year, it was applied to 26 percent of government proposals, but the proportion increased to 77 percent in 1996/97.[25] Most government departments have used SEA, based on guidelines provided by the Ministry for the Environment and Energy, to assess the environmental implications of their policy proposals. Proposals are subjected first to a general scoping exercise based on a checklist. When it is found that the environmental effects could be significant, the proposal is subjected to a full assessment. In 1998, SEA was also applied to the budget in a major exercise coordinated by the Ministry of Finance, but that involved all ministries.[26]

One study of the Danish SEA system concludes that the scope of assessments and the quality of final SEA statements have tended to vary, with statements sometimes being as short as a paragraph or page. Over time, it is noted, the quality of environmental assessments has improved and a more systematic approach is now being taken.[27] The OECD, in its review of Denmark's environmental performance, notes that: "Efforts made by Denmark to apply strategic environmental assessment (SEA) to government bills and proposals and to the national budget are innovative and exemplary. The greening of government operations was one of the major elements in the SEA of the 1998 national budget. With green auditing, action plans by many State institutions and public procurement plans, progress is real in Danish administrations."[28]

However, it has also been noted that, while SEA has been frequently applied to the energy and transport development sectors, environmental bills, action plans and other environmental initiatives have tended to receive the most comprehensive assessments.[29] That the assessment of policy proposals in nonenvironmental policy may not be undertaken as rigorously as is desirable can also be inferred from the OECD's recommendation that the government should "pursue and further develop strategic environmental assessments, notably with respect to sectoral policy proposals and the national budget, in order to promote and evaluate progress towards sustainable development" and "continue and strengthen the integration of environmental concerns in planning and policies relating to agriculture, transport, energy and fisheries, as well as in new spatial planning concepts."[30]

In the Netherlands, the environmental assessment of legislative proposals was introduced in 1995 with the so-called E(nvironment)-test. The test is carried out on the basis of a short questionnaire, and under guidance from the Environment Ministry. Although initially intended to apply to all policy proposals, application has been confined to draft legislation and regulation. At first, the test was implemented in a flexible and low-key manner, with a minimum of guidance and procedural requirements. However, after a review of the test in 2001 concluded that the test appeared to have a negligible effect on decision-making, new procedures were issued in 2003, prescribing a two-stage process of scanning and appraisal.[31] Still, the test does not cover all policy proposals that have a potentially important impact on the environment, and as the institutional backing and capacity supporting its implementation have not been significantly strengthened, doubts remain about its effectiveness.

By contrast, the separate SEA system that the Netherlands has introduced for plans and programs has been judged to have had greater value and effectiveness. It is an EIA-based system prescribed for specified plans and programs, follows a mandatory process allowing for public input in the scoping and review stages, and provides for review of the quality of the information by the independent EIA Commission. It has been applied to national plans for waste management, electricity generation, and water supply, among other things. Subjected to reviews every five years, the system has been found to be generally positive and effective. The introduction of the SEA directive of the European Union is not expected to enhance the Dutch system; rather, it has raised some concern that the more minimalist approach contained in the directive may erode the effectiveness of the Dutch system when transposed into more flexible rules.[32]

The latter issue points out the importance of the institutional backing and capacity with which an SEA system is endowed. Whether and how (serious) SEA is implemented depends largely on whether it is prescribed rather than voluntary, and on the existence, position, and power of SEA advocates. Merely providing for SEA, even by law, does not guarantee that it is undertaken in more than a rudimentary or even symbolic way, or even at all, as the Australian and New Zealand experiences show. Although these two countries have legislative provisions for SEA, the provisions in Australia have never been used at the federal level.[33] In New Zealand, SEA is applied only on the basis of generic rules for environmental assessment, without specific mechanisms, and then only at the local and regional level of government.[34]

SEA, as a separate mechanism for advancing policy-external integration, is still a relatively new phenomenon. It is therefore not surprising that no generally accepted approach or "best practice" has yet emerged. Moreover, given the significant differences between project-based decision-making and the wider realm of policy-making, it is doubtful that the methodology that has evolved for EIA is suitable and appropriate for integrating environmental concerns into the policy process. Sheate et al. also have expressed the view that the inheritance of EIA has, in the past, acted as a constraint on the development of more appropriate SEA methodologies, because of the focus on technical detail.[35] Policy development involves much more than the rational assessment of specific proposals, and is fundamentally about collective decision-making regarding the direction, goals, and objectives of groups of people who, in most cases, have different interests, values, and views on these matters. Ensuring integration of environmental values and interests in public policy, although requiring knowledge, primarily demands the incorporation of these values and interests into the collective goals and objectives, and the adoption or development of appropriate and sufficient means for achieving these. Moreover, given the interconnections between policies and their synergistic and cumulative impacts on the environment, policy integration requires a common framework that provides guidance to environmental integration within policy areas and sectors. This is where the importance of green planning comes in, to be discussed in the next chapter.

That SEA is, fundamentally, a political process that involves, or should involve, deliberation about the place of environmental values and objectives within and across policy areas is increasingly recognized in the literature. For instance, Dalal-Clayton and Sadler note the mutually supportive nature of SEA and the national sustainable development strategies, with the latter providing a "key framework for giving effect to SEA and more integrative approaches."[36] Others refer to the objectives-led SEA as a form of assessment whereby proposals are assessed on the extent to which they impact on, and contribute to, formulated objectives.[37] The notion of sustainability impact assessment or sustainability assessment (SA) has emerged as a mechanism for assessing how policy proposals across the spectrum of policy areas impact on the goals and objectives that have been formulated by governments in such strategies. In some circles, sustainability assessment is seen as means of integrating the wide range of assessment tools (including CBA, regulatory impact assessment, and SEA) that have evolved over time.[38] Although SA is still very much in its infancy, it may well become a popular tool in the future, given the dominance of the discourse of sustainable development internationally. I will therefore discuss it shortly in the next section.

SUSTAINABILITY ASSESSMENT

Sustainability assessment has been described "as a process by which the implications of an initiative on sustainability are evaluated, where the initiative can be a proposed or existing policy, plan, programme, project, piece of legislation, or a current practice or activity."[39] Sustainability assessment can be seen as a form of integrated environmental assessment that encompasses environmental, social, and economic assessment, based on the three pillars commonly identified with the notion of sustainable development. Given that sustainable development is increasingly seen and adopted as an overarching cognitive framework for integrating environmental, social, and economic policies, the emergence of SA as a generic means for assessing proposals against this framework can be considered a logical next step in the evolution of assessment thinking and practice.

While applications of SA are still rare, the idea seems to have gained greater traction in some policy areas than others. In particular, the area of trade policy has been the subject of a variety of initiatives aimed at the promotion and application of SA, notably in North America and the European Union. In the early 1990s, the European Community assessed the environmental implications of the anticipated internal market. And the governments of Canada and the United States undertook environmental assessments of the proposed North American Free Trade Agreement (NAFTA). Although these reviews were mainly focused on the potential environmental effects of the agreement, these included some social aspects like safety and health issues. In 1994, the Canadian government undertook a post hoc assessment of the Uruguay Round and in 2000 NAFTA was also subjected to post hoc assessment by the North American Commission for Environmental Cooperation, the body set up in conjunction with the agreement. *Ex ante* assessments have been done, among other, by the U.S. government of proposed trade agreements with Chile and Singapore, and by the European Union, of its position in the new round of trade negotiations under the World Trade Organizaton.[40] The United States, Canada, and the European Union have institutionalized integrated assessment or sustainability (impact) assessment (SA) for trade agreements, and a range of other countries have applied such assessments on an ad hoc basis.[41] Various other studies have been done by nongovernmental organizations and academic institutions.[42] Altogether, these developments indicate that there is considerable and high-level interest in SA in the context of trade liberalization.

Although SA of trade agreements is becoming a more widespread practice, there is no commonly accepted standard or method for undertaking it. The OECD has produced several reports on methodologies of trade reviews.[43] In 1998, The World Wildlife Fund (WWF) published its recommended methodology for the assessment of trade liberalization agreements, and the UNEP also issued several reports on this topic.[44] The approaches taken vary on a wide range of points, including the subject, the scope, and the analytical framework and methods used. While opportunities for public participation are a feature of most approaches, they all have gaps and weaknesses, especially with regard to subject, scope and methodological rigor, and their use of indicators.[45] They often take a narrow view on what should be included, and only from the point of view of the country by which it is undertaken, not necessarily considering the social and environmental effects on other countries.[46]

But arguably the greatest weakness of SAs of trade agreements lies in the fact that most, if not all, take a "trade first" approach to the assessment, and do not conduct the assessment from an environmental or sustainability framework.[47] This means that they do not start with the question how such policies can or should be *designed* or changed to ensure environmental protection or sustainability, but take nonenvironmental policies or proposals as a starting point. While it might be deemed desirable that SA should be anticipatory and objectives-led, involving the assessment of proposals against the background of goals and objectives that have been formulated in the context of a government's sustainable development strategy, many governments appear to apply SA in the EIA-based tradition, whereby (positive and negative) impacts are identified but not placed in a policy context. In practice, SA then becomes the sum of three different assessment processes (based on a range of different methods) to identify environmental, social, and economic impacts, rather than a mechanism for advancing and integrating (policy) objectives.[48] Thus, SA, like EIA, is fundamentally reactive in nature and does not assess or address the driving forces underlying nonenvironmental policies.

Even if SA is objectives-based, however, it does not necessarily guarantee the integration of environmental concerns into nonenvironmental policy. As discussed in chapter 3, the dominant idea of sustainable development as encompassing environmental, social, and economic objectives usually leads to the interpretation of integration as the trading off between these three categories of objectives, which in many cases conflict with one another. Consequently, it is quite possible, if not likely, that environmental objectives lose out, as economic and social interests and objectives often enjoy stronger political support and priority. Pope et al. refer to several examples of SA applications in Western Australia in which environmental concerns were overridden by nonenvironmental interests.[49] SAs do not guarantee that environmental or social concerns are given the weight in decisions that social and environmental advocates expect or seek. Economic and political interests may still outweigh social and environmental interests, depending on the "politics of trade." Perversely, SAs may help to legitimize trade agreements, as it can be claimed that social and environmental concerns have been considered and integrated, even if in reality only lip service is paid to such concerns.

This does not mean that SA should be rejected out of hand and that it cannot or will not improve environmental performance within policy areas or sectors. Studies indicate that SA of trade agreements, if conducted *ex ante* and meeting certain criteria, has the potential to identify and prevent social and environmental harm.[50] Having a formal system for the SA of trade agreements, for instance, seems preferable to a reliance on just broad government statements of commitment toward the integration of trade and environmental interests, which often appear to be hollow and largely symbolic, as in Australia and New Zealand.[51]

What this means and amounts to is still an open question. On the one hand, SA can function as a means for opening up the process of discussion (and even decision-making) about the merits of trade liberalization, and for incorporating environmental concerns into trade policy. On the other, it is possible that SA will be used to justify and legitimize an ongoing process of trade liberalization, through multilateral and bilateral agreements, at most mitigating environmental and social impacts. The former possibility is emphasized by proponents of SA who interpret it mainly as a social communication and reflexive learning process that leads to the "transformation of the basic (economic, social) beliefs of the actors and institutions" and consequent changes in goals, objectives, and policies.[52] An indication of the latter possibility can be found in the report of the OECD's workshop on methodologies for the environmental assessments of trade liberalization agreements, in which it is noted that "when assessments point to possible negative environmental effects arising from trade agreements, the appropriate response is not to halt the process of liberalization but rather to develop appropriate environmental policy responses."[53] How SA functions depends foremost on the specific arrangements by which it is institutionalized, and on who implements it. Given that the debate about SA appears to be dominated by officials and experts, it seems most likely that it will evolve into a comprehensive form of EIA-based SEA, shaped and implemented mostly by these groups within the prevailing political and legal parameters.

It is doubtful, however, that, on its own, SA will lead to a fundamental transformation or greening of nonenvironmental policies—in particular, of economic, energy, transport and agriculture policies. Other means or processes will be required to green the hard core of such policies, so as to make these compatible and properly integrate them with environmental imperatives. One other generic means that is increasingly advocated and used to integrate environmental considerations into a wide range of policy areas is economic instruments.

ECONOMIC INSTRUMENTS

Economic instruments[54] are a class of policy instruments that enjoy growing support, both within the area commonly regarded to fall within the realm of environmental policy (such as pollution control) as well as a generic means of integrating environmental concerns into nonenvironmental policy areas. Although initially the advocates for economic instruments were mainly found among economists, increasingly these policy tools have found favor also with environmentalists and governments. However, their adoption for environmental purposes still is relatively modest, and not without issues, controversy, and opposition. Here the discussion will concentrate mainly on the (potential) merits of economic instruments as tools for promoting policy-external integration. In particular, the "politics" associated with economic instruments will be highlighted as a crucial factor affecting their viability as well as desirability.

Economic instruments can be broken down into three main categories: charges and taxes, positive incentives/subsidies, and market creation.[55] Charges and taxes, such as on waste disposal, on the use of resources, on products, and on emissions of pollutants, have been used most in European countries, some already for a long time.[56] Similarly, positive financial incentives/subsidies are also not new instruments, and have been used by governments for many years, especially to encourage and support economic activities—notably, in agriculture, transport, and the production of nonrenewable energy. Some instruments in this category, like deposit-refund systems, have been used to promote the reuse of resources before the notion of environmental policy became common. Market creation is a relatively novel instrument, and was first introduced in the United States in the 1970s.[57] However, referring to economic instruments generally as "new" instruments seems odd, as most have been around for at least thirty years, and some for much longer.[58] What may be new is the level of interest that these instruments started to attract during the 1990s, in the environmental literature as well as from governments; this new level of interest can be attributed largely to political-economic factors.

The promotion of economic instruments as new and better instruments for environmental policy, and as a means of environmental integration, may be motivated primarily by political and economic rather than environmental reasons. Their attractiveness to governments appears to have grown with the rising costs of environmental regulation and the need to find additional sources of revenue to compensate for a declining tax basis as a result of tax cuts, especially for higher incomes.[59] The shift from direct (income) tax to indirect taxes has also been advocated on economic grounds (reducing "distortion" in economic decisions). As the OECD notes: "The use of economic instruments is likely to increase as governments and industry are subject to increasing pressure to implement cost-effective approaches to meet their economic and environmental policy goals."[60]

The growing interest in and attraction of economic instruments is often attributed to their purportedly inherent advantages, as proclaimed in the theoretical literature. From a theoretical-economic perspective, the main strength of economic instruments lies in their cost-effectiveness. Economic instruments lead economic actors to adopt the most cost-effective means for addressing environmental problems (where the marginal costs of measures equate with their marginal benefits). Moreover, they are also claimed to provide incentives for ongoing innovation (to further reduce pollution and the costs of environmental measures) and thereby to create new employment (the "double dividend"). Although they are credited with stimulating environmentally desirable behavior, they also are said to leave choice with economic actors (enhancing their "freedom"). Last but not least, they are a means of generating (government) income that can be used to cover the costs of environmental management. Economic instruments are often contrasted with the "traditional" regulatory or "command and control" approach used by governments, which is, by implication or explicitly, deemed to be less cost-effective, stifling, rigid, and financially burdensome.

However, as many authors have pointed out, advocates of economic instruments have a tendency to compare apples with oranges. Comparing the theoretically possible advantages of economic instruments with "real life" "command and control" practices, economic instruments may indeed show to advantage. However, when their actual implementation and performance is assessed, the claimed advantages of economic instruments always fall (far) short of their alleged potential. Evaluations of actual uses of economic instruments commonly produce a mixed bag: while they are often credited with having produced economic and, in some cases, environmental gains, these appear to be much less than the promise held up in theoretical models.[61] Although environmental taxes can, and sometimes have had, significant impact on emissions,[62] the level at which they are set is often insufficient to influence significantly behavior or practices.[63] The Dutch water quality charge[64] and the Danish waste tax[65] have been referred to as examples of economic instruments that have been successful in producing significant environmental gains, but in most cases environmental taxes appear to be too low to provide a sufficient incentive to behavior change.[66] Most emission charges and taxes seem still to be designed primarily for revenue-raising purposes, in high- as well as low-income countries.[67] Environmental taxes are usually set at levels that internalize only a fraction of the environmental costs brought about by the activity that is taxed, and/or the costs of abatement.[68]

Subsidies can be used to encourage positive environmental practices and behavior. Subsidies, perhaps better labeled "positive financial incentives," come in different forms, including tax breaks, price subsidies, and financial support for research and development. Governments have used positive financial incentives to promote, for instance, public transport, recycling, energy efficiency and conservation techniques, conversion to organic growing, and the development of renewable energy technologies. Although economists often warn against the use of subsidies because of their "distorting" effects on prices and efficient resource allocation, there is a place for such tools if properly designed and targeted.[69] Subsidies have played an important role, for instance, in boosting the development of wind power, as the experience in some countries, notably Denmark and Germany, shows.[70] However, most governments are reluctant and modest in providing such incentives; in some countries where such subsidies were used, they have again been abolished.[71]

By contrast, governments have been much less reluctant and cautious providing subsidies for industries and activities that have (had) enormous negative environmental effects, such as for mineral production, forest logging, fishing, agriculture, energy exploitation, and transport. It has been estimated that, for the period of 1994–98, worldwide subsidies to natural resource, industry, and energy sectors comprised more than one trillion US$ per year, 68 percent of which is provided by governments of OECD countries.[72] Whatever positive effects environmental charges and taxes achieve, these are offset or even negated by the continued use of subsidies for activities that cause considerable environmental harm. Although there has been some movement toward phasing out subsidies,[73] especially in the context of international talks and agreements on "free trade," they are strongly entrenched politically. Therefore, despite the overwhelming economic, social, and environmental arguments against most of these subsidies, abolishing them is quite a challenge, even in countries where governments officially proclaim their support for free trade.

Tradable permits or quota systems imply the allocation of tradable rights to a quantity or proportion of a resource (such as fisheries or water) or to a certain level of emissions or discharges (pollution). The overall level of resource use or pollution is set by the government, based on what is deemed acceptable or desirable. Buying and selling of permits or quota arguably promotes the optimal use of the permits or quota. As overall limits can be based on ecological sustainability criteria, tradable permit or quota schemes can integrate the issue of scale or limits more effectively than environmental taxes or charges. They therefore seem compatible with the view of those who argue that economic activity should be reembedded into the ecological context.[74]

Tradable permit or quota systems should not be confused with the property rights or free-market environmentalism approach, which advocates the privatization of resources based on the view that the combination of private property rights and the market ensures the optimal allocation and use of resources.[75] This effectively eliminates the role of government in resource decision-making, and thus contributes to the neoliberal aim of moving toward a minimal state. Although this approach assumes that the market will integrate environmental concerns if and when these are important to economic actors, the record of market failure provides not much basis for optimism in this respect. As Kinrade notes, ownership (property rights) does not guarantee the protection of noneconomic values (as land management practices on private land demonstrate), and what may be an optimal level of pollution from an economic point of view may not be sustainable from an ecological perspective.[76] By contrast, permit and quota systems remain under government control and ownership, and allow for the setting of levels considered to be environmentally necessary or desirable. However, although formally not property rights, permits and quotas de facto are assets that can be bought, sold, and accumulated, and that may end up being concentrated in a few big companies.[77] Unless the government sells such rights or charges rents, all or most of the revenue that they generate is appropriated by the permit or quota holders, not the government, which, from an economic point of view, blurs the distinction between permits/quota and private property rights.

The introduction of tradable permit and quota systems has been confined to relatively few countries and to a limited range of applications, and still seems to be at an experimental stage. The United States has been the main center for experimentation for trading schemes (in emissions, lead), and, in 1992 became the home for the world's largest tradable permit system designed to cut sulphur dioxide (SO_2) emissions.[78] In Europe, where there has been a prevailing preference for the use of taxes rather than trading schemes, as far as the use of economic instruments is concerned, there has been a growing interest in this approach, especially in the United Kingdom.[79] To meet their emission reduction targets under the Kyoto agreement, several countries, including Denmark, the Netherlands, and the United Kingdom, adopted proposals for putting in place greenhouse gas emissions trading systems and, in 2005, a CO_2 emissions trading scheme became operative at the European Union level.[80] With regard to tradable quota systems for resources, so far few countries have introduced such schemes. In the area of fisheries, New Zealand led the way with the introduction of a system of individually tradable quotas in 1986, an example followed by several other countries.[81] Local trading schemes for water resources have been introduced in a wider range of countries, including parts of Brazil, India, Mexico, and Australia, but also these are still not widespread.[82] Since the 1990s, what has become more common with regard to water is the (semi)privatization of the resource in the hands of multinational companies. This has happened especially in low-income countries, where a few Western corporations dominate the market.[83]

The environmental results of the use of tradable permit schemes, mostly in the United States, have been referred to as "not very impressive."[84] For Australia, it has been noted that tradable permit schemes "do not significantly enhance environmental outcomes or improve pollution abatement performance."[85] Air pollution schemes appear to have been most successful, but water pollution control schemes generally not, while individually tradable quota systems in fisheries have delivered mixed results.[86] Moreover, where positive results have been achieved, it is difficult to attribute these solely to particular economic instruments, given that such instruments are normally part of a broader policy package, and given the influence of other developments.[87]

The discrepancy between the promise (in theory) and practice of economic instruments is often blamed on politics, which causes decision-makers to adopt "flawed" and "suboptimal" designs that often fail to satisfy the "ideal model outlined in environmental economics."[88] Taxes introduced commonly depart from the "Pigouvian" model because of the influence of political-institutional factors.[89] Much of the literature on economic instruments appears to take the view that an expansion of their use is desirable, and refers to political and other obstacles as negative factors that prevent more effective or large-scale application. The relatively low number of post hoc evaluations and meager evidence of their positive (economic, environmental, and social) outcomes does not seem to deter advocates from proclaiming their superiority. In 2003, a study of their introduction in eight countries found it "puzzling" why it has taken so long for the superiority of the new instruments to be accepted and acted upon.[90] Their growing adoption by governments is often portrayed in positive terms, while continued reliance on "command and control" or "old" forms of regulation is put in a negative light.[91]

The use of such terminology points to the political and ideological dimensions of the debate on and practice concerning economic instruments. The language and classifications used in this context are far from objective or neutral. As Jacobs notes, the "common practice of calling regulatory instruments 'command and control,' with its pejorative connotations, is simply propaganda."[92] Charges and taxes require determining levels, need to be collected, and often entail little if any freedom for those on whom they fall. Permit and quota schemes depend on rules for allocation and trade, and also require monitoring to ensure compliance. Decision-making on all such issues involves allocating costs and benefits, affects people and interest groups differently, and is therefore highly political. Views on the merits of economic instruments are influenced by who benefits and who bears the costs, and ideology, and may vary from instrument to instrument.

From a political-economic point of view, it is not surprising that economic instruments enjoy different levels of support from groups in society. Charges and taxes, unless compensated for by other means, increase costs and prices for industries, consumers, or the public, and can have inequitable, regressive effects, which is unlikely to make them popular. Subsidies obviously are of immediate benefit to those who receive them. Not surprisingly, interest groups will try to influence the choice of instruments, and their shape, depending on how they are affected.[93] Differences between the (relative) political power of groups can make the difference between the adoption or rejection of a charge or tax.[94] Businesses usually take a more favorable view of trading schemes, as these are perceived to impose lower costs, can generate income, or even amount to being granted ownership of, or valuable rights to, resources, as has been mostly the case.[95] However, the distribution of advantages of permit and quota trading schemes depends to a large extent on their design, and they are often very uneven within an industry sector, accruing disproportionately to bigger companies.[96] Obviously, this gives little reason to smaller companies to provide strong support to such schemes.

Many environmentalists are much less favorably disposed toward trading schemes, especially if these amount to privatization, as they object to the commodification of collective environmental goods, and/or prefer public ownership and management, which is (nominally, even if not always in practice) subject to democratic control. Environmentalists tend to be more positive toward the use of environmental taxes, but some also feel uneasy about these, as taxes may not be effective enough (if set at low levels), or, more fundamentally, because taxing environmentally and socially damaging behavior is seen as morally unacceptable (amounting to a license to pollute, or to paying fines for sinning).[97] Tradable permits and environmental taxes have been compared to the medieval practice of selling indulgences by the Catholic Church.[98] They have also been opposed because such instruments may diminish opportunities for democratic debate about the underlying issues.[99]

Ideologically, the shift from so-called command and control to economic instruments can be seen to fit well with the political agenda of those who advocate a reduction of the role of the state and the adoption of governance, new styles of governing "whereby hierarchical government structures are increasingly giving way to public-private partnerships" and that blur the boundaries between the public and private spheres of decision-making.[100] But while the purported aim of governance may be to enhance democracy, it may de facto increase the power of economic actors, in particular of major corporations, and assist in the (semi)privatization of publicly owned resources and assets.[101] Dryzek condemns economic instruments as having antidemocratic effects, since they "help to establish more firmly an economically rationalistic world, one populated by *homo economicus* rather than *homo civicus*." "*Homo economicus* is not good for democracy."[102]

Because of the political-economic obstacles that stand in the way of a much more significant level of "internalizing externalities" into the prices of goods and services, it is unlikely that environmental taxes, on their own, even if accompanied by tax reduction in other areas, will soon become a much more important mechanism for economic-environmental integration. At most, such taxes can only be increased very gradually, to lessen the pain and reactions that they can bring about. This is commonly acknowledged also by the advocates of ecological tax reform.[103]

Whether economic instruments contribute to environmental integration also remains doubtful. While they may induce actors to change their practices or behavior, they do so, economic theory tells us, for economic, not environmental, reasons. By implication, if or when the economic incentives weaken or disappear—for instance, because the economic gains have been exhausted (the "optimal" savings have been achieved) or economic developments (such as rising incomes or declining market prices) erode the effect of a tax or charge—actors may revert to their previous practices and behavior. Environmental values are only recognized and taken into account to the extent that they have been translated into monetary values. Economic incentives do not, by themselves, instill environmental consciousness or values into the cognitive frameworks of actors. At most, therefore, they are complementary tools for the greening of policies, behaviour, and practices.

VOLUNTARY AGREEMENTS

Since the 1980s, many governments, including Denmark, the Netherlands, Canada, the Czech Republic, New Zealand, and the United States, have relied on voluntary commitments of, or agreements with, industries or industry sectors, including reducing CO_2 emissions.[104] In Japan, an early leader in this area, the first "pollution control agreements" were concluded in the 1960s, and now total more than 30,000.[105] In 2002, the European Commission proposed comprehensive rules for drawing up voluntary agreements with industry sectors across the European Union to achieve environmental goals without recourse to legislation.[106] With neoliberal ideology becoming a strong and even dominant political force, first and foremost in Anglo-Saxon countries but then in much of the world, voluntary agreements, and more generally cooperation ("partnerships") between governments and business, sometimes also involving environmental or community groups, became a preferred approach, while regulation, often dismissively labeled as "command and control," fell out of favor.[107] This was confirmed at the World Summit in Johannesburg in September 2002, where "partnership" became the prevailing catchphrase.[108]

However, not everyone is convinced about the merits of voluntary agreements. For a start, there is doubt, backed by evidence, about the effectiveness of voluntary agreements. Even in the Netherlands, a traditionally cooperative society where voluntary agreements ("covenants") have become a preferred tool, their success has been variable. Although many covenants have led to emissions reductions, targets have not always been achieved, and they appear to be not so effective in the transport and agriculture industries.[109] In the fourth Environmental Policy Plan (NMP4) of the Netherlands, it is recognized that a more rigorous assessment of the effectiveness of covenants is required.[110] The reliance on voluntary agreements to reduce CO_2 emissions—for instance, in Canada and New Zealand—has not produced much, if any, result. Moreover, it is not clear to what extent voluntary agreements have led or contributed to technological innovation directed at reducing environmental impact. Based on several criteria, including impact, a comparative study of twelve voluntary agreements found a mixed bag.[111] An OECD study concluded that the environmental effectiveness of such agreements was questionable, as only in a few cases had such agreements contributed to "environmental improvements *significantly different* from what would have happened anyway" (emphasis in the original). Moreover, from a wider economic perspective, their economic efficiency was found to be generally low, as they rarely include mechanisms to equalize marginal abatement costs between producers.[112] Their main advantage lies in the flexibility that they provide to individual industries, offering greater scope for a more lenient treatment than economy-wide policy measures.

Although, to some extent, the limitations of voluntary agreements might be overcome by introducing particular mechanisms or conditions, there are also more fundamental concerns about a heavy reliance on an approach that provides much scope for industry to influence environmental policy. As the OECD study notes, the questionable environmental effectiveness of voluntary agreements "*could* indicate that a significant degree of "regulatory capture" has taken place" (emphasis in the original).[113] Often, voluntary agreements are worked out behind closed doors between industry and government, excluding environmental and community groups from the process. Even if the latter get a chance to participate, the emphasis on technical and economic issues (feasibility) and the sheer imbalance in resources between industry and community/environmental groups give industry the advantage in defining what is deemed realistic. And given that emphasis and imbalance, voluntary agreements bring with them a narrow view of the environmental *problématique*, a focus on emissions and technical aspects rather than on underlying political-economic and sociocultural issues. At most, therefore, voluntary agreements prod industries to partially clean up their act. But they can also function as a mechanism for delaying the introduction of more demanding (and possibly more effective) policies and rules by governments.

CONCLUSION

While strategic environmental assessment, sustainability assessment, economic instruments, and voluntary agreements are receiving growing support among governments, their outcomes and potential in terms of integrating environmental values and interests into nonenvironmental policies appear to be limited, for the reasons discussed above. SEA and SA are relatively new mechanisms or approaches that lack commonly agreed-upon methodologies and even meanings. Applications are still rather tentative, almost experimental by nature, and practices vary widely, differing also in the extent to which assessments and assessors are assigned importance, authority, and resources. As yet, the actual impact of these mechanisms on the adjustment or development of policies seems very modest. Also, given their roots in the idea and practice of EIA, there is a tendency for these tools to be applied after the fundamental parameters of policies have been determined rather than to function as inputs into the design of policies. Economic instruments, by contrast, have a longer history of use and are inherently part of policy design. However, their use for greening nonenvironmental policies is constrained primarily by political-economic factors. As the "internalization of externalities" implies higher prices or costs, this inevitably incurs opposition from those affected. Moreover, the effectiveness of economic instruments is circumscribed by autonomous economic developments and is dubious with respect to bringing about enduring changes in the driving forces (values, views, attitudes, interests, needs) behind behavior, as they reaffirm economic rather than ecological or social rationality.

Although these mechanisms create opportunities for drawing environmental considerations into the development of nonenvironmental policies, they do not, on their own, provide any guidance about what green policies are. The latter depends on ideas and criteria (cognitive frameworks) for determining what green or good policies are, and that provide a basis for assessing, and recommending changes to, existing policies. Although advocates and practitioners of these tools may create the impression that determining what is good or bad about policies can, or even should, be done by experts or professionals that use quasi-scientific or objective methods, analogous to what is often claimed with regard to the mechanisms used for cognitive-external integration, their application is always based on value judgments. Often, such judgments are politically and ideologically inspired, reflecting the interests and views of those who practice these methods. Whether and to what extent policies can be deemed to adequately integrate environmental concerns depends on substantive ideas about what green policies are.

Environmental integration into nonenvironmental policies, therefore, requires more than the application of tools such as those discussed in this chapter. Some idea or vision about what constitutes "green" economic, energy, transport, and agricultural policies, for instance, is required. Greening assumes that for every sector that (potentially) impacts significantly on the environment, policy goals and objectives are developed and adopted that incorporate environmental interests to the extent that those impacts are prevented or minimized to a level that is deemed acceptable. It also assumes that such policies are properly implemented and evaluated, and that any shortcomings or defects lead to readjustments that are considered desirable, in line with the notions of the policy cycle and policy learning.

Governments now commonly proclaim to be committed to the integration of environmental considerations into nonenvironmental policy areas. What they are doing to ensure that such efforts are compatible and coherent is the topic of the next chapter.

5

Policy-Internal Integration

INTRODUCTION

In the preceding chapter, the limited nature and effectiveness of the generic means used by governments to advance policy-external environmental integration were described and illustrated. One of the main limitations of these approaches lies in the fact that they do not and cannot by their very nature offer an overarching framework for policy integration. Generic methods are mainly means for identifying environmental issues, values, and interests that existing or future policies may generate or affect. Given the interdependence and interactions between policy areas and sectors, and the potential for incompatibilities and conflict between environmental integration efforts to emerge, there is a need for a broader policy framework that provides direction and a common basis for evaluating as well as developing such efforts. This challenge is referred to here as policy-internal (environmental) integration, as it expresses the need for internal consistency of integration efforts within the broad range of policies.

In this chapter I will discuss a range of broader policy frameworks that governments have used to promote policy-internal integration. To begin, some frameworks that are relatively limited with regard to their environmental inclusiveness will be discussed briefly. These frameworks may offer some degree of integration with regard to some issues or policy areas, and therefore have value and should not be discarded, but they are inadequate as overarching policy frameworks that provide guidance to all policies that (potentially) impact significantly on the environment. The policies based on these frameworks are also mostly reactive, directed at mitigating environmental problems rather than at addressing their sources or causes. Related to that, they fall short in providing a positive framework for guiding policies, in a concerted way, toward an environmentally sustainable future. By comparison, green planning offers a potentially more inclusive and more promising form of policy-internal integration, and one that has been adopted already in most countries around the world. Most of this chapter, therefore, focuses on green planning, analyzing and discussing developments, issues and obstacles, and limitations. The main argument is that, although green planning holds much promise as a form of policy-internal integration, its effectiveness has been constrained, in practice, by a weak political-institutional support basis and by cognitive limitations.

LIMITED FORMS OF POLICY-INTERNAL INTEGRATION

As noted in chapter 1, recognition of the need to tackle pollution in a more integrated way, to prevent it from being shifted from one medium (air, water, land) to another, led to the development of the idea and practice (in some countries) of integrated pollution control (IPC). That environmental problems need to be addressed in a more integrative way has also come to be accepted with regard to many other environmental issues, and has led to a wide variety of approaches that have integration in their label, such as integrated pest control, integrated waste management, and integrated coastal management. In the United States, comparative risk assessment (CRA) was introduced by the EPA as a framework for setting priorities among environmental problems.

However, the degree of environmental inclusiveness of most of these approaches is very limited. As their labels suggests, some of these approaches focus only on one environmental problem, such as "pests" or "waste." Although they represent a move toward a more integrated approach to these problems (for instance, by considering and addressing a range of pests together, or by addressing a variety of forms of waste), they are by their very nature not very environmentally inclusive. That does not mean that they are not worthwhile pursuing. On the contrary, as their focus is clear, as they bring together expertise and resources, and as they are likely to involve a more strategic approach and better coordinated action, such policies are likely to be more effective than their isolated counterparts. However, by their vary nature they do not provide, and are not meant to provide, an overarching policy framework for most or all environmental problems. Their effectiveness may also be constrained by the fact that they usually focus on *reducing* problems, often by some technical and managerial means, and do not address underlying causes or driving forces, which may lie outside of the area of expertise and responsibility of those charged with the responsibility for the management of the problem.

Integrated pollution control is a more environmentally inclusive form of policy-internal integration. Many countries, with Sweden being an early leader, have taken steps toward IPC as it became apparent that nonintegrated pollution-control policies and measures for air, water, and land often simply shifted pollution from one medium to another. Since many environmental issues can be seen as pollution problems, IPC is (potentially) a very comprehensive form of policy-internal integration.[1] In practice, however, IPC often appears to take quite a narrow approach to the problem of pollution. It sets out to identify the "least harmful" way to dispose of pollutants—accepting that *some* level of pollution is likely to be technically or practically inevitable—whether in water, air, land, given available treatment methods. This can occur on the basis of mainly environmental considerations (the "best practicable environmental option" approach), or while taking into account the economic costs (and benefits) of options (the "best practicable means" approach).[2] While it may set out to control the immediate sources of pollution ("end of pipe"), it is not directed at addressing the underlying causes of pollution, such as those related to decisions about the design of products and production methods; decisions about the means of transport, urban, and regional planning (including the location of industries); and economic decisions and policies.

Moreover, the notion of environment and environmental policy that guides IPC is rather narrow and does not cover many important environmental issues. Although IPC may address concerns about ecosystems as well as human health inasmuch as they arise from pollution, it does not consider the other sources of pressure on these environmental dimensions, in particular those associated with resource use—for instance, soil erosion and the overexploitation of water and other resources (such as energy, forests), population growth and distribution—and issues associated with the design and construction of the human environment (roads, urban development).

In short, IPC may provide a comprehensive but still not very environmentally inclusive framework for environmental policy integration, providing little if any guidance to agriculture, transport, energy, urban development, and economic policies. Although IPC is a step forward from fragmented approaches to pollution control, its effectiveness is compromised by the lack of attention to factors and driving forces behind the proximate sources of pollution, such as decisions about the design and production of new products with potentially damaging environmental effects and the continuing expansion of production and consumption that, over time, tend to negate the gains achieved by IPC.

CRA has been described as an application of RA to policy "designed to provide a framework for systematically evaluating risk reduction programs and budgets for the purpose of ascertaining whether different approaches or different priorities might go further or faster to produce environmental improvements."[3] It is thus a means toward getting the "most bang for the (risk management) buck." The main driving force behind the development and adoption of CRA, in the United States, was growing political concern about the rising costs of pollution control measures and a desire to increase the cost-effectiveness of such measures.[4] Although CRA has also been adopted outside the United States, it has not spread as widely as EIA or CBA. However, its appeal is likely to grow as the costs associated with combating environmental problems continue to rise, especially in countries and at times where governments are under growing budgetary constraints.

The limitations of comparative risk assessment, inasmuch as they derive from a narrow interpretation of the environmental *problématique* and environmental issues (all reduced to a particular notion of "risk"), have already been discussed in chapter 2. In theory, the notion of risk used in CRA can be expanded to encompass most if not all environmental issues, including risks to the (sustainable) use of resources, and to the integrity of ecosystems, and risks to broad notions of human well-being, including those associated with urban development, in the short term as well as in the long term. In practice, CRA often focuses on the more immediate threats to those who participate in the assessment, and on threats that can be quantified and translated into monetary terms, to calculate and rank options on their costs and benefits. Given funding constraints and the need to set priorities when facing numerous environmental issues and competing demands, CRA can be a useful tool. However, it does not provide much more than a ranking order of environmental issues in terms of threats and costs, and of the likely returns for every dollar invested in addressing them. Although this could imply a strategic analysis of the linkages between environmental problems and their underlying causes, CRA does not go that far. In practice, CRA appears not to be concerned with identifying and addressing the causes and driving forces behind environmental problems, but more with determining how much money should be spent on the various environmental demands upon environmental agencies, to justify their expenditure and to accommodate conflicting political pressures. Also, as noted in chapter 2, the focus on risks as a basis for determining environmental priorities gives a rather negative, problem-oriented orientation to environmental policy. It does not put forward a positive vision or program for guiding policies across the spectrum toward a future state of the environment that society aspires to.

Compared to these two forms of policy-internal integration (IPC and CRA), green planning potentially offers a more positive approach. The remainder of this chapter, therefore, will focus on green planning and assess to what extent its promise as a form of policy-internal integration has been fulfilled.

WHAT IS GREEN PLANNING?

Green planning offers, at least in theory, a comprehensive, environmentally inclusive, and source-oriented approach to policy-internal integration. The term "green planning" is used here to refer to a range of comprehensive policies adopted by governments under a variety of labels, such as sustainable development strategies (SDS), national environmental action plans (NEAP), national environmental policy plans (NEPP), or green plans. Early green planning initiatives developed in the 1980s, but they became common practice during the 1990s. Most governments have now adopted some form of green planning. However, the extent to which green planning has taken root and been developed into a more or less effective framework for policy integration varies between countries and governments.

As noted in chapter 1, green planning stands for the idea that there is a need for some kind of overarching policy framework to guide the development of all policies that have (potentially) significant impact on the environment. Such a framework provides *substantive* guidance to the environmental policy integration efforts across policy areas and sectors, in the form of common premises, goals, objectives and targets, to ensure that the efforts undertaken are complementary and mutually supportive. This is needed because conflict between policies, serving different interests and objectives, is a common feature of policy-making in modern pluralist societies, and does not necessarily disappear if or when environmental concerns are integrated, as discussed in the previous chapter. Green planning can therefore be conceived as an effort directed at finding or developing common ground between policy areas, *based on environmental parameters, imperatives, or goals,* to avoid or minimize environmental harm (potentially) caused by decisions and practices within individual policy areas. Green planning is environmental policy development at a higher level, defining the parameters on which other policies should or must be developed, not unlike the way monetary policy and financial-economic policy circumscribe or influence policy development across policies.

It is important to emphasize the *substantive* nature of green planning to distinguish it from other forms of integration. Green planning is a form of *policy*, involving the formulation of goals and objectives (and possibly targets) by governments, as an expression of government intent, and includes what governments *do* (or intentionally do not do) to pursue or achieve those goals and objectives. It should therefore be distinguished from institutions or institutional frameworks, which are formal and informal *rules* that prescribe, prohibit, or guide behavior and practices. Institutions may be introduced or changed as a result of government policy (for instance, in the form of legislation), and in support of government policy, but not all institutions are the result of, or represent or support, government policy. Governments are themselves bound by institutions (such as constitutions), and inherit a mass of legislation enacted by their predecessors, much of which can be at odds with the goals, objectives, and intentions of the government of the day. Institutional environmental integration, although it can be the result of government policy, also binds, limits, or guides existing governments, whereas green planning is a form of policy (integration) that can be more readily changed, or even dropped, by governments, in line with their priorities. Therefore, the extent to which, and how, green planning has been *institutionalized* (supported by environmental-institutional integration) is of fundamental importance to its long-term effectiveness.

The distinction is also important since sometimes countries are put forward as leaders in green planning, whereas, according to the interpretation advanced here, they are not. For instance, Johnson refers to New Zealand as a leader in green planning because of its Resource Management Act, an integrative piece of environmental legislation.[5] However, as the RMA does not contain or express environmental goals, objectives, or targets for guiding environmental policy integration across policy areas or sectors, and does not reflect the intentions, goals, and objectives in that respect of governments, it is not a form of *policy* integration. Rather, it is an instance of institutional-environmental integration (with its own merits and shortcomings) that has attracted considerable attention and, as such, will be discussed in chapter 7. When it comes to green planning, however, New Zealand has not been a leader but a rather poor performer.[6]

Sometimes, green planning is interpreted or defined in terms of *process* characteristics. For instance, public participation is often regarded in the literature as a key feature of green planning.[7] However, although public participation may be an important or even crucial condition for *effective* green planning, it is debatable whether that means that green planning is *by definition* participatory, to any degree. Green planning practices differ greatly on the extent to which they involve public participation, which could raise the question whether those with no or little provision for public participation deserve the label "green planning." To avoid such squabbles, it may be better to identify fewer core characteristics of green planning as a form of policy and to distinguish these from conditions that can be seen as desirable or essential characteristics of the *process* by which it should be practiced, for a variety of reasons including effectiveness and legitimacy. This implies that green planning can and does occur by different processes, and that there is scope for debate about what makes it more or less effective and desirable.

In this context it may also be important to point out that while green planning is a form of more comprehensive, integrated, and strategic policy development, it does not represent an effort toward "rational-comprehensive decision-making" as interpreted by the traditional critics of the latter.[8] According to these critics, it is simply not realistic, and undesirable or even dangerous, to base decisions on an analysis of all options and their consequences, and on an unambiguous and coherent set of goals and objectives. This assumes a level of rationality in decision-making that is not humanly, organizationally, and politically possible; to try to impose such an "ideal" is bound to be flawed and risks being undemocratic. In practice, these analysts argue, government decision-making is incremental and messy, involving limited knowledge and lots of politics. While I do not wish to revisit the debate between proponents of rational decision-making and incremental decision-making, which has been overtaken by more recent views that rationality (knowledge, science) and values and interests (politics) both have a place in policy development, it is important to make the point that green planning, as defined here, is no less rational and political than the financial-economic policy frameworks adopted by governments as a basis for integrating financial-economic concerns across policy areas, and for guiding them toward what is considered to be economically possible and/or desirable ("economic imperatives"). Whether green planning, as a policy framework, is feasible and adopted has more to do with politics and the relative importance and power associated with values and interests than with its proclaimed limitations or impossibility as a form of policy.

Another issue relevant to the interpretation of what green planning is about is whether it is, or should be, about advancing sustainable development. Earlier green plans focused mostly on environmental matters,[9] but the trend has been toward making sustainable development the fundamental goal of green planning, and toward the adoption of sustainable development strategies. As discussed in chapter 3, the adoption of sustainable development as an overarching cognitive framework for government policy comes with the risk of marginalizing environmental interests, and of subordinating them to social and economic interests. Whether that happens depends largely on how the notion of sustainable development is interpreted and translated into policy objectives. There is good reason for hanging on to the concept of environmental integration as a basis for greening sustainable development policies and practices.

A related point is that green planning, and environmental integration in general, involves making trade-offs between competing or conflicting values and interests. While this is inevitable, it does raise the question whether integration is anything more or else than the bargaining and compromising that is common to most, if not all, policy formation. This issue is usually treated as a matter of priorities: environmental interests should be assigned a high level of importance relative to other interests even though that does not imply that they always "win."[10] However, the term "integration" implies more than assigning weightings to different or competing elements; it suggests that they become parts of a whole (system) in which the parts contribute interactively to the functioning of the whole. If elements continue to compete or conflict with the functioning of the whole, they cannot be properly considered to be integrated. If green planning is to function as an overarching environmental policy framework, the goals and objectives of all policy areas should be brought in line with the core functions identified as essential to the functioning of the environment system. Although this may be very difficult or even impossible in the short run, this point should not be lost in the debate about trade-offs or priorities. To justifiably use the term "environmental integration" means that there must be at least a move toward eliminating the need for trade-offs by bringing all human decisions and practices, and the policies that guide these, in line with environmental requirements that are seen as fundamental to the continued and proper functioning of the environment as a whole, including the part played by humans.

Based on these considerations, green planning is defined here as policy based on environmental parameters, imperatives, or goals, that is also comprehensive, integrative, long-term, strategic, and laid down in a public document. "Comprehensive" refers to the inclusion of a broad range of policy areas, ideally all that impact significantly on the environment. "Integrative" refers to the development of an overarching framework of environmental goals, objectives, and targets that are "translated" into goals, objectives, and targets for individual policy areas included in the plan. As it is unlikely that these overarching goals and objectives can be achieved within a few years, green planning requires a longer time frame than one term of government; it requires, say, from five to twenty or even fifty years. The "strategic" feature of green planning relates to the sequencing of steps to achieve the long-term goals and objectives, and to the selection of means. Given the many and complex linkages between problems, causes, objectives, and obstacles, strategizing involves identifying the most promising, effective, and efficient way to make progress. Determining a strategic path poses a considerable analytical challenge that includes physical and technical considerations, and also economic and political ones. Finally, these four features of green planning are laid down in a public policy document (plan or strategy), making the government's intentions and commitment explicit and transparent.

It almost goes without saying that green planning cannot be a one-off exercise, a master plan that makes governments and societies rigidly beholden to once-chosen options. Obviously, information and knowledge on environmental conditions, ideas, and technological means evolve, and it would be silly not to regularly update green plans in the light of such developments. This does have implications for the institutional arrangements for green planning, an insight that has not always dawned upon policy-makers, as we will see later in this chapter.

THE EMERGENCE AND SPREAD OF GREEN PLANNING

As the emergence of and rationale for green planning ties in with the factors and actors that gave rise to the move toward environmental integration in general, there is no need here to elaborate much on this matter. It suffices to highlight two main points: first, that international initiatives, calls, and demands have been very significant driving forces for environmental integration, including green planning; and second, some countries and governments have been more willing to pick up green planning, and become leaders in this field, than others.

The importance of international agency behind the emergence of environmental integration has been noted earlier, even though the term itself has not gained widespread currency. But the desirability and need for the development of comprehensive and integrated policies to guide environmental integration across environmental and nonenvironmental policy areas was already recognized by environmental professionals and advocates who operated at the international level in the 1970s. Faced with the need to accommodate nature conservation and "development" interests, especially in the context of low-income countries, the International Union for the Conservation of Nature took a more integrated policy approach in its *World Conservation Strategy*, adopted in 1980, the first major international-level document that also introduced the notion of sustainable development.

Although the role of international actors in the emergence and adoption of green planning may, at face value, be seen as positive, it should be judged more judiciously in the light of further considerations about the motives behind this push and the implication that, in many instances, governments appear to have adopted green planning not for domestic environmental reasons or motives but because of external pressure and demands. Since 1987, the World Bank started to promote the development of National Environmental Action Plans (NEAPs), and required their adoption as a condition for its loans since 1991.[11] Despite this, Falloux and Talbot claim that the adoption of NEAPs was a demand-driven process led by African governments, and that they were "authentically national efforts" undertaken with the financial support and encouragement of a wide variety of donors.[12] Nonetheless, the International Development Association (IDA), a World Bank affiliate, urged IDA borrowers to complete National Environmental Action Plans, something most of them had done by 1994.[13] The motivation behind this push for green planning by the bank may have at least as much to do with creating a safe environment for foreign investment in low- and middle-income countries as with environmental reasons.

So, although some countries have been early adopters of green planning, they have not necessarily done so out of their own volition. Madagascar, Lesotho, and Mauritius were among the first countries to develop a National Environmental Action Plan,[14] but these moves should be seen in the light of what has been said above.[15] Although higher-income countries have not been pressured into adopting green planning to the same extent, international influence often did play a role. The Brundtland report and *Agenda 21*, adopted at the United Nations Conference on Environmental

Development (UNCED) conference in Rio de Janeiro in 1992, both called upon governments to adopt sustainable development strategies, and are often referred to as having been instrumental in the adoption of green planning by governments. By 2003, some 140 countries had adopted official green plans or sustainable development strategies, up from less than ten in the late 1980s. Green planning appears to have become a global norm, and it has been argued that "by 1997 a point had been reached where it would have been difficult for any single country to openly refuse to adopt a national programme for sustainable development or to oppose a corresponding decision within the United Nations."[16] By the end of 2003, only four OECD countries—Mexico, New Zealand, Turkey, and the United States—had not yet adopted a national development strategy or announced that they would do so in the near future.

Notwithstanding the widespread adoption of green planning, it has never been able to get a strong foothold in the United States and some other countries. The reasons for the differences in the adoption of green planning may have much to do with the nature of the political systems and dominant policy styles. However, although green planning has been taken up in many countries, this does not mean that it has been applied with equal vigor and success everywhere. Some authors note that in many low-income countries sustainable development and other strategies have remained paper exercises, simple wish lists without much if any effect, whereas in high income countries they have often been in the nature of "one-shot processes with little in the way of monitoring and no follow-up revision."[17] Why this is so is a question that requires analysis of both negative and (relatively) positive experiences and developments. A number of studies have been undertaken to this end, providing insights into the reasons for the failure of (relative) success of green planning efforts, and offering ideas about how performance can be improved.[18]

The aim here is not to discuss extensively the developments of green planning around the world, or to summarize the many factors and conditions that have been identified in the literature as essential for good or successful green planning. Rather, the focus is on two main issues that, in my view, pull together many of the limitations and challenges of green planning with regard to environmental integration. The first relates to the political-institutional basis of green planning efforts, the second to its cognitive basis.

Regarding the first issue, the adoption, longevity, and relative effectiveness of green planning are affected by its political-institutional support basis. Arguably, the biggest challenge in this respect is not to get governments to adopt a green plan, as most have at some point in time, but to promote or ensure its durability and survival, especially given the frequent changes of government and the short-term political horizon demarcated by the type of democratic political system that prevails in much of the world. Even in the Netherlands, where green planning appears to have enjoyed a high level of political support from across the political spectrum, and has been institutionally entrenched, it seems to have lost, in recent years, much of its strength and appeal as a guide for environmental policy integration.

In regard to the second issue, many of the limitations associated with green planning relate to the cognitive basis or frameworks on which it rests. Since green planning is about creating an overarching policy framework that provides *substantive* guidance to environmental integration, it requires a cognitive basis on which environmental issues are interpreted and explained. The direction, degree of environmental inclusiveness, and clarity of the guidance provided by green plans depend to a large extent on that cognitive basis, including the interpretation of environmental problems and/or the notion of sustainable development. Crucial, in this context, is whether and how the underlying causes or driving forces are identified and defined. As discussed in chapters 2 and 3, ideology and politics inherently play a role in the process of interpretation, even if undertaken from a rational or scientific perspective. The politics of interpretation therefore spills over into the politics of green planning.

The next sections will discuss these challenges in the context of the contrasting experiences in Canada, Australia, and the Netherlands. Canada and Australia have been chosen because in both countries green planning had a promising start, but proved to be confined to one-shot exercises and came to grief after a relatively short time. By contrast, green planning in the Netherlands has been long-lived and is widely regarded as most advanced, providing a model for other countries. But even here, the challenges and limitations of green planning have become apparent. The differences between Canada and Australia, both large countries with federal systems and an Anglo-Saxon political tradition, on the one hand, and the Netherlands, a small unitary state with a cooperative policy style, on the other, provide additional reasons for the selective attention given to these countries.

THE SUPPORT BASIS FOR GREEN PLANNING: THE NETHERLANDS, CANADA, AND AUSTRALIA

Although green planning may be considered a good idea, it needs active agents to be put into practice. Perhaps more importantly, to be more than a one-shot exercise, it needs a strong and enduring political support basis. Its introduction and continuation presume political support, but this fluctuates over time. Building and strengthening the political support basis for green planning, to the point that it becomes institutionalized and can survive the vagaries of politics, is arguably its biggest challenge. But institutionalization is no guarantee for its effectiveness or even survival. To a large extent, this depends on the views, skills, and relative power and capacity of the advocates of green planning vis-á-vis those who have little or no sympathy for it. Related to that, its power basis and effectiveness relies on the extent of support in, and the involvement of, the wider society. If the ownership basis of green planning is small, even if at a high level, it is politically vulnerable and unlikely to survive in the longer term.

While green planning in the Netherlands has become an enduring affair, it has proved to be a one-off experience in Canada and the Australia. The difference suggests that the political-institutional support basis for green planning in the Netherlands has been stronger than in the other two countries. While the green plans produced in Canada and Australia died unspectacular deaths after changes in government and political leadership, green planning was institutionalized in the Netherlands, where it was made a legal requirement upon governments to produce or revise a plan every four years.

Work on the first Dutch National Environmental Policy Plan (NEPP) started in 1986, following the production of two Indicative Multi-Year Environmental Programs and a growing recognition from the early 1980s that environmental policies required a higher degree of integration. Further impetus to the introduction of a green plan was provided by the release of the country's first state-of-the-environment report, *Concern for Tomorrow*, in 1988, which painted a gloomy picture. NEPP1 was adopted in 1989, putting forward the "desire to solve or gain control of environmental problems within the duration of generation."[19] The main objective, to "maintain the environment's carrying capacity on behalf of sustainable development,"[20] was translated into many specific objectives and targets, often quite ambitious (emission reductions up to 90 percent) for the main problem areas ("themes"), and for several points in time up to 2010. In 1990, NEPP Plus (more an amendment to the first) was introduced to set out the targets for some policy areas for which none had been formulated. In 1994, a second plan was adopted (NEPP2) that focused mainly on problems and issues associated with the implementation of NEPP1, as it had already become apparent that it would be hard to achieve some of the targets. NEPP3, adopted in 1998, elaborated further on implementation issues and emphasized the need for greater flexibility, cooperation, and facilitation in the search for efficient solutions, as well as the importance of science and technology. As it became increasingly clear that some targets would be difficult to meet, an additional 2.6 billion guilders was allocated to several problem areas. NEPP4, adopted in 2001, evaluates the environmental policy record of the past thirty years, focuses on seven of the more intractable environmental problems, identifies new risks, and shifts the horizon to 2030 (and, for some issues, to 2050).

A fifth policy statement, entitled *Toekomstagenda Milieu*, said to introduce a new approach to the implementation of NEPP4, was released in 2006.[21]

In Canada, work on the Green Plan started in 1989, and resulted in its formal launch by the federal government in December 1990. It covered a period of five years and was accompanied by Can$3 billion of new spending.[22] The government proclaimed that the aim of the plan was "to make Canada, by the year 2000, the industrial world's most environmentally friendly country."[23] The plan had two major foci. The largest part focused on programs designed to address specific environmental problems. A smaller part, but theoretically the more important one, focused on the need to encourage behavioral changes in the decision-making systems of government and society.[24] Following its adoption, the government started on some thirty-six initiatives directed at implementing the plan.[25] However, by 1995, the government had lost interest in the environment and sustainable development.[26] Initially, the intention was to revise the plan every three to four years, but this was not built into the design of the plan.[27] After a change of government in 1995, the plan died, and has not been revived since.[28] Although subsequent Canadian governments have been "cautiously supportive" of sustainable development,[29] by 2007 Canada still had not adopted a national sustainable development strategy.[30]

In Australia, moves toward green planning came under the label of the "ecologically sustainable development" (ESD) process. The ESD process started in June 1990 with the release by the federal Government of a public discussion document on a proposal to develop a National Strategy for Ecologically Sustainable Development (NSESD).[31] An important feature of the process was the consensual approach toward the development of the strategy, involving about 150 participants from a broad range of sectors and involving representatives from public and private organizations. Nine working parties produced reports for the sectors of agriculture, forestry, fisheries, manufacturing, mining, energy use, energy production, tourism, and transport. Further reports on intersectoral issues and the greenhouse issue were presented by the three chairs. The final strategy was released by the end of 1992.[32]

Although the adoption of the NSESD strategy has been followed by the introduction of many other strategies and programs that have taken sustainable development as their main principle, these evolved largely independently from the strategy. The implementation of the strategy itself was patchy, unsystematic and uncoordinated, and has been mostly in the nature of more studies, inquiries, and reviews.[33] The strategy has never been revisited and updated by the federal government, making it, like Canada's Green Plan, a one-shot exercise. Therefore, the ESD strategy, as an overarching national green plan that provides guidance to the operationalization of sustainable development across states and sectors in Australia, appears also to have died.[34]

Despite the differences between the Dutch experience, on the one hand, and those in Canada and Australia, on the other, similarities can be identified in the processes by which plans were introduced, and in some of the difficulties that the advocates of green planning faced. Politicians and bureaucrats played a key role in the initiation and introduction of green planning in all three countries. In the Netherlands, moves toward environmental policy integration originated within the Environment Department in the early 1980s, when two environmental policy statements ("More Than the Sum of the Parts" and the first "Indicative Environmental Programme," respectively released in 1983 and 1984) were produced that highlighted the need for greater integration.[35] Although these efforts reflected a recognition that, at all levels of government as well as across sectors, policies affecting the environment needed to be harmonized to be effective, it also was deemed desirable to avoid a restructuring of government responsibilities, or the creation of a "Super Environmental Ministry."[36] The Environment Department was the driving force behind these developments, but a key role was played also by Peter Winsemius, who was the minister of the environment between 1982 and 1986. Winsemius, who had a background in science as well as business management, encouraged the Environment Department to rethink its approach to environmental policy. During this period, many of the concepts underlying the National Environmental Policy Plan, such as "themes" and "target groups," were developed.[37]

Political leadership was a key factor also in the initiation of the Canadian and Australian green plans. In 1989, the minister for the environment, Lucien Bouchard, with the personal support of the prime minister, set out to formulate a coherent framework for Canada's environmental policy. Although largely an in-house job of Environment Canada (the Department of the Environment), the government of Brian Mulroney saw reason to support the development of a green plan in a climate in which public concern about the environment had reached new heights. Also, given the prominent role played by Canadians in environmental issues in the international arena, there was thought to be a need to bring Canadian domestic environmental efforts in line with its international image.[38] In Australia, the initiative for the NSESD came from Prime Minister Hawke, who arguably became an environmental convert one year before work on the strategy started.[39] As in Canada, reasons for the initiative had much to do with the growing electoral significance of environmental issues at the time, and with a perceived need to respond to international developments—in particular the publication of the Brundtland report.[40]

A common difficulty, which underlies the need for strong political leadership, was the lack of enthusiasm for, if not straight opposition to, green planning among nonenvironmental government agencies. Although officials from a range of government agencies were consulted or involved in the process of developing the green plans of the Netherlands and Australia, these agencies continued to hold strong reservations, particularly at the higher level. In the Netherlands and Canada, where relations between the environment department and other government agencies were quite strained, especially at the higher level, opposition could only be overcome by strong support from the environment minister and prime minister.[41] In Australia, reservations held among top-level officials about aspects of the NSESD led to amendments being made to the document at the final stages of the process.[42] Suspicion about green planning being used by the Environment Department to extend its influence over the policy domain of other government agencies is a common concern, inciting traditional departmental jealousy and protectionism regarding mandates. Tact and diplomacy, and even the adoption of a cooperative approach to the development of a green plan on the part of the environment agency, is not, in itself, sufficient to overcome these institutionalized barriers to environmental integration. Even when green plans are formally underwritten by a range of government ministers (as in the Netherlands), the actual level of cooperation that has gone into their production, or that takes place in their implementation, is less than this shared underwriting perhaps suggests.

Reservations regarding genuine interdepartmental policy development were not confined to nonenvironmental agencies. In the Netherlands, integration between physical environmental planning and pollution control policy, both policy areas within the domain of one government department (but served by different branches), has proven to be extremely difficult. The idea of producing a common, integrated policy statement for both areas also stumbled upon reservations on the part of the minister for the environment, who wished to retain full control over the development of environmental policy.[43] As interdepartmental policy development inevitably involves compromise, and environmental concerns are still treated as sectoral concerns rather than common concerns by most nonenvironmental agencies, environmental agencies are indeed often caught between a rock and a hard place. To overcome departmental resistance, they depend on strong leadership, which almost inevitably leads to the government and/or the environment agency becoming, or being perceived as, the owners of a green plan. On the one hand, policy integration depends on other agencies accepting co-ownership (at least for those environmental concerns that are most closely associated with their mandates), but this may imply that those concerns will not receive the weight or priority that they deserve from the point of view of those in the environment agency. On the other hand, a noncooperative (or less cooperative) strategy in these matters may result in a serious backlash against the environment agency when the political tide turns, as happened in Canada.[44]

Although green planning is often referred to, or thought of, as a manifestation of a move toward more participatory environmental policy development, the actual degree of public involvement in the production of green plans or strategies in the three countries discussed here has been rather limited. Arguably the process by which the Australian NSESD was produced was the most participatory compared to the processes relied upon in the other two countries, but even in the case of Australia genuine participation was confined to a relatively small group of representatives from organizations (most of them nonenvironmental), whereas opportunities for public comment, let alone input, were very limited.[45] In Canada, a draft document was made available for wider public comment and discussion, but only at a late stage, and the feedback received was of little consequence.[46] Often, the process of Dutch green planning is described as participatory and cooperative, but this requires qualification.[47] In the process leading up to the adoption of the first plan, participation by nongovernment (target) groups was invited at a late stage, and was focused on persuading these groups to accept the plan and to take responsibility for implementing the targets that had been formulated.[48] In the preparation of the second and third plans, the degree of participation and input increased, but was still limited in the sense that objectives and targets were declared nonnegotiable. The focus remained on implementation, and the main mechanism used was meetings with selected stakeholder groups, with little or no opportunity for wider debate and input from the general public. Even in the Netherlands, where the environmental policy plan enjoys considerable public support, there is no sense of ownership of green plans among societal groups.[49]

Apart from these similarities, there are also important differences that may help explain why green planning gained a stronger political support basis in the Netherlands than in the other two countries. These differences relate to relative environmental pressures, the role of scientists, policy styles and traditions, and political systems.

One possible explanation for the stronger support basis for green planning compared to Canada and Australia may lie in (perceived) differences in environmental pressure. Environmental pressures and problems in the Netherlands, a small, densely populated, and highly industrialized country, are likely be perceived and experienced more readily by its citizens than in the much bigger countries of Canada and Australia. Statistically, there is some evidence to suggest that small and densely populated countries score higher on environmental performance than big countries with a low population density.[50] However, as the populations of Australia and Canada are largely concentrated in relatively small parts of both countries (and therefore may experience similar degrees of environmental pressure), the importance of this fact should perhaps not be exaggerated. Nonetheless, it is plausible that the widespread support for the first Dutch green plan had much to do with a high level of concern about environmental pressures in the Netherlands. In 1988, the Rijksinstituut voor Volksgezondheid and Milieuhygiene (RIVM), a scientific bureau involved in environmental research, produced the first comprehensive study of the Dutch state of the environment.[51] The report contained alarming findings, and caused a wave of concern throughout the Dutch community. No such reports were published in Canada and Australia prior to the release of their green plans, which were treated with considerable skepticism by environmental groups in both countries.

An additional factor in this context is that the Dutch National Environmental Policy Plan relied heavily on this scientific assessment of the size and scale of the problems and tasks ahead. Independent scientists provided the hard data on which the case for ambitious environmental objectives and targets was based, and lent an appearance of objectivity and even necessity to the plan. Widespread recognition that drastic action was required lifted the Dutch plan above party politics, and gave it the status of a commonly accepted beacon for what was required to address the serious environmental problems in the Netherlands. Scientists provided a level of legitimacy to the objectives and targets of the green plan (even though these were less ambitious than what they had indicated was required to bring about a sustainable Netherlands) that is hard to match by politicians and bureaucrats. By contrast, departmental interests and politics (perceived gains and threats associated with the plans) played a much bigger role in the preparation of green plans in Canada and Australia than in the Netherlands. Arguably, this also indicates that there is greater scope in the Netherlands for the development and acceptance of science-based rational-comprehensive policies, which depoliticize issues, than there is in both other countries.

However, this may not apply to all issues and policy areas, and may have been more related to the perceived seriousness and urgency of the problems in the Netherlands, creating a crisislike climate in which strong leadership is usually more appreciated than political wrangling. As noted above, departmental politics is also alive and well in the Netherlands, and did affect the preparation and implementation of plans. But what may be relevant in this respect is that, in the Netherlands, there is a stronger tradition of cooperative policy development than in Canada and Australia. It has been argued that the capacity to develop innovative and effective policy (including green plans) is associated with a cooperative or corporatist policy style, whereas an adversarial policy style is seen as an obstacle in this respect.[52] The Netherlands is usually regarded as falling into the former category, whereas Australia has a tradition of adversarial politics (the period under Bob Hawke being more of an exception), with Canada occupying a position in between. This does not mean that policy development in the Netherlands is more democratic in the sense of offering greater opportunities for (direct) public participation in decision-making. In the Dutch policy tradition, which has been described as corporatist, consociational, or based on the "polder model," participation is commonly confined to the representatives of recognized interest groups, with decisions often reached behind closed doors.[53] In the 1990s, debate about extending this model to include environmental groups in decision-making led to the adoption of a "green polder model" by the government.[54] However, some politicians and top officials do not regard the involvement of environmental groups as crucial to the success of the National Environmental Policy Plan, and see the business sector as a more important player in that respect.[55]

As for the role of business, it has been argued that, in some cases, the support for green planning has been higher among business leaders than in the upper echelons of government departments.[56] To a large extent, this can be attributed to the potential advantages to business associated with green planning, notably a greater predictability of the regulatory environment. Business support also appears to be stronger when there is a heavy reliance on a cooperative approach in the implementation of green plans (voluntary agreements, partnerships, covenants), as it provides flexibility to industry in the selection of the most cost-effective means by which targets are met.[57] However, it has been argued that, to lead to meaningful environmental outcomes, a reliance on the cooperation of business needs to be set within a clear and strong policy framework, encompassing objectives and targets that are nonnegotiable, and that it needs to be backed up by a threat with regulatory measures if progress toward these is unsatisfactory.[58] Where such a framework is absent, as is the case in Canada and Australia, a reliance on voluntary and cooperative measures may bring about few if any results.

Finally, the differences between political systems may help explain why it is much harder to have green planning stick in Australia and Canada than in the Netherlands. Given the shared power arrangements in federal systems between national and state or provincial governments, with the latter often strongly safeguarding their prerogatives, it is plausible that the development and maintenance of a green plan poses an even bigger challenge in a federal system than in a unitary state. However, it can also be argued that federalism provides a convenient cover for governments at both levels (central and state or provincial) behind which to hide a lack of serious commitment to green planning. In Australia, there appear to be no legal or structural impediments to the central government adopting a much stronger stance, and taking the lead, on environmental matters. Rather than federalism per se, *politics* holds the key to explaining the difficulties associated with environmental politics, including green planning.[59] In Canada, where the power of the provinces is greater than that of the states in Australia, it may indeed be more difficult for the central government to ensure the implementation of green planning at lower levels of government, but also here, it can be argued, this has been used as a convenient ground for a "passing the (environmental) buck" to the provinces and as an excuse for weak central government action.[60]

Yet, it is undeniably true that, to succeed, green planning requires the cooperation between governments at all levels, as well as the cooperation of groups in society, including the business sector. As the implementation of green planning depends to a large extent on lower levels of government, which often have control over the licensing of development projects and operations that have an immediate impact on the environment, their involvement in, and commitment to, green planning is of considerable importance. Arguably, this is more problematic in federal than in unitary political systems. States (in Australia) and provinces (in Canada) are mostly in control of the exploitation of natural resources in their areas and, in most cases, are development-oriented.[61] However, on a smaller scale, such problems also occur within unitary systems of government, and even in a small country like the Netherlands. A common issue in all political systems is the (perceived) need or tendency of lower levels of government to attract investment to maintain or improve economic conditions within their area. This is of particular concern to the governments of those areas that are having difficulty in this competitive struggle, and when investments and population, and consequently markets and services, tend to concentrate increasingly in a few (metropolitan) areas. These developments are particularly pronounced in countries like Australia and Canada, but even in a small country like the Netherlands some provinces have held a longtime status as problem areas in this respect (with higher levels of unemployment).

Despite their importance to the implementation of green planning, or perhaps because of the difficulties referred to above, lower levels of government have not played a significant role in the development of the green plans in the countries discussed here. Predominantly, the drafting of green plans or strategies has been a central government affair, involving some consultation with representatives of lower levels of government among other interested parties. Notwithstanding this, support for green plans has varied among states, provinces, or regions, depending on whether there were perceived benefits associated with its acceptance (as in Canada, where a considerable amount of funding accompanied the Green Plan), and/or on the level of environmental pressure and support for environmental matters within those areas (as in some Australian states). But even where lower levels of government have adopted their own green plan or strategy (as is compulsory for the provincial councils in the Netherlands), integration between these plans and the central government's green plan has been weak and problematic.

Although green planning has been institutionalized in the Netherlands, this has not been a guarantee for continued strong political support. As in many other countries, the political priorities of Dutch governments have shifted to other areas such as the economy, social problems, and the threat of terrorism. The preparation of another green plan, and environmental issues in general, has not been a priority for the conservative Dutch government that came to power in 2002, which can be read from the fact that it did not even appoint an environment minister.[62] In large part, this is in line with a considerable drop in the ranking of environmental concerns in the priorities of citizens. In a survey held in 2005, combating global warming was ranked at number fourteen, and reducing air pollution at nineteen, lagging way behind the top priorities of improving health care, employment, maintaining purchasing power, maintaining pensions for the elderly, and reducing crime. This does not imply, however, that the Dutch are willing to compromise environmental policies, as 59 percent of the respondents also wanted the government to adopt stricter or much stricter environmental policies.[63]

In conclusion, the introduction of green planning has been the result primarily of the combined forces of political leaders and government officials. Although this happened (in the Netherlands, Canada, and Australia) at a time when public concern about environmental issues reached new heights, the initiative or demand for green planning did not come from society, and neither has there been much public involvement in the actual drafting of green plans. However, it appears that the level of support for green planning is not primarily determined by the extent of public input into the process; this was demonstrated in the Netherlands, where the level of public consultation about the first plan was minimal, but the level of support for the plan widespread and high. By contrast, in Canada and Australia skepticism among environmentalists about the green planning efforts was strong. Arguably, key factors explaining these differences are the important role played by scientists in providing a strong scientific basis for the Dutch plan, which lifted it (almost) above politics and the bargaining processes by which policies usually come about, and a sense of urgency. However, as the sense of urgency waned and other priorities took over, the level of government commitment to green planning has also declined. That green planning is still alive in the Netherlands is a measure of the importance of institutionalization.

Whether green planning is actually fulfilling its role as an overarching framework for environmental policy integration is a question that requires more than survival and institutionalization, however. This we will assess in the next section, where we will focus first and foremost on developments in the Netherlands, as it is the country with probably the longest sustained effort toward policy-internal integration.

GREEN PLANNING AND THE POLITICS OF INTERPRETATION

How much, and what kind of, guidance a green plan provides to the integration of environmental concerns across policy areas or sectors depends on a range of qualities or characteristics. Most obviously, it depends on the degree of specificity of the objectives and time frames it contains. Although general principles, aims, and goals can provide direction, they may also leave much scope for interpretation in terms of what and how much needs to be achieved. Time frames are important in that they provide clarity about when outputs or outcomes are expected to be realized. Arguably more important, and underlying the capacity to specify clear objectives, targets, and time frames, is how the plan interprets or defines the nature of the environmental *problématique* and the underlying causes, variables, factors, or driving forces. As discussed in earlier in this book, this is not just a matter of scientific analysis. While scientific research, information, and explanations play a crucial role in identifying and understanding environmental problems, interpretations are never value-free. Often, scientists can be found in opposing camps arguing in favor or against environmental measures.

Dutch green planning is widely regarded as being most advanced, both in terms of the guidance it provides in the form of specific objectives and targets for most environmental problems and in terms of its solid cognitive basis. The first National Environmental Policy Plan formulated more than two hundred specific objectives and targets, and a time frame of twenty years ("one generation") for achieving them. Objectives and targets were derived from the first Dutch state-of-the-environment report (*Concern for Tomorrow*), prepared by independent scientists. It laid out not only the (bad) environmental condition the Netherlands found itself in, but also the scale of the reduction of pollution that was required to move the country toward a more sustainable situation. The objectives and targets adopted, although often lower than the reductions of 70 to 90 percent that the scientists had indicated were required, were still very ambitious.[64]

Another important strength of Dutch green planning lies in its cognitive basis. From the start, independent scientists have played a key role in the collection and analysis of information on the environment, producing annually a state-of-the-environmental report. The reports also provide an assessment of effects and effectiveness of the policies adopted. The frequency, rigor, clarity, and frankness of the reporting are qualities that enable policy adjustments to be made on an annual basis, and in sync with the budget cycle. The scientific agency producing the reports, the RIVM, also publishes a range of other reports, providing more detailed information on the environment or aspects thereof. Altogether, the excellent information basis and analytical environmental capacity in the Netherlands enable green planning to be based on specific problems, objectives, targets, and time frames, and for policy responses to be adapted when and where this is deemed necessary or desirable.

The high degree of specificity in Dutch green planning thus provides clear guidance to governments and other actors in society. The environmental *problématique* has been made comprehensible and manageable, clustered around eight main "themes," by identifying the immediate sources of the problems, by allocating responsibilities for addressing them, and by formulating specific objectives, targets (usually in quantitative terms), and time frames. Thus, Dutch green planning can be said to make sustainability "concrete," translating it into specific, mostly biophysical, conditions and measures.

Although Dutch green planning has been successful in significantly reducing emissions of many pollutants, and appears to be on track to meet many of its targets, it has also run into some intractable problems. In some areas, notably agriculture and emissions from traffic, meeting the set targets has proven to be difficult if not impossible with existing policy. Despite the big reductions in emissions from industry sources, the quality of much of the air, water, and soil has not significantly improved, and still poses a considerable threat to the health of humans and other species, many of which continue to decline.[65] In part, this is because a considerable proportion of the pollution is imported from surrounding countries. However, for many pollutants, the Netherlands exports more than it imports.[66] The country also has a large ecological footprint; using two-and-a-half times its own size for the consumption of forest and agricultural products alone, thus contributing to growing environmental pressures in other countries.[67] But even within its own borders environmental pressures continue to mount with the continuing growth of production, transport, infrastructure, and urban development.[68] It looks unlikely that the Netherlands will be able to achieve its Kyoto target of reducing greenhouse gas emissions by 6 percent by 2008–12 without purchasing reductions from other countries.[69] The country is also struggling to meet a range of European Union environmental standards, and has lost its status of a leader in the European context.[70] It appears that the easiest and least costly ways of reducing emissions have been used ("the low hanging fruit has been picked") and that achieving further reductions will be a lot harder and more expensive. Already, the Netherlands spends about 3 percent of gross domestic product (GDP) on environmental policy, about twice as much as other European Union member states.[71]

The difficulties encountered by Dutch green planning are an indication of its limitations, notably with regard to addressing the underlying causes and driving forces of environmental problems, domestically and internationally. Addressing these underlying factors implies the need to integrate environmental imperatives into and across all policy areas that have significant impact on the environment. Also, in the Netherlands green planning has had only limited effect in terms of bringing about sectoral (external) environmental integration, and it continues to face big structural obstacles.

Although the Dutch green plans, especially the first and the fourth, discuss underlying issues, causes, and driving forces behind environmental problems, and talk about the need for structural change, they are much less specific on this front than with regard to the description of the biophysical problems, objectives, and targets. In NEPP1, the need for structural changes was translated into three main policy objectives and strategies: energy extensification, integrated chain (life cycle) management, and quality improvement (of products and processes).[72] In practice, this amounted to the promotion of technological measures and innovation, by means of a range of policy tools that include covenants, economic incentives, and the threat of regulation. Given the emphasis on the biophysical nature of environmental problems, and on the role of the government as a catalyst for inducing technological innovation, the Dutch approach has been described as technocratic,[73] and as an example of ecological modernization.[74]

The approach is based on the assumption that solutions to environmental problems can be found within the existing political-economic and sociocultural order. Although science and technology are seen as a source of environmental problems, they are also hailed as holding the key to their solution. Ecological modernization, as discussed in chapter 3, is promoted as both environmentally and economically beneficial. In theory, ecological modernization could mean more than technological innovation and could imply "reembedding" economic practices into social and ecological contexts, even toward futures that challenge the underlying tenets of "modernity."[75] However, in practice, governments that embrace ecological modernization focus mostly on the promotion of technological innovation that has economic as well as environmental benefits.

That resolving the environmental *problématique* may involve and require more than reducing emissions and increasing resource efficiency is something that has started to dawn upon some governments. The fourth Dutch National Environmental Policy Plan admitted that environmental problems prove to be persistent and intractable, and that a new vision and approach were required. Central in this plan is a focus on "quality of life" issues and on the importance of linking environmental policy efforts to the living environment of people (the why question behind environmental policy). The plan states that emission reduction targets mean little to people, and that further progress in environmental policy depends on the extent to which people acknowledge the connections between their own quality of life and the quality of the natural environment, locally and globally. Consequently, the notion of sustainability underlying Dutch green planning is broadening. Whereas, initially, sustainability had been defined mainly in biophysical terms (and admissible levels of emissions), it has come to incorporate social and economic values. To achieve sustainable production and consumption systems, people need to be able to define, and become committed to, patterns of sustainable living. Environmental concern needs to be socially internalized.[76]

The fourth plan also recognizes that the institutions needed to internalize environmental concerns, nationally and internationally, are either nonexistent or not strong enough, and that reforms of a systemic nature ("transitions") are necessary. As a promising concept, the plan advances "transition management," which is directed at influencing or steering developments within and between interconnected subsystems (such as the energy sector and agriculture). This is interpreted as implying, among other things, the formulation of clear policy frameworks (short, medium, and long-term goals), the internalization of environmental costs in prices, the introduction of systems of tradable property (emission) rights, and the promotion of research and technological innovation based on the principle of sustainability.[77]

The extent of (systemic) change advocated in the policy can hardly be called radical, however, and may be more justly qualified as tinkering than as fundamental change. Although the analysis underlying Dutch green planning, especially in the first and the fourth plan, puts the environmental problems in the Netherlands in a broader context, identifying sociocultural and political-economic factors, including inequality, short-term thinking, institutional barriers, and "systematic" causes, in practice the focus has been mostly on finding technical solutions by cooperative, managerial, and economic means. This orientation is made even more explicit in the *Toekomstagenda Milieu* released in 2006, which restates the environmental challenge as an opportunity for promoting technological innovation and economic growth, with a focus on transitions required in the energy sector.[78]

To conclude, green planning in the Netherlands has produced demonstrable and significant achievements, mainly with regard to reducing or mitigating pollution. It has been institutionalized and provides for an ongoing process of comprehensive environmental policy development. However, signs are that it has run up against its own limitations (in particular its focus on the physical aspects of pollution), and increasingly encounters structural obstacles to further improvement. Although the need for structural changes to address these obstacles has been recognized in several green plans, it is not evident that this recognition has been translated into practices that reduce, let alone eliminate, environmental pressures at the source. The solutions sought are confined mainly to technological and managerial means that produce environmental and economic benefits. Underlying this reluctance to dig deeper are vested interests that accept change only to the extent that their interests are not threatened. The OECD notes that policy integration is constrained by the desire "not to endanger major economic development objectives, for instance in agriculture, infrastructural development, and transport," and adds that "[e]nvironmental considerations still appear to be of marginal importance in decision-making relating to major infrastructure."[79] Even within the large and multifaceted ministry that has the main responsibility for environmental matters, environmental integration is problematic.[80] As, in the early part of the twenty-first century, economic, social, and security issues started to dominate the political agenda, environmental concerns, and their integration across policy areas, have been relegated to a backseat.

CONCLUSION

In this chapter, efforts toward the development of overarching frameworks for environmental policy integration at the national level—in particular, green planning—have been discussed and analyzed. The importance of such frameworks lies in the need to promote or ensure coherence and consistency between external policy integration efforts; efforts aimed at the integration of environmental concerns into a broad range of policies regarding sectors that harbor many of the main sources of environmental pressure. Green planning, at least in theory, holds promise as a means of providing substantive coordination to policy integration efforts, prescribing objectives and targets for each sector in line with its contribution to environmental problems and to common and overarching environmental goals, objectives, and targets that are considered to be necessary or desirable (increasingly in terms of sustainability).

In practice, however, most green planning efforts fall (far) short of this promise. One of the main problems facing green planning is a lack of continuity. Most green plans have been in the nature of one-shot exercises that failed to maintain sufficient political support over time, especially after changes of government, and consequently met early deaths. A concomitant weakness of many of these efforts is that they have not been institutionalized, and therefore have lacked a strong legal and organizational basis. The experiences in Australia and Canada illustrate these weaknesses, aggravated by the federal and adversarial nature of their political systems. By contrast, in the Netherlands, green planning attracted broad and strong support from across society and the political spectrum, largely because of the alarming, science-based assessment of the environmental situation in the Netherlands. This provided a strong enough basis for its institutionalization and continuity. However, although the quality of Dutch green planning efforts is widely admired and has delivered significant results, it also has limitations, and it faces strong structural obstacles that constrain environmental integration at a more fundamental level, where many of the causes or driving forces behind environmental problems are located. Although some of the Dutch plans refer to the need for systemic or structural change, they do not outline specific programs or courses of action for bringing about such change, or a clear vision or picture of the structures that need to be put in place. Vested economic, bureaucratic, and political interests, and the decline in the status of environmental problems on the political agenda in recent years, further constrain environmental integration at that level. So, although Dutch green planning, in many respects, has been exemplary and provided a model for other countries, among other things because of its institutionalization, its effectiveness in providing an encompassing basis for policy integration across sectors has been, and still is, limited.

The Dutch experience indicates or illustrates that environmental integration is not only required at the cognitive and policy level but also at the structural or systemic level. The interpretation of environmental problems, and the formulation and adoption of policies, is guided or channeled by institutions (rules) that prescribe, circumscribe, encourage, or prohibit human behavior and action, with regard to the environment but also in the economic, social, and political spheres. The extent to which, and how, environmental integration efforts, at the cognitive and policy level, are institutionalized strongly conditions their effectiveness, and even survival. But to address the underlying sources or driving forces behind many environmental problems, environmental considerations or imperatives also need to be built into nonenvironmental institutions, in particular the systems and rules that guide or channel behavior and actions in the economic, political, and social spheres. Although this is not just a task for governments, but the subject of a broader political debate and struggle, many governments have introduced institutional changes or innovations that purport to entrench or strengthen environmental interests. The next chapter discusses and evaluates institutional changes formally aimed at the greening of dominant institutions, notably in the political and economic sphere (institutional-external integration). In chapter 7, I will discuss institutional reforms and innovations that aim to direct or guide behavior and actions more comprehensively, across areas or sectors, toward what is deemed environmentally required or desirable. These are referred to as forms of institutional-internal integration.

6

Institutional-External Integration

INTRODUCTION

Institutions can be described as relatively enduring formal and informal rules that guide or channel people's behavior.[1] Much of human behavior is guided by rules rooted in social and cultural values, beliefs, and traditions. Institutions forge a link between collective values and beliefs, and human action. Institutions shape individuals but are in turn subject to change because of the actions of individuals, evolving in an interactive process. They are constraining as well as enabling. Rules channel behavior by prescribing what is important, desirable, and allowable. They are enforced by social control mechanisms such as social esteem and condemnation. Social and cultural institutions, together with the belief systems in which they are rooted, are passed on from generation to generation through processes of socialization, and therefore are often of an enduring nature. To varying degrees, institutions have expressive and symbolic value, and are important reference points for the collective identity of a group.[2] However, collectively, people also change institutions and create new ones, to give weight to particular views, norms, and goals.[3]

In modern societies, many institutions have been formalized in political-legal rules, including constitutions, other legislation, legal rights, and organizations. Formal institutions also reflect and express social and cultural values, and thus are often seen as important in themselves, but they also constitute the rules by which societies make collective decisions.[4] They assign rights, roles, powers, and responsibilities, and formulate the rules by which decisions are to be made and implemented, and conflicts addressed. Although they often present themselves, or are presented, as "given," passed on from generation to generation, they are in fact socially constructed. And as they assign and embody weight and power to values, interests, and groups in society, they are fundamentally political and, in pluralistic societies, often the terrain and subject of political struggle. Frequently, institutional reform is sought as a means of enhancing or maintaining the influence of groups or individuals, and of strengthening the social and political status of particular values and interests.

Most political, economic, and social institutions have been created for other than environmental reasons, and therefore more or less disregard environmental values and interests; they even are significant sources of environmental pressures and problems. Indeed, the state, the economic system (notably capitalism) and dominant (materialistic) values and norms are widely regarded in environmental circles as the main culprits of the environmental *problématique*. Whether and how these institutions can and should be changed to incorporate adequately environmental concerns is therefore also major topic of debate in the literature.

Since the early 1970s, most governments have established agencies with special responsibility for environmental matters, have passed new environmental legislation, have created a ministerial portfolio for the environment, and have adopted rules or guidelines for assessing the environmental implications of new projects and/or policies. However, the introduction of special rules and organizations for protecting the environment does not guarantee that environmental concerns are adequately integrated into nonenvironmental spheres, for several reasons that we will discuss below. Nor do these institutions necessarily provide coherence and consistency to environmental integration efforts, both within and outside governments, an issue that will be discussed in the following chapter.

Although most governments have established environmental institutions, only a few, notably in Canada and the United Kingdom, have undertaken deliberate institutional reforms directed at the greening of nonenvironmental political-bureaucratic institutions, commonly referred to as the "greening of government." The reform of government institutions with the aim of integrating environmental considerations across the "whole of government" proves to be a daunting challenge, not in the least because it poses a threat to strong and long-established vested interests.

Given the dominance of economics and economic institutions in the present world, their greening arguably is of even greater importance. However, apart from relatively modest moves toward the introduction of economic instruments and ecological tax reform, which have not brought about anywhere near a greening of the economic system, the efforts of governments have been quite modest. Perhaps most significant in this area is green accounting, as it provides a broader framework for valuing economic behavior and practices, and consequently for policies and decisions, but this form of environmental integration is still in its infancy. Increasingly, governments also support the integration of environmental considerations into economic institutions by means of environmental labeling schemes, such as environmental management systems (EMSs), although the adoption of such schemes is driven mostly from within the business sector. Potentially significant also is the introduction, in some countries, of mechanisms for assessing the environmental implications of (proposed) free-trade agreements, but again this form of integration appears not to have much, if any, influence on the main institutional driving forces that promote economic growth and trade, which arguably are also the most important drivers behind many environmental problems. Although there has been growing support for the view that capitalism can be greened (mostly by technological innovation), few governments appear to be willing or able to corroborate this view by significant institutional reform.

Increasingly, neoliberal governments have actively sought to make social institutions (such as labor laws, trade unions, retail opening hours, and media programming) subservient to economic institutions ("imperatives," "the market"). Similarly, it can be argued that, at the institutional level, moves toward the integration of economic and environmental interests have been more in the nature of subordinating environmental values to economic interests rather than of a greening of economic institutions. Governments appear unwilling or incapable to "interfere" with market-based institutions such as the media and the advertising industry that influence or even shape notions of desirable lifestyles or the "good life." Government efforts in this area are largely confined to "educational" programs and campaigns (such as on road safety, the risks of smoking, antilittering, recycling), and at picking up the tabs for the "externalities" of "free market" practices, and do not address the structural sources of these problems.

This chapter focuses on government moves toward the greening of political and economic institutions. First, I discuss the initiatives toward the "greening of government." Before assessing, in particular, the merits of the efforts of the governments of Canada and the United Kingdom, some of the more general limitations and obstacles facing environmental agencies in this area will be discussed. Second, moves toward green accounting and the adoption of labeling schemes as forms of environmental integration in the economic-institutional sphere are dwelt upon. The conclusion reflects on the significance of these institutional-external integration efforts in the light the broader environmental integration challenge.

THE GREENING OF GOVERNMENT

Since the early 1970s, governments across the world have created agencies with responsibility for "the environment" and passed an array of environmental legislation. Many of these institutional reforms are aimed at the promotion of environmental protection in particular policy areas—for instance, by creating legislation and agencies for pollution control (often separate for pollution of air, water, and land), (hazardous) waste management, and the protection of natural areas. Responsibility for the implementation of legislation and regulations often has been assigned to specialist agencies. To the extent that legislation of this type, embodying or supporting environmental policy, does affect areas of policy and practice that are not environmental but that do (potentially) affect the environment, such as the production of goods or transport, it is indeed a form of external integration.

In most countries, over time, the creation of separate environmental laws and agencies for a wide array of environmental problems has produced a fragmented system of environmental management, the shortcomings and effects of which, in particular with regard to the displacement of environmental problems, have been widely recognized and documented, and have been already discussed earlier.[5] Here the focus is not on the environmental outcomes and effectiveness of environmental institutions, but on the question whether and to what extent they have brought about the greening of nonenvironmental institutions. Despite their fragmentation, it is possible that environmental institutions contribute to the integration of environmental concerns in, for instance, agencies and legislation that guide or govern policies and practices in energy, transport, and agriculture.

However, as environmental legislation is commonly implemented by environmental agencies, its effect on nonenvironmental institutions is usually very limited. For instance, emission standards for transport may be set and enforced by an environmental agency, but this may have very little if any "greening effect" on the institutions (agencies and legislation) governing transport policy. Indeed, it can be argued that the delineation of particular areas of responsibility as "environmental" effectively serves to insulate nonenvironmental institutions and policies from interference by environmental agencies. It simply reinforces the view that environmental values or interests are separate from other values and interests, and that integration, if required, involves balancing rather than institutional change. As long as nonenvironmental agencies meet certain environmental requirements, they can continue to pursue their dominant nonenvironmental objectives, even if doing so generates more or new environmental pressures. Environmental policies and institutions rarely touch, let alone "green," the core institutions that guide nonenvironmental practices.

An example can be found in the institutionalization of EIA. As noted in previous chapters, the effectiveness of forms of cognitive-external integration like EIA, CBA, and/or RA depends in large measure on how they have been institutionalized. However, as discussed in chapter 2, these forms are fundamentally limited by their scope and nature. They do not alter the institutional frameworks that guide behavior and action in nonenvironmental spheres to the extent that environmental interests are incorporated at the early stages of decision-making or design, so that environmental damage is prevented. Usually, environmental interests are considered, weighed, and "balanced" against other interests after decisions or designs have been determined on nonenvironmental grounds. Proper environmental integration, I argue, requires also the (re)design of institutions in a way that they are made congruent with what is deemed environmentally necessary or desirable.

As discussed in chapter 4, the means used by governments to advance environmental integration in nonenvironmental policy sectors or areas remains highly problematic and largely ineffectual. Economic, energy, transport, and agricultural policies, even where strategic environmental assessment or economic instruments are used, continue to be developed within their own institutional frameworks and policy networks. They are driven by sectional interests and objectives, and based on cognitive frameworks that emphasize the importance of growth and expansion and that pay scant, if any, attention to environmental considerations—or, if they do, they assume the compatibility of this "imperative" with environmental protection.[6] Environmental institutions, including environmental ministries or departments and environmental laws, rarely challenge this assumption, and usually lack the means and teeth to ensure that environmental concerns are integrated at the design stage of the policies. The relative power and weight of environmental institutions vis-à-vis economic and social institutions is often such that the former are not in a position to require or bring about environmental integration.

Environmental agencies are relative newcomers to the bureaucratic arena. Many other government ministries and departments have a longer established record, greater experience, more formal power and status, and possess considerably greater capacity (including knowledge, databases, personnel, and financial resources). By comparison, central environmental agencies, especially those endowed with general (policy advice and/or coordination) mandates, are commonly relatively small, underresourced, and less experienced. Their efforts often encounter intransigence and resistance, if not outright hostility, nourished by vested interests, departmentalism, bureaucratic rivalry, and personality conflicts. Against such odds, it is not surprising that environment agencies struggle to effectively achieve or advance environmental integration. For this reason, deliberate efforts toward "greening government," such as those pursued in Canada and the United Kingdom, are rare and worth special attention.

As discussed in chapter 5, Canada's initiative toward the greening of government came in the wake of the demise of its Green Plan. When, in 1995, the newly elected Liberal government effectively dropped the plan, it looked at some other means by which to establish its environmental credentials. Rather than develop its own green plan or radically overhaul environmental policy, the government turned to institutional reform that put the responsibility for integrating environmental concerns on government departments. The *Guide to Green Government*, signed by the prime minister and all members of the cabinet, was adopted to assist departments in developing sustainable development strategies. As a complementary initiative, The *Greening of Government Operations* sought to promote more efficient resource use by government departments and a green procurement policy.[7] The *Guide to Green Government* presents the principles of sustainability, identifies decision-making tools and principles to promote sustainability, and specifies the steps that need to be undertaken in the preparation of a strategy (departmental profile, issue scan, consultations, goals, objectives and targets, action plan, and measurement, analysis, and reporting of performance, following the rational policy model). It asks departments to assess their policies as well as their programs and projects on the implications for sustainability. Given the size of federal government (224,000 employees, 21.4 million hectares of land under direct management, 59,000 buildings and facilities, more than $8 billion in annual purchases of goods and services, and 25,000 motor vehicles),[8] the greening of these operations is significant on its own.

The Green Government initiative was backed institutionally by amendments to the Auditor General Act (1995) and the creation, also in 1995, of the Office of the Commissioner for the Environment and Sustainable Development, via amendments to the Auditor General Act. These introduced a requirement for departments to table sustainable development strategies every three years, for the first time in 1997, and provided for the auditing of these strategies by the commissioner.[9] About 50 percent of the office's time is taken up by its auditing function, with the remainder spent on a broad range of environmental issues, often focusing on the implementation of policies.[10] By 2005, three rounds of strategy development had been completed.

Whether and to what extent the requirement upon government departments to adopt sustainable development strategies has brought about a greening of their policies and practices remains a matter of debate. The first round of strategies provoked considerable critique and skepticism about the effect and meaningfulness of this requirement. In his first audit report, the commissioner noted that almost all departments failed to establish clear and measurable targets, and that many strategies "appear to represent less a commitment to change in order to promote sustainable development than a restatement of the status quo."[11] One commentator pointed out that the sustainable development strategies had been produced mostly by junior officials, and that they did not have any follow-up or weight in what departments are doing.[12] Others, however, were more optimistic and expected that, over time, the strategies would become more meaningful, and their influence possibly profound.[13]

As yet, these expectations do not appear to have been borne out. In its 2004 report on Canada's environmental performance, the OECD notes that "in most cases sustainable development strategies developed by various federal departments or agencies consist in repackaging current and planned activities and have little bearing on budget allocation."[14] Several of the commissioner's audit reports found that strategy commitments were generally not measurable or meaningful; that management systems supporting the strategies were weak; leadership from senior managers was often missing; that there was too much focus on current and planned activities and not enough on long-term results; and that performance reporting was incomplete and inconsistent.[15] Commenting on the round of strategies produced in 2004, the commissioner noted that "[w]hile the overall quality of the strategies had improved somewhat since 2001, the quality of the 2004 strategies still varies widely. Every strategy has room for improvement."[16]

The extent to which these institutional changes can be expected to bring about the greening of government is circumscribed by several limitations and constraints. The first limitation is that the requirement to adopt and implement sustainable development strategies does not apply to all branches of government, with some significant exemptions granted to, among other, Crown Corporations.[17] The policies and practices of these institutions have a significant direct and indirect impact on the environment, and their exclusion from this requirement creates a major gap, especially in the area of economic-environmental integration. It also does not apply to provincial governments, which collectively possibly have an even bigger environmental impact. A second important limitation is that, even where and when departmental strategies lead to environmental policy integration, these efforts are not guided by an overarching federal green plan. Although, before every round, the government sets forth some priorities, these were different every time and lacked a consistent rationale.[18] Consequently, departments are not given specific objectives and targets for reducing environmental impacts in their areas or sectors, in line with an overall plan, and consequently there is no basis for assessing whether their efforts and achievements are sufficient in the context of Canada's overall environmental (or sustainability) needs or aspirations. As discussed in chapter 5, Canada no longer has a federal green plan or sustainable development strategy to guide and coordinate efforts toward this challenge.

In the absence of clear national environmental objectives and targets, departments are largely free to determine their own greening objectives in their strategies. Consequently, it is not surprising that many of the strategies are not very ambitious. Many appear to be oriented more toward the greening of the departments' internal household operations rather than of their *policies* that guide and affect the practices of target groups. As the assessment of departmental strategies by the commissioner is based primarily on the commitments made by the departments themselves, attention is focused more on issues like whether departments have adopted and implemented environmental management systems (like the ISO 14001 standard), than on whether and how their *policies* have integrated environmental concerns. Although the former issues can be significant, given the size of government and its use of resources, it is the latter questions that lie at the core of the greening of government. Interpreting the greening of government mainly in terms of the adoption of environment management systems or green procurement policies surely limits this challenge but also tends to overshadow what greening government fundamentally is about.

The weakness or modest nature of these external-institutional integration efforts is also reflected in the feeble organizational and political backing that they receive. Even when and where departmental efforts are found to be very weak, there is nothing the commissioner can do, apart from shaming departments in reports. The role and power of the commissioner are confined mainly to monitoring and reporting, within the wider constraints of the Auditor General Act. And as integrating environmental concerns into the policy process is foremost a political matter, forcing government departments in this direction is indeed not a task for the commissioner but for elected government officials. However, thus far, governments have shown no inclination to be willing to significantly strengthen institutional-environmental integration. Although deputy ministers in each department are responsible for the strategies, the accountability for the strategies at the senior management level needs strengthening.[19] In 2004, the government created a deputy ministers' Environment and Sustainable Development Coordinating Committee, to ensure that departments collaborate on sustainable development, and for coordinating the strategies' crosscutting issues, but the committee did not develop a federal strategy, had no full-time secretariat, did not meet for over a year, and had no plans for meeting.[20] A new Deputy Ministers' Policy Committee on Environment and Sustainability was formed in the spring of 2005 with, among other things, the task to oversee the production of the next generation of departmental strategies as well as the elaboration and implementation of a national framework on environmental sustainability. But the strong political leadership needed to put environmental concerns into the heart of government institutions appears to be lacking. Even with regard to "green procurement," a rather limited aspect of government greening, governments have been dragging their feet.[21] The commissioner notes that a recurring theme in the efforts of the federal Canadian government appears to be a "chronic inability to see its own initiatives to completion."[22]

Whether and how much Canada's government institutions have been greened as a result of these initiatives is a question that is open for interpretation. On the one hand, there is no doubt that the environment and sustainability have been firmly put on the agenda of most government agencies. On the other hand, environmental concerns appear to have been interpreted and integrated in narrow, limited, variable, and varied ways, with little if any impact on nonenvironmental policies and practices, and on environmental outcomes.

In the United Kingdom, government initiatives directed at the integration of environmental concerns into nonenvironmental institutions begun following Margaret's Thatcher environmental "conversion" in 1988, and the appointment of Chris Patten as secretary of state for the environment.[23] A contributing factor was also the growing electoral support for the greens (15 percent of the vote in June 1989 in the European elections). In September 1990 a white paper, *This Common Inheritance: Britain's Environmental Strategy*, was published, followed by five annual progress reports. The white paper's significance lies not so much in its substance (it presents options rather than a course of action) as in the institutional innovations that it brought about. Among them were the creation of "green ministers" in each government department, publicly accountable for the environmental performance of that ministry; the guidance provided by the Department of the Environment on environmental appraisal of policy decisions and green housekeeping; the establishment of discussion groups with business, local government, and NGOs; the introduction of a reporting obligation for departments, required to give an account of progress in implementing their strategies; and the establishment of two ministerial committees, later fused into one, the Ministerial Committee on the Environment.[24]

The United Kingdom thus provides an example of the institutional reform pathway rather than of green planning, despite the adoption of the white paper. Although, in 1994, the government adopted a sustainability strategy (*Sustainable Development: The UK Strategy*), it has been argued that this document "cannot properly be described as a "strategy" at all," as it also involved mainly institutional initiatives, notably the establishment of the Government's Panel on Sustainable Development, the UK Round Table on Sustainable Development, and a citizen's environment initiative (later renamed "Going for Green").[25] The significance of these developments lies in the processes that they establish rather than in their policy objectives, which are rather vague and complacent.[26]

The process of institutional reform continued after the election of the Labour government in 1997. Labour introduced a range of new institutional mechanisms toward bureaucratic-environmental integration to "ensure that environmental considerations are fully integrated into all areas of policy in order to achieve sustainable development in a joined up way."[27] Among these was the establishment of a Sustainable Development Unit within the Environment Agency, which turned out to be a catalyst for action by other departments.[28] Labour continued the practice of appointing "green ministers" in all the main central government departments to promote the integration of the three strands of sustainable development (economic, environmental, and social), but established also a Parliamentary Environmental Audit Committee (EAC) to consider to what extent the policies and programs of government departments and nondepartmental public bodies contribute to environmental protection and sustainable development. In 2000, a new Sustainable Development Committee was created out of previously existing advisory bodies, with the task to monitor progress on sustainable development and to build consensus on actions toward it across sectors. The Labour government also put considerable effort into the development of indicators and has introduced a more robust framework for monitoring and reporting.[29] Altogether, the extent of institutional change directed at the promotion of sustainable development and bureaucratic-environmental integration that has occurred in the United Kingdom looks impressive.

However, to what extent these changes have produced meaningful results, or will do so in coming years, is not clear. In its sixth report, released in 1999, the EAC made the comment that it was "particularly disappointing that there is so little evidence of environmental appraisal of new policies," and that, although the green ministers had started to make a difference, departments still had a long way to go with regard to assessing and reporting on their environmental performance.[30] In 2005, one author notes that "[a]lthough this process of 'greening government' has ensured that 'non-environmental' departments have increasingly had to consider environmental issues, attempts at integration have arguably been less than successful. The SDU, which was to be established in the Cabinet Office, ended up in the DETR (and then the Department for Environment, Food and Rural Affairs, DEFRA), which meant that it had much less coordinating authority."[31]

Green ministers have been largely ineffective, and many government departments hardly appear to pursue environmental integration, producing few if any environmental assessments of their policies. And if they do pursue it, then they do so only halfheartedly, paying lip service to sustainable development objectives.[32] Government departments, notably Transport, Finance, and Agriculture, strongly opposed the adoption of the white paper and the strategy.[33] While the EAC plays an important role in reminding the government of its commitment toward environmental integration and sustainable development, and has assessed government performance on a range of issues and policies, it has not been able to effectively assess environmental integration efforts of government departments.[34] As in Canada, the absence of an overarching framework of measurable objectives and targets makes it difficult to evaluate the significance and adequacy of the integration efforts undertaken by government bodies, individually as well as collectively.[35] Also, commitment to environmental integration and sustainable development at the senior management level has been noted to be lacking.[36]

Short-term political rationality continues to pose a considerable obstacle to the implementation of environmental integration, even when formal government policy appears to indicate strong commitment in this direction. For instance, despite the adoption by the UK government, in 1998, of an integrated transport strategy (*A New Deal for Transport: Better for Everyone*) that "represented a sea change in thinking," many of its "policy goals were watered down or abandoned as Prime Minister Blair became increasingly concerned that the proposals were 'anti-car' and would jeopardize the votes of key sectors of his electorate."[37] More fundamentally, it has been argued that the view of the Blair government toward environmental integration has been one where environmental concerns are added onto existing policies rather than properly integrated, which is seen as too big a challenge.[38]

The experiences in both Canada and the United Kingdom demonstrate that vested interests and political and bureaucratic rationality continue to militate against environmental integration even if it is institutionally supported. Creating agencies and rules specifically to promote environmental integration does not appear to be sufficient, as many or most of the preexisting institutions, with their entrenched interests, and the rationality underlying the government system, are not fundamentally changed by these "add-ons." Arguably, institutional change at a more fundamental level is required. As it is sometimes argued that governments are "prisoners" of the economic system,[39] arguably the greening of the economic system is a prerequisite for, or essential complement to, the greening of the political system.

THE GREENING OF ECONOMIC INSTITUTIONS

In preceding chapters, several forms of economic-environmental integration already have been discussed, such as the sustainability assessment (SA) of trade agreements, and the use of economic instruments (both in chapter 4). Although these tools can contribute to positive environmental outcomes, depending largely on how they have been institutionalized, they also are fundamentally limited in the extent to which they can be said to green economic decisions and policies, and are, at most, modest starting points for the greening of economic institutions.

It can be argued, therefore, that greening economic policies and practices requires environmental integration at a more fundamental or systemic level. Although the efforts toward economic-environmental integration that have been undertaken so far may have (had) some impact on mitigating or even reversing environmental damage, they are seen as inadequate by those who place economics into an ecological and social context. This is because these efforts, and economic theory and decisions in general, fail to appreciate the shortcomings and inappropriateness of valuing social and environmental values only in monetary terms.[40] They also do not take into account the physical-environmental basis of economic activity. In Daly's graphical depiction, prevailing economic theory and decisions fail to place the "economics box" within the larger "environment box," and assume an infinite resource and waste absorption capacity. This "preanalytic vision" needs to be replaced by a view of economics as being dependent on, and circumscribed by, environmental space, and by an economic model that takes into account physical-environmental limits and impacts of economics.[41] From this point of view, infinite material growth (growing material throughput) is not possible, but qualitative change (development) is. As the economic subsystem already takes up too much space of the ecosystem, it is necessary to reduce the level of material throughput, especially in the high-income countries that are responsible for a disproportionate share in the use of resources.

However, the ideas advanced by ecological economics have only had modest influence on practical policy development, and have thus far failed to displace the dominant economic paradigm.[42] To what extent the (capitalist) economic system needs to be, and can be, reformed remains the subject of much disagreement. As pointed out in chapter 3, the original idea underlying ecological modernization is that environmental problems can be effectively addressed by technological and managerial measures within the prevailing economic system, thus not requiring fundamental change of economic institutions. Although stronger versions of EM see a need for institutional change, views differ on how much and what kind of change is required or desirable. What a green economic system looks like, or could or should look like, is still unclear and open to debate. Socialism, widely written off as an alternative to capitalism since the fall of the Berlin Wall, was never seen by many environmentalists as a green economic system in the first place, given its fundamental commitment to "industrialism" and economic growth, which it shared with capitalism. However, despite the proclaimed "end of history," and the contemporary dominance of neoliberal ideology, capitalism continues to be contested, notably from left and green ideological positions. Here the aim is not to discuss the variety of views on this matter, but to identify what governments have done or are doing to green economic institutions.

Some of the ideas developed by ecological and other economists have found some resonance with governments. In particular, the idea that accounting systems should be changed to take account of environmental values and effects has received considerable attention and follow-up. Arguably, at the macroeconomic level, "green accounting" (including natural resource accounting) has the potential to strongly influence economic policies, decisions, behavior and practices. Some other efforts are focused on institutional greening at the microeconomic level—for instance, by promoting or requiring the adoption of environmental management systems (EMS) and labeling systems. However, whether and to what extent these initiatives have led or lead to a greening of economic institutions is highly questionable.

As Daly and other economists have pointed out, existing ways of accounting for economic activity and growth count expenditure on all kinds of "negatives," such as the cleanup costs for environmental damage, as "positives" that add to the gross domestic product, and therefore provide a poor indication of changes in societal well-being. To correct for these anomalies, Daly and Cobb proposed an alternative system for measuring economic progress, the index of sustainable economic welfare (SEW).[43] The SEW has provided the basis for the development of an amended measure of welfare, the genuine progress indicator (GPI).[44] An application of the GPI measure shows that, in the United States, GPI has declined since the 1970s while GDP continued to rise. However, one critique of the GPI is that it does not reflect the value of nature's services except when they are lost,[45] and work has continued on better ways of accounting for economic activity and its effects on social and environmental well-being, including by the development of sustainable development indicators.[46]

Norway and France have been pioneers in green accounting, each developing its own versions of natural resource accounting. Norway started with the development of environmental accounts in the 1970s, notably for energy, air quality, fish, forestry stocks, and some minerals. The initial idea of developing natural resource accounts for all natural resources was abandoned for economic, political, and theoretical reasons. Instead, the focus has been on developing accounts for resources and issues where it was considered to be most important and useful. Data on energy flows, in particular, have been used in econometric models for economic and environmental analyses.[47] Natural resource accounting in France, known as a system of national patrimony accounts, was taken to a highly sophisticated level, linking resource use with (ecosystem) effects and sources (agents). The aim of the system, which recognizes the importance of ecological regions, is to be able to provide decision-makers with information about the amounts that can be extracted from ecosystems without surpassing "threshold values" and diminishing the resource bases.[48] It seems, however, that the French approach has not received a great following in other countries and remains largely "a French speciality."[49]

The environmental accounts system used in the Netherlands consists of physical accounts based on the concepts of environmental pressures (indicators) and themes (problem areas). This enables them to be linked with the Dutch National Environmental Policy Plan, which uses themes as a basis of its green planning efforts, as described in chapter 5. The main aim of the system is "to provide an information system that can be used to help researchers and policy-makers determine the 'trade-offs' between environmentally sustainable development and other macroeconomic objectives."[50] Although it is admitted that it is difficult to measure the environmental effects associated with a single theme (given interactions between processes), the accounts make transparent the contribution of the different economic actors to the pressures in absolute and relative terms and, at an aggregate level, the system presents the interrelations between macroeconomic indicators and the environment (by theme). It also takes into account the import and export of emissions (pollution transactions with the rest of the world).[51]

That the prevailing national accounting system does not adequately take account of environmental values and effects has also been recognized at the international level. In the 1980s, a number of workshops on environmental accounting was organized under the auspices of the United Nations Environment Programme and the World Bank.[52] In 1992, *Agenda 21* called upon governments to include an environmental dimension into their accounting systems, indicating that green accounting has become a tenet of "soft law."[53] Since then, many governments have introduced some form of "green accounting" (including resource and pollutant flow accounts, natural resource balances, and environmental expenditure accounts). One new measure, the human development index (which corrects GDP for health and education attainment measures, but which does not correct for environmental/resource impacts) gained international currency. The system of national accounts (SNA), which was developed in the 1940s, has been subjected to two major rounds of review, leading to the publication of handbooks for integrated environmental and economic accounting in 1993 and 2003.[54]

However, as yet, there is no international consensus on how the existing, United Nations–based SNA should be amended to account for social and environmental changes, in part because of the complexities involved, but also because of strong resistance from national accountants and neoclassical economists.[55] Much of the disagreement, according to Bartelmus and Seifert, relates to whether to use physical or monetary measures for weighting the importance of environmental impacts. Different views on the relative merits of physical/ecological and monetary/economic approaches have become polarized and persist.[56] National accountants take the view "that the reputation of 'official' statistics has to be protected against the vagaries of analytical debates" and prefer to stick with established approaches. "At least for now, they have relegated any modifications of the national accounts to 'satellites' or preferably to 'research.' "[57] The United Nations system for integrated environmental and economic accounting (SEEA) embraces both physical and monetary accounts and seeks compatibility with the system of national accounts adopted worldwide, but also reflects ambivalence on this point, showing in fact a predilection for physical accounting.[58]

Whether a fully integrated account system based on monetary valuation is necessary or even desirable from the point of view of environmental integration remains a subject of debate. Arguably, for reasons of environmental integration, physical accounting systems that enable the identification of the sources of environmental pressures, as well as the total scale of problems, are more useful, as they enable policy-makers to target their efforts better. This is probably more important and productive than forcing all environmental values and activities into a fully integrated monetary accounting system, which not only distorts environmental reality but which subjects it to predominantly economic ways of thinking. Such approaches may embed the environment into prevailing economic institutions rather than reembed economic institutions into what is considered to be environmentally necessary or desirable. For that reason it may be better not to fully integrate environmental physical accounts with national income accounts.[59] As demonstrated by some authors, hybrid accounts, as provided by SEEA-2003, can provide a basis for attributing "environmental consumption" to activities and residents, and take account of the environmental effects of imports and exports ("the environmental balance of trade"). Analyses based on such an accounting system appear to be more useful for policy purposes (to address the sources of environmental pressures) than highly aggregated indices expressed in single units, monetary or physical.[60]

However, there is no guarantee that satellite or hybrid accounts *actually* inform or influence policy. Although, in the literature, the impression is often conveyed that green accounting will alter environmental policy, it is not evident that it has contributed, or can or will contribute, to the greening of economic and other policies that affect the environment. Atkinson notes, "Somewhat alarmingly . . . , much of the green accounting literature pays very little attention to how the revised accounts will actually be used."[61] It has been noted that in Norway "the accounts related to fish stocks, forests, minerals and soil have not been used extensively, partially because of a lack of interest by policy-makers in these types of resources and partially because of a lack of appropriate theoretical and econometric models."[62] Information provided by those accounts may be used first and foremost to assess the economic costs of environmental policies rather than for steering economic policy toward environmental objectives. As Nese notes, in Norway some accounts have been discontinued in part because of their limited use for *economic* policy (emphasis added).[63] Accounting systems can provide information that is more or less useful for the development or change of policy, but the systems are not themselves drivers of policy. What information is collected, and how it is interpreted and used, depends on decisions that are colored by judgment, informed by environmental, economic, and political considerations.

While green accounts may be used for some economic or environmental purposes by governments, this does not necessarily imply that economic practices and behavior affecting the environment are changed or influenced in a green direction. As Bartelmus points out, there is a considerable discrepancy between green accounting efforts of governments and corporate accounting practices. Much of the effort at the macroeconomic level toward physical accounting is ignored at the microeconomic level, where companies that have embraced environmental reporting follow different models.[64] To close the gap between macro-level and micro-level environmental accounting, the "voluntarist" approach that most governments have adopted may need to be replaced by a "substantive interventionist form of regulation."[65]

Work on green accounting overlaps with the development of sustainability indicators, which also have become the subject of considerable effort at the national and international levels. Presumably, green accounting is or needs to be guided by criteria for sustainability, including ecological and social criteria for the use of renewable and nonrenewable resources (which I have referred to in chapter 1 as the resource dimension of sustainability). However, work on sustainable development indicators is also still very much in progress, and as yet there is no internationally agreed standard. As noted earlier, the resource dimension of sustainability is often interpreted mainly or exclusively in traditional economic terms, including a certain level of economic growth measured by GDP. Other interpretations are based on the application of the notion of "natural capital," but differ with respect to whether, or to what extent, human-made capital can be considered as a substitute for natural capital, giving rise to "strong" and "weak" notions of sustainability.[66]

Because of the complexities and disagreement involved, green accounting is still a work in progress, and any hope that the existing system of accounting will be replaced by an environmentally based system seems premature.[67] In the meantime, many countries continue to operate different "green accounting" systems, largely separate from the SNA system. More importantly, most governments and international organizations continue to base their economic policies largely on the notion of GDP as the main indicator for their economic performance and, often explicitly, for the well-being of their countries.

Following on from the observations above about the weak links between the macro level and the micro level in environmental accounting efforts, it can be argued that this is characteristic of a general reluctance on the part of many governments to change the institutions that guide economic decisions, practices, and behavior at the micro level. In capitalist economies, especially when guided by the neoliberal "free market" doctrine, this does not come as a surprise. Nonetheless, as it is claimed that within such an institutional framework it is possible to integrate environmental concerns, it is important to assess the merits of the (modest) institutional changes that are expected to bring this about.

In many countries, governments have started to promote, introduce, or regulate certification and labeling schemes—for instance, for organic agriculture and energy efficiency, and for enhancing the environmental performance of businesses in general. Perhaps most prominent in this respect is the adoption of environmental management systems, often seen as evidence for the greening of economic institutions at the micro level. As such schemes may have international ramifications (including implications for trade), they have been the subject of international standardization.[68] The two main systems that have evolved are ISO 14001 (launched in 1996 as part of a series of ISO14000 standards), developed by the International Standards Organization (ISO), a nongovernment organization, and the European Union's Eco-management and Audit Scheme (EMAS). Both are voluntary schemes.

The number of organizations adopting an EMS has been growing rapidly, though more so in some countries than in others. By April 2006, more than eighty-eight thousand ISO 140001 certificates had been issued, compared to more than four thousand EMAS certificates. Although initially more than half of the ISO 14001 certified organizations were located in European countries, by 2006 Japan and China were the countries with the highest number of certified facilities, together accounting for 30 percent of all registrations. By contrast, American companies are less inclined to adopt the standard. EMAS, being a European Union standard, has received a much smaller following, even in the European Union. Germany on its own accounts for about half of the certificates issued under EMAS.[69]

The stated aim of environmental management systems is to improve environmental care by organizations. The main means by which this is sought are organizational structures and managerial processes, not by requiring particular environmental standards or objectives. Although such systems do expect companies to set environmental goals (as a basis for continuous improvement), the goals are determined by the companies themselves. EMS standards do not set specific limits upon energy or resource consumption, levels of emissions, or levels of performance other than those based on national compliance. They only require "a commitment to continual environmental improvement through the management system loop and do not aim for environmental protection."[70] Although the EMAS scheme is sometimes claimed to be superior to the ISO 14001 standard because, on top of the same or similar requirements, it requires companies to produce environmental reports (which are not required under the ISO 14001 standard), both systems leave it to the organizations themselves to determine how ambitious they want to or can be in their environmental objectives.[71]

Assessing the effectiveness of environmental certification and management schemes is problematic, as much of the information available is of questionable reliability. Much of the research undertaken relies heavily on information provided by the companies themselves, and in particular on those within companies who carry responsibility for the EMS and who have a vested ("micropolitical") interest in proving the positive results of the systems.[72] Hard data on environmental benefits are often lacking and, if available, are not comparable across companies or useful for determining overall results, because of differences between information systems and methods. An American longitudinal study that concluded that the adoption of an EMS does result in (modest) improved environmental performance relied on organizations that volunteered to participate, on (a handful of) self-selected indicators, and on self-reported data that were not independently verified.[73] Two studies that relied on independent data led to contradictory conclusions.[74] Many of the improvements reported by companies are of a managerial, technical, and "end-of-pipe" nature, and few companies appear to be engaged in more innovative practices, such as the redesign of products or production processes that could be referred to as ecological modernization.[75]

An even stronger indictment of the merits of EMSs is that companies that have adopted a formal standard, whether ISO 14001 or EMAS, do not show demonstrably superior environmental commitment compared to those who have not.[76] As the responsibility for EMSs tends to be put in the hands of experts, they often fail to invoke the involvement of employees. Corporate culture appears to be a more important factor in influencing the extent to which environmental care is adopted and spread throughout an organization.[77] The authors of one study conclude that environmental management systems "have not yet proven their capabilities to lead companies to improved ecological performance, let alone to sustainability."[78] At best, they provide a modest basis for mitigating the environmental footprint of companies; at worst, they are means used to ward off more serious and effective government measures directed at regulating economic practices.

Although the adoption of an EMS by a corporation may give the impression of environmental commitment, the rationale for doing so appears to be more hard-nosed. First, they pay off economically, often within one to two years after their adoption, although information on this point also should be treated with caution.[79] Second, by promoting compliance with existing regulatory environmental requirements, they reduce the risks of costs and negative publicity associated with not meeting legal environmental standards. Contrary to the common perception that companies that adopt an EMS are "ecopioneers," most that sign up are not "above average" environmental performers.[80] This makes sense, as it is in such companies that the scope for financial gains and reducing risks (of noncompliance) is probably the biggest. Regulatory drivers appeared to be the primary motivations behind the adoption of environmental management systems in the United States.[81]

Many environmentalists are skeptical about the greening efforts of businesses, and dismiss them as "greenwashing."[82] Although some companies appear to express a genuine commitment toward addressing environmental problems (rather than denying them)—for instance, with regard to reducing CO_2 emissions and waste[83]—it has been pointed out that the scale of these efforts, financially, pales in comparison to these companies' expenditures on other activities, such as new investments or advertising.[84] Since the late 1980s, when demands for more effective environmental government action reached a high, the business sector has become a lot more sophisticated in responding to, and undermining, the demands and actions of environmentalists. In particular, businesses have adopted strategies directed at redefining environmental problems and sponsoring the development of (policy) solutions that are business-friendly, including voluntary approaches or self-regulation like environmental management systems, and by funding conservative think tanks and academics.[85] By taking on board the need to address environmental issues, the business sector has been able to (at least temporarily) ward off more stringent government measures, and to deal with these issues on its own terms, and to its own advantage. For instance, critics of the "partnership" approach that so dominated the discussions at the World Summit in Johannesburg see it as a means for business to expand its grip over (often publicly owned) resources for its own commercial ends, rather than as the integration of environmental concerns into the economic institutional framework.[86]

From an environmental policy perspective, then, the greatest significance of environmental management systems may be that they encourage compliance with regulations. The adoption of such systems does not imply that organizations will go beyond the minimum of what is legally required, and there is no evidence to suggest that, overall, companies that have adopted an EMS are superior environmental performers compared to companies that have not done so. Although the adoption of an EMS can, in some ways, be interpreted as the integration of an environmental dimension into an organization, it does not, as noted above, necessarily *bring about* the creation of a corporate environmental culture, which has been identified as a more important factor for the environmental performance of an organization. But this also means that the extent to which an EMS contributes to the greening of business, or most businesses, depends on the nature and degree of regulatory requirements. Environmental management systems, therefore, are not an alternative to regulation but a means by which the implementation of and compliance with government policies can be promoted.[87]

The same argument has been advanced with regard to other labeling schemes, such as the German Blue Angel scheme, and schemes administered by the Forest Stewardship Council, the Marine Stewardship Council, and the International Federation of Organic Agriculture Movements. While hard data on the environmental effectiveness of these schemes, with the exception of the organic agriculture scheme, are largely lacking, it has been argued that "it is generally accepted that many types of ecolabels are not likely to be successful in the absence of complementary public and private policies."[88] Where labels are supported by regulatory standards (for instance, for energy efficiency or noise), and/or by public procurement policies, they are more likely to attract a greater following. On their own, labeling schemes are unlikely to green the great majority of consumers or producers.

More fundamentally, however, even though environmental management systems and other labeling schemes may produce some improvement in the environmental performance of some companies, the extent to which these efforts lead to a greening of economic institutions is quite limited. They do not alter, but operate within, an economic system that requires continuous growth, and they do not address the issue of scale referred to above. Although some or even many companies may improve their environmental performance,[89] such gains are likely to be reduced or negated by the cumulative environmental impacts of economic expansion, especially in sectors and economies that rely heavily on material throughput. To achieve a greening of the economic system, such efforts will need to be accompanied by more structural and macro-level reforms.

THE GREENING OF ECONOMIC INSTITUTIONS: LIMITS AND OBSTACLES

Although countries and governments differ in this respect, few if any governments appear willing or able to fundamentally change the dominant, capitalist economic institutions for environmental reasons. Whereas, under the influence of neoliberal ideology and international pressure, in the past two decades governments have considerably changed economic and social institutions to promote a narrow notion of national economic health (defined foremost in terms of a growth of GDP and low inflation), they have been much more reluctant to change economic institutions for environmental and social purposes. Although in many countries there have been moves toward a greater use of economic instruments and environmental taxes, overall these have been modest, and so have their effects. But even if used on a larger scale, the aforementioned measures are likely to have limited effect, as they are more in the nature of *correcting* behavior and practices rather than *steering* or *directing* them.[90] Governments appear very reluctant to engage in the latter, and to change, for environmental purposes, the rules that guide economic actors (producers, consumers, financiers), as exemplified in the reliance mostly on voluntary schemes, codes of conduct, and "partnerships." The effectiveness of such approaches with regard to environmental integration, however, remains dubious. Even if they lead to some mitigation of environmental pressure, they do not address the systemic factors and driving forces behind economic decisions and behavior. Thus, the integration between economics and environment, although widely recognized by governments as being important, happens mainly to the extent that it is economically advantageous, and is much more problematic where and when "win-win" situations do not exist or have been exhausted.

A variety of factors can be identified that underlie the apparent inability and unwillingness of governments to green the dominant economic institutions. First, as suggested above, they continue to be wedded to what has been referred to as a preanalytic economic vision that does not recognize environmental limitations[91] and that regards competition and the principle of the "survival of the fittest" (Adam Smith's "invisible hand") as the best guide toward the collective good. In practice, this means that collective and long-term interests are either ignored or discounted. Consequently, government efforts in this area are not guided by a cognitive framework that re-embeds the economy within environmental and social parameters, but by a conception of economics that continues to subject and colonize the social, environmental, and political spheres. Second, underlying and associated with the predominance of this economic ideology are political-economic interests that are powerful enough to shape and maintain this hegemonic economic discourse, through the media, education, and think tanks, among other things. These interests have also been able, in many countries, to colonize or capture the most important state agencies that shape the economic policies, including ministries of finance and/or economic policy, and reserve banks. Third, many other government agencies have institutional mandates that are oriented toward the promotion of interests that demand or benefit from economic growth, including departments of agriculture, energy, and transport. Such agencies usually have more resources and power than government agencies that have environmental protection mandates. In liberal-democratic states, political and bureaucratic rationality remains biased toward serving special, fragmented, short-term, and often conflicting interests, and is not directed at the protection of common and long-term interests.[92] Fourth, with the intensification of economic globalization, which itself is shaped and influenced by political and economic actors, the ability of governments to control the economic situation in their countries, and to more fundamentally change or shape economic institutions and policies for environmental and social purposes, is increasingly compromised. Their economic well-being is to a large extent determined by global market forces, especially financial capital (referred to by Thomas Friedman as the "electronic herd").[93] This does not mean that governments no longer play a crucial role in the management of their economies: state capability still is an important factor in international competition.[94] But it does mean that the greening of the economic system increasingly has become a global challenge, one that involves also the reform and (re)design of international economic institutions.

Finally, underlying these four factors is the bigger and more fundamental issue of capitalism and its connections with the dominant political systems. The issue, basically, comes down to two questions: "Can capitalism be greened?" and "If it can, what is the role of governments?" Both questions deserve much deeper discussion than can be provided in this book, which focuses intead on what governments have done to advance environmental integration, and more particularly on the means they have used. It is my aim to elaborate on these questions, and the factors that shape the broader context of the "politics of environmental integration," in a separate volume. Here I will confine myself to a few comments.

First, there is no agreement on these questions, in large part because they are fundamentally political-ideological by nature. Some analysts seem to think that, subject to a few changes, capitalism can be made sustainable. Buttel, for instance, argues that "[a] few major policy changes that might obtain wide consensus could have a major impact in inducing a shift in the direction of sustainability."[95] Porrit also thinks that a "sustainable variant of capitalism" is possible, at least in theory, but that its realization is "very, very difficult."[96] Others take a more pessimistic view. O'Connor's short answer to the question whether capitalism is sustainable is "No," and the long answer "Probably not,"[97] whereas Kovel's view on the matter can probably be summarized as "Definitely not"[98] and Pepper unequivocally states that green capitalism is an "impossible dream."[99] Not surprisingly, people's views on whether capitalism can be greened are influenced by their interpretation of capitalism and its links with the dominant political system, and by whether they deem it desirable or necessary to change or abolish it, for environmental and other reasons.

Second, whether or not capitalism can be greened or must be replaced by another economic system, there is virtually no choice but to start the process of change from within. Given its (now) worldwide dominance, the few alternative economic systems that (still) exist alongside capitalism (either in Cuba and North Korea, or in the form of cooperatives and alternative or "green" money schemes in other countries) cannot escape having to operate within a wider capitalist economic system. However, that does not imply that there is no alternative to capitalism or that capitalism cannot and will not be changed beyond recognition. Like all human institutions, it is likely to have a limited "use by" date and can and will be changed by human agency based on changing conditions, interests, and perceptions.

Third, and related to the first two points, *how* capitalism will be changed depends mainly on politics and the relative power of competing groups and interests. Although ideas about what a green economic system looks like are important, political-economic factors and developments largely determine their viability and uptake. In the light of history, the creation, if ever, of a green political-economic system is less likely to come about in incremental steps and by gradual reforms then it is to happen through a period of political upheaval and rapid and radical change.

In short, there are limits on how much greening of economic institutions can be expected of governments within the existing political-economic order. However, this does not imply that advocates of environmental integration should give up pushing governments in this area, and even less that they should abandon their own efforts toward the development of ideas, models, and practices aimed at the creation of a green economic system. Such efforts can make a (more or less) significant difference in mitigating environmental harm. They also provide a basis for learning about important elements or essential building blocks for a green economy.

CONCLUSION

Over the past thirty years, governments have introduced many institutional changes aimed at environmental protection. Much of this change has been in the form of the creation of specialized environmental institutions, organizations as well as laws. Although these institutions can and do play a role in the integration of environmental considerations into nonenvironmental institutions, their power and effectiveness is generally limited vis-á-vis those institutions, as reflected in the low degree of policy-external integration discussed in chapter 4. Moreover, nonenvironmental institutions remain wedded to structures, rules, and functions that do not have environmental interests at their core, and that often conflict with such interests. To achieve more significant integration into nonenvironmental policies and practices, therefore, requires a greening of nonenvironmental institutions. In this chapter, we have looked at what governments have done or are doing in that respect.

Institutional measures formally aimed at the greening of government, as adopted in the Canada and the United Kingdom, arguably have the potential to have a significant impact on the policies and practices of nonenvironmental agencies, if indeed they bring about the integration of environmental considerations into the rules and operating procedures of these agencies. If bureaucratic rules and procedures require environmental goals and concerns to be addressed at the design stage of policies and decisions, there is the potential of this leading to a more genuine greening of government policies. However, as decisions on *how* to consider environmental interests are left largely to the nonenvironmental government agencies themselves, these greening efforts often amount to modest adjustments at most, and token gestures at worst. They do not fundamentally alter the goals, interests, responsibilities, and functions that lie at the core of nonenvironmental agencies, which often continue to be at odds with those of the environment. Moreover, to ensure that these integration efforts by individual government agencies are sufficient and complementary, they need to be accompanied at the policy level by an overarching and integrated green plan. However, in Canada, green planning has died, and in the United Kingdom the sustainable development strategies adopted by the government provide not much specific and strong guidance in nonenvironmental policy areas. Thus, the efforts to green government in both countries, arguably leaders in this area of integration, continue to flounder. Green planning needs a strong institutional basis, legal as well as organizational, to support efforts toward the greening of government, a condition missing in most countries.

In the economic-institutional sphere, government efforts toward environmental integration possibly have been even more modest than in the political-institutional realm. Green accounting is still in its infancy, and there are few indications of it being used by governments to guide the development of economic and other policies. And although it can provide governments with information about the impact of economic activities on the environment and the resource base, it does not, in itself, offer a set of rules or goals for economic policies and activities. Whether and how green accounting will be used depends on other political-economic institutions and factors, including the dominant rules and norms regarding the role governments (states) can and should play in economic affairs, and on the willingness of governments, influenced by politics, to intervene in economic activities and to change the economic-institutional framework.

The modesty of government efforts aimed at the greening of the economic system hints at the existence of a range of structural political-economic obstacles, some of which could only be touched upon in this chapter. Fundamental questions remain about the compatibility between capitalism, now globally dominant, and environmental imperatives, and about whether capitalism can be greened. A closely related question is what can be expected of governments, given their role in the functioning of capitalism and the nature of the prevailing political systems, with regard to the transformation toward a green economic system.

As noted above, apart from the political-economic obstacles, the greening of nonenvironmental institutions is further complicated by a lack of clarity and agreement on what green political, economic, legal, and social institutions are. Arguably the biggest of all environmental integration challenges is to design or even sketch an institutional framework that encompasses the different institutional spheres and can promote or ensure their environmental rationality and compatibility. The greening of political, economic, and social institutions are not separate tasks, independent from one another. The success of greening efforts in one sphere depends in large measure on those in other spheres, and on the extent to which they are moving in the same direction and create synergies. What governments have done in this respect is the subject of the next chapter.

7

Institutional-Internal Integration

INTRODUCTION

As explained in chapter 1, institutional-internal integration refers to efforts toward creating (greater) coherence and consistency in environmental management by the (re)design, introduction, or reform of institutions, rules as well as organizations. The rationale behind institutional-internal integration is twofold: first, as environmental institutions evolved in an ad hoc, reactive, and fragmented manner, and generated issues in terms of overlap, consistency, efficiency, and effectiveness, increasingly governments recognized a need for rationalization and integration. In the literature, the term "internal environmental integration" is sometimes used to refer exclusively to the integration of environmental institutions. Here the term is used in a broader sense to include institutional reforms or innovations aimed at providing (greater) coherence to *all* policies, decisions, and actions affecting the environment, including those in nonenvironmental areas, as well as to efforts directed at the greening of institutions. The justification for using the term in this broader sense is that providing greater coherence and consistency in environmental management is not just a challenge or task for environmental institutions. Increasingly, governments recognize the need for external integration, as discussed in previous chapters. However, efforts in this respect are not necessarily consistent with each other, which may adversely affect their effectiveness. The second rationale behind institutional-internal integration is that most political, economic, and social institutions that have evolved within societies and countries do not have environmental values and interests at their core, and therefore often contribute to or cause environmental problems. If environmental problems are to be prevented rather than mitigated, as is now mostly the case, institutions need to be adapted or redesigned on the basis of some overarching environmental parameters, ideas, and prescriptions to ensure that they are greened in the same direction. Both rationales, fundamentally, come down to the same thing: the need to promote, at the institutional level, (greater) consistency and coherence between *all* environmental integration efforts.

Governments have adopted a variety of approaches to promote institutional-internal integration. First, based on the first rationale mentioned above, some governments have introduced changes to the environmental-institutional framework to reduce or overcome the problems associated with fragmentation. The reforms introduced in New Zealand during the 1980s and early 1990s, which attracted considerable international attention, are a good example of efforts in this area, and will therefore be discussed below. Second, many governments have institutionalized environmental rights, duties, and/or principles, in many cases at the constitutional level; their aim can be seen as providing touchstones for environmental integration across policy areas and institutions, including those oriented toward nonenvironmental goals. Third, and perhaps most widespread, is the practice of institutionalizing principles that are inherently integrative by nature, notably sustainable development (SD), the polluter pays principle (PPP), the precautionary principle (PP), and the environmental integration principle (EIP). Fourth, many governments have created organizations specifically with the task to provide advice or guidance on the integration of environmental concerns across policies and institutions, such as roundtables and national sustainable development councils.

To the extent that other forms of environmental integration, such as green planning and the greening of government initiatives, have been institutionalized (backed up by legislation and/or dedicated agencies), such forms can also be considered to be instances of institutional-internal integration. However, as pointed out in chapter 5, in many countries green planning has not been formally institutionalized, with the result that often it has been a one-shot exercise. Greening government initiatives in Canada and the United Kingdom, by contrast, have been institutionalized but are not clearly and strongly guided substantively by overarching goals and objectives. As a result, the integration efforts of government agencies tend to be uncoordinated and are not necessarily coherent and consistent. As both of these forms of integration have already been discussed in previous chapters, they will not be elaborated upon further here.

THE INTEGRATION OF ENVIRONMENTAL INSTITUTIONS

In recognition of the limitations and problems associated with the fragmentation of environmental institutions, often leading to the displacement of environmental problems rather than their resolution, governments have moved toward their integration. In this respect, Sweden and the United States have been early leaders. In 1969, Sweden was one of the first countries to adopt a more integrated approach to pollution control with the introduction of the

Environmental Protection Act.[1] Swedish efforts in this area later stalled and were only revived again in the late 1990s. Similarly, in the United States, the adoption of the National Environmental Policy Act (NEPA) in 1970 marked a significant step in the direction of providing an overarching legal framework for environmental integration by concentrating responsibilities for pollution control into one agency, the Environmental Protection Agency (EPA). However, environmental policy development in the United States has remained notoriously fragmented and even problematic within the EPA, as traditional divisions of responsibilities remained largely intact.[2]

Some countries, such as Japan, the Netherlands, and Sweden, have introduced environmental framework laws (or basic environmental laws) as a means of providing guidance to legislation on a range of environmental issues. Japan adopted a Basic Law for Environmental Pollution Control in 1967, which was revised in 1970 and replaced, in 1993 by the Basic Environmental Law. Although the 1967 act has been referred to as an ineffective, symbolic policy, it provided a basis for other, stricter laws regulating pollution and introduced formal provisions for participation.[3] The 1993 act broadened the scope of the framework legislation and adopted sustainability as a goal.[4] In the Netherlands, the first environmental framework legislation was adopted in 1980 (Environmental Protection—General Provisions Act), and was followed, in 1993, by the introduction of the Environment Act, aimed at the harmonization of previous environmental legislation.[5] However, also under the latter, separate laws for regulating environmental issues (among which, three alone for water) continued to exist, some of which were not covered by the Environment Act; this led to an acknowledgment by the ministry that further integration is desirable.[6] Sweden adopted environmental framework legislation with the introduction of the Environment Code in 1994, which was considered to have several weaknesses.[7] It was followed by a more comprehensive code, amalgamating fifteen acts, in 1999.[8] The Swedish code goes further than the framework legislation in Japan and the Netherlands in that it actually consolidates (integrates) a raft of different pieces of legislation providing specific rules and sanctions covering different environmental areas rather than just orienting them toward the same goals or principles.

New Zealand, arguably, has gone further than most countries in creating of an overarching legal-institutional framework for environmental management. Between 1984 and 1990, the fourth New Zealand Labour government initiated a process of institutional and policy change that left virtually no area untouched. Based on the ideas and principles associated with "New Right" thinking, the government transformed and halved the public service, corporatized and then privatized most state-owned companies, and reframed most policies based on the notions of public choice, agency theory, and the "new public management." The main principles on which the reform were based were the separation between commercial and noncommercial activities, the separation between policy, regulatory, and management functions, and enhanced accountability, transparency, and efficiency.[9]

Based on these ideas and principles, the institutional framework for environmental management was also drastically changed. In 1986, a Ministry for the Environment with a broad environmental policy mandate was established; it was made responsible for advising the government on all environmental matters, not just pollution control. The ministry is not burdened with the implementation of policies, responsibility for which has been largely devolved to local and newly established regional councils and a handful of specialized agencies. Responsibilities for nature conservation and the management of national parks, previously also scattered across a range of agencies, were concentrated into a Department of Conservation. More than seventy environmental laws were consolidated into the Resource Management Act (RMA) 1991, which has the sustainable management of resources as its main goal. The act provides an integrated framework for decision-making about all activities that potentially impact on the environment and, in theory, for the development of environmental policy at all levels of government. An independent environmental watchdog, the Office of the Parliamentary Commissioner for the Environment (PCE), was established to keep an overview of the functioning of the whole environmental management system, and to advise Parliament on how gaps, shortcomings, and limitations in the system could be addressed. The office was a world first in environmental-institutional learning of a systemic nature.[10]

However, New Zealand's environmental-institutional framework, despite the significant degree of integration, has several fundamental shortcomings and limitations. Some of these are related to the RMA, others to different aspects of the framework. First, the RMA does not guarantee that environmental concerns receive the weight that many environmental advocates think they deserve, and does not provide a level playing field for environmental and development (economic) interests. Second, the act has little to offer with regard to the integration of environmental values and concerns into national level policy development and government decision-making, and across ecological, social, and economic sectors at all levels. Third, the *effects* orientation of the act encourages a reactive rather than an anticipatory approach to environmental problems, and fails to address their underlying causes or factors.

Although the act requires proponents of development initiatives to undertake an environmental assessment, it is up to councils and citizens to prick holes in these assessments. Neither proponents nor the consultants that they often use (and pay) to undertake environmental assessments can be relied upon to comprehensively, adequately, and objectively report on the environmental effects of proposals. Although sometimes regional councils challenge proposals approved, supported, or initiated by district and city councils, it is often up to environmental and citizens' groups to contest the sustainability of proposals and the decisions by Councils. However, decision-making, by councils as well as the Environment Court, the appeal body, is dominated by legal and scientific considerations, and cases are won or lost primarily on the evidence provided by expert witnesses.[11] As proponents, often businesses, usually have significantly greater resources at their disposition to pay for expert witnesses than environmental and citizen groups, the playing field is far from level. A modest government fund created to provide legal aid to such groups does not compensate for the big differences in this respect. Moreover, there have been several instances where court costs have been imposed on environmental groups that lost appeals in court, providing a further deterrent to challenging decisions.

Although the act encourages the use of mediation procedures to settle conflicts out of court, this can lead to other inequities. It is not uncommon for such settlements to involve financial compensation to those who are considered to be adversely affected by proposed developments. But only those who take part in such a settlement process are compensated, whereas many other people who may be equally affected, but do not formally object, do not receive compensation. This practice of "buying consents" opens the door to abuse on both sides, and can compromise the purpose of the act, as material personal gain may prevail at the expense of environmental values that offer no financial benefit to the parties involved.

A second limitation of the RMA is that it provides no prescriptions or guidance for environmental integration at the national level, other than requiring the formation of a National Coastal Policy Statement. The act does not require that government policy within or across sectors be developed on the basis of the principle or goal of sustainability. The act does not address many of the causes of environmental problems that relate to growing energy use, the expansion of the dairy industry, transport, economic growth, and new technology. Although sustainability increasingly is incorporated into a range of government policies as a guiding principle, many of the pressures underlying environmental problems continue to rise unabated. It also remains beyond the capacity of local and regional government to address such problems, other than through end-of-pipe measures.

A third, and fundamental, limitation of the RMA is that it is focused on managing environmental *effects* rather than on the causes or driving forces behind environmental problems. The effects-orientation was introduced deliberately to move away from the rule- and activity-based planning regime that prevailed before the act was introduced, and which was seen as lacking flexibility, as stifling development, and as ineffective in that environmental effects were inadequately accounted for. Under the new act, in principle, proposed land-use-based activities are allowed to go ahead as long as their environmental effects are considered to be acceptable. Although this may sound like an ideal marriage between developmental and environmental interests, it can only work in practice if there is a basis of complete and unambiguous environmental knowledge and information, especially about the cumulative effects of all existing and newly proposed activities, and if there is consensus on what is sustainable. The "first come, first served" approach that has been followed has meant that the environmental effects of proposals have been assessed independently from each other, and has allowed resource and environmental pressures to cumulate over time. Only recently, in the wake of growing conflicts and concerns about environmental deterioration and resources, has the central government started to recognize the need for more comprehensive and integrated plans for the management of resources.

However, moves in this direction are not helped by the large gaps in knowledge and information about New Zealand's environment. The lack of a comprehensive and integrated system of environmental monitoring and reporting is another significant weakness in New Zealand that has been noted, among other, by the OECD in its assessments of New Zealand's environmental performance.[12] The first state-of-the-environment report, published in 1997, and international data bases on the environment, such as those compiled by the OECD, revealed many gaps on New Zealand because of a lack of data. Although, more recently, significant advancement on this front has been achieved and, in 2007, the Ministry for the Environment produced a second state-of-the-environment report based on a new set of core national environmental indicators, the system and capacity still need strengthening to ensure coherent and consistent monitoring and regular and independent reporting, from the local level to the national one.[13]

But arguably the greatest gap in New Zealand's environmental-institutional framework that impacts adversely on institutional-internal integration is the lack of institutional provisions for green planning. Although New Zealand governments have, at several points of time, made some moves toward developing strategic environmental planning, these have been weak and inconsequential. New Zealand does not have a Sustainable Development Council or similar body that carries responsibility for the development and updating of a green plan, and green planning has not been made a formal requirement upon central government. Government support for green planning has been very low at most, and even modest attempts have failed to survive changes of government. Although, under the Local Government Act, councils are required to develop long-term community plans, these are not developed within a national-level policy framework. New Zealand's capacity for developing a long-term, comprehensive, and integrated environmental policy is poor, and governments appear to lack the commitment toward significantly strengthening it.[14]

Thus, New Zealand's efforts toward environmental institutional-internal integration, although comprehensive, fail to guide policies and practices toward common goals and objectives, even within the environmental realm, let alone in the nonenvironmental sphere. They have also failed to halt the deterioration of New Zealand's environment, especially with regard to biodiversity, the quality of freshwater, the quality of soils, the buildup of traffic, and the generation of waste, and to stem the driving forces behind environmental pressures related to economic and population growth, translated into urban expansion and the growth of transport, energy use, and agriculture.[15] The New Zealand example demonstrates the limitations of a mainly legalistic approach to institutional integration, and more generally of institutional integration that is unaccompanied by a comprehensive environmental policy framework (policy-internal integration). On its own, institutional integration does not ensure that environmental integration occurs, or occurs in coherent and consistent ways. Much depends on the role, functions, and power assigned to environmental advocates, especially those whose main aim or role it is to promote environmental policy integration across all policy areas. While institutional-internal integration is essential to support moves toward policy integration, it cannot substitute for the latter.

The New Zealand experience also shows that institutionalizing sustainability as a principle does not guarantee environmental integration. As the institutionalization of principles, often linked with environmental rights, has become a more common practice around the world, we will look into this form of institutional-internal integration separately in the next section.

THE INSTITUTIONALIZATION OF ENVIRONMENTAL RIGHTS AND DUTIES

The previous section has shown that rationalizing and integrating environmental legislation as a means of promoting environmental integration is not necessarily effective. In many countries, it is also not easy to achieve, because of political and bureaucratic obstacles and opposition. By contrast, the adoption by governments of high-level environmental principles appears to be much less problematic; environmental principles, rights and/or duties have been incorporated into many constitutions. As constitutions provide an overarching legal-political framework for the actions of governments, arguably the integration of environmental values or considerations at this level is also highly significant. It potentially has implications for the actions of all government agencies and policy areas, and could provide a basis for citizens to challenge the failure or inadequacy of government efforts toward environmental integration. It has also been argued that the incorporation of environmental rights in constitutions can promote the coordination of environmental protection measures, function as a unifying basis for the integration of various laws, and provide an overarching legal-normative framework for directing environmental policy.[16] However, whether this is so is a question that requires research. Research is also needed to determine whether and how the institutionalization of environmental rights, duties, and principles outside constitutions (such as in bills of rights and in standard legislation) contributes to environmental integration in practice.

The incorporation of environmental concerns into constitutions has become a widespread practice. Indeed, most countries now have included references to the environment in their constitutions. In 2005, Earthjustice reported:

> Numerous constitutions of the nations of the world guarantee a right to a clean and healthy environment or a related right. Of the approximately 193 countries of the world, there are now 117 whose national constitutions mention the protection of the environment or natural resources. One hundred and nine of them recognize the right to a clean and healthy environment and/or the state's obligation to prevent environmental harm. Of these, 56 constitutions explicitly recognize the right to a clean and healthy environment, and 97 constitutions make it the duty of the national government to prevent harm to the environment. Fifty-six constitutions recognize a responsibility of citizens or residents to protect the environment, while 14 prohibit the use of property in a manner that harms the environment or encourage land use planning to prevent such harm. Twenty constitutions explicitly make those who harm the environment liable for compensation and/or remediation of the harm, or establish a right to compensation for those suffering environmental injury. Sixteen constitutions provide an explicit right to information concerning the health of the environment or activities that may affect the environment.[17]

From this overview it becomes apparent that the integration of environmental concerns in constitutions has taken a variety of forms. Some refer to duties, either of governments or citizens, or both. Others state environmental rights, but differ in the rights mentioned and/or how they are formulated. Some contain very short and general clauses, while others have extensive sections. An example of the former can be found in the Dutch constitution, which states (in Article 21), "It shall be the concern of the authorities to keep the country habitable and to protect and improve the environment."[18] By contrast, the Brazilian constitution contains one of the most extensive environmental clauses, and specifies a range of obligations upon the authorities.[19] The Chinese constitution, like the Dutch one, has only one article referring to the environment (Article 26), but includes some very specific duties: "(1) The state protects and improves the living environment and the ecological environment, and prevents and remedies pollution and other public hazards. (2) The state organizes and encourages afforestation and the protection of forests."[20] In other countries, such as Norway and South Africa, constitutions or human rights charters formulate the environmental rights of citizens, but do not refer to an obligation on the part of authorities to protect or enhance the environment.

A commonly made distinction is between procedural environmental rights and substantive environmental ones. The former are rights that enable individuals to defend or pursue their rights to a clean environment, and may include the right to information, participation in decisions, and due process (access to courts). Many procedural rights overlap with other human rights, like the freedom of expression and the freedom from violence and torture. Substantive environmental rights are often summarized under a general right to a clean and healthy environment, but can be very specific, such as the right of access to water and sanitary services. As views differ on what substantive rights are or what they should entail, and as such rights can be seen to put (policy) obligations on governments, they are more controversial than procedural rights, and more difficult if not impossible to achieve political agreement on.

Although the integration of environmental concerns into constitutions has become a widespread practice, this does not mean that it is unproblematic. As Hayward notes, there seems to be little controversy about the claim that constitutions should say *something* about the environment, but there appears to be greater reluctance to include individual environmental rights alongside other fundamental individual rights.[21] Many governments, including those of Japan, the United Kingdom, Germany, France, Italy, Australia, Canada, China, and the United States, have not included individual environmental rights in their constitutions.[22] Although the case for including such rights may seem persuasive,[23] apparently governments of many Western governments still need to be convinced on this point.

One of the arguments often raised against the inclusion of environmental rights in constitutions relates to doubts about the meaningfulness of doing so. Some of the states where environmental rights have been constitutionally recognized are not known as model democracies or for their human rights records. Hayward notes that "states with the most extensive environmental rights on constitutional paper often compare unfavorably with other states with regard to their actual record in enforcing those and other rights."[24] Eckersley argues that "there are dangers in overworking and devaluing the international rights discourse or offering vague formulations at the national level that are unlikely to be justiciable or enforceable."[25] Arguably, this helps to explain why countries that regard themselves as standard-bearers of democracy are reluctant to join in a practice that seems to diminish rather than enhance the significance of constitutions.

However, this reluctance can also be explained on other grounds. There is nothing to prevent governments that take democracy seriously from institutionalizing environmental rights in meaningful ways. On the contrary, in countries where human rights are of more than symbolic significance, and can be legally enforced, the incorporation of environmental rights has the potential to significantly assist environmental advocates in their political and legal battles. The other side of this coin is, of course, that this may adversely affect nonenvironmental interests. Ironically, the potential of such rights to trump competing claims that now often prevail through mechanisms aimed at "utility maximisation"[26] (including EIA, CBA, and RA), may be a more important reason why governments in the self-proclaimed more genuine democracies resist, under the pressure of vested nonenvironmental interests, the incorporation of environmental rights in constitutions. Their reluctance may be explained not so much by concerns about the erosion of the value of rights but about their potential effectiveness.

The potential for environmental rights, especially substantive rights, to conflict with other rights and interests has also fed reservations about formalizing such rights on the part of some human rights activists and protagonists of "development." It is sometimes feared that environmental rights could be used to block development and protect the environment at the expense of humans. At the same time, human rights are sometimes seen to promote an "anthropocentric" attitude toward the environment, not necessarily offering protection to nonhuman species and ecosystems. One author refers to a philosophical and ethical debate that has "deep ecologists rail[ing] against the anthropocentric nature of human rights and seeking to protect the environment *from* people, rather than *for* people" (emphasis in the original).[27] But although there can be tension between human and environmental rights, they can also complement each other. As noted above, some human rights (such as to due process of law, freedom from violence, and the right to participation) can assist in, and are essential to, the protection of environmental rights.[28] However, as Hayward notes, this should be no reason for relying solely on human rights for environmental protection, as the latter is not a primary aim of the former, and as efforts to invoke civil and political rights in the pursuit of environmental claims have been few and have met with mixed success.[29] More fundamentally, he argues, environmental rights are, in themselves, as important as other human rights: "[I]f it is accepted that *any* human rights ought to be constitutionalized as fundamental rights, then it must be accepted that the right to an adequate environment ought to be among them."[30]

Whether and to what extent the adoption of environmental rights and duties brings about environmental integration in and across institutions, policies, and practices, and in a complementary, coherent, and consistent way, remains a largely open question. Much depends on how they are interpreted and implemented. As yet, however, there is a paucity of information and studies about the implementation of both rights and duties. Hayward notes that although many African countries have a constitutional right to an adequate environment, most of these have yet to interpret or apply them.[31] In Latin America, where many countries have also adopted such rights under the influence of international law, a significant body of environmental public-interest lawyers has emerged. But to what extent this has resulted in the enforcement of environmental rights and the greening of state institutions is unknown.[32] It seems that the best-documented and most interesting instances of the protection of environmental rights and duties are to be found in the Indian subcontinent and the Philippines. In India, Pakistan, and Bangladesh, judges, in the absence of express environmental rights, have used various constitutional rights, such as the right to life, to protect people from environmental harm. In the Philippines, logging concessions were canceled by a judge following a class suit representing children and generations yet unborn.[33] But, in its 2005 report, Earthjustice also notes that "[c]orporations, international institutions, and governments contribute to the environmental harms that result in human rights violations, yet the existing enforcement systems at the international, regional, and domestic levels seldom hold any of these actors fully accountable for causing such harm."[34]

Notwithstanding these difficulties, the incorporation of environmental rights and duties into constitutions and charters is significant in that it provides formal recognition of their importance at the highest level, and a basis for delegitimizing authorities and actions that blatantly disregard the environment. Although their enforcement may be problematic, constitutional environmental rights and obligations also can be seen to reflect, and contribute to, a growing recognition of environmental values in society. Politically, they provide legitimacy to the efforts of environmental advocates to expose and address environmental abuse. Increasingly, the institutionalization of environmental rights and obligations, alongside human rights, has become a matter of international efforts.[35] Institutionalization at that level—if that were to happen—is likely to enhance their symbolic and political importance, and may assist in further sensitizing governments toward taking them more seriously.

But whether and to what extent environmental integration is effectively advanced by the adoption of individual environmental rights and/or environmental duties upon governments remains largely unclear and dependent on politics. In this context, the distinction between procedural and substantive rights, and whether the latter are in the form of duties (on governments, corporations, and other organizations and citizens), is potentially important. In the case of procedural environmental rights, integration relies first and foremost on the extent to which *individuals* are willing and able to pursue and protect their rights. This puts the onus on environmental advocates, and is likely to involve long and costly processes, with uncertain outcomes and, if successful, at most a reactive and partial form of environmental integration related to the particular issue involved. The same applies to the defense of substantive rights where these have not been specifically formulated as duties upon governments. Only when substantive rights have become legal duties upon government might one expect a more proactive and concerted approach to their implementation, across policies and programs. However, whether this occurs depends largely on political and economic factors, and on the extent to which governments are held accountable for their performance by other public actors (such as an administrative court or constitutional watchdog). If they are, the political weight behind the implementation of government duties could be (made) considerably stronger than that behind the enforcement of individual rights.

In conclusion, although the inclusion of environmental rights and duties in constitutions is of symbolic and moral significance, their practical effect with regard to the integration of environmental concerns into nonenvironmental institutions and policies cannot be assumed but needs to be demonstrated. Also, environmental rights and duties do not have to be constitutionalized to have significant consequences. For instance, normal legislation providing for public access to information, or requiring companies to publicly disclose information (such as emissions or toxin-release inventories), has proved to be of great importance to public and environmental groups in their efforts and campaigns, while emission inventories have created an incentive for companies to reduce emissions.[36] More generally, however, the degree to which environmental protection and integration are promoted by governments depends more on political-economic factors than on formal constitutional statements, as discussed in previous chapters. On their own, constitutional rights and duties may do little to achieve the integration of environmental concerns into nonenvironmental institutions, policies, and practices.

THE INSTITUTIONALIZATION OF INTEGRATIVE PRINCIPLES

The institutionalization of environmental principles arguably has been the most widespread and common form of institutional-internal integration. In particular, the notion of sustainable development (SD) has become a global principle or norm, and arguably has achieved hegemonic status among the environmental discourses expected to be adopted, institutionalized, and implemented by all governments. However, as discussed in chapter 3, SD is a very stretchable concept that can be and has been interpreted in different ways, some of which imply more a "balancing" of interests than environmental integration. Here, the discussion will focus on whether the way SD has been institutionalized in a few high-income countries functions as an overarching institutional framework for environmental integration as defined in chapter 1. The same question will be asked for the polluter pays principle (PPP), the precautionary principle (PP), and the environmental integration principle (EIP), which are sometimes seen as implementing principles of SD, but which also have been institutionalized separately, nationally and internationally, as guiding principles for integration.

The Netherlands, Norway, and Sweden have been referred to as "enthusiastic" supporters of sustainable development.[37] This has manifested itself in a variety of ways, including formal statements and the adoption and implementation of policies or strategies that have sustainability or sustainable development as their central goal, as discussed in chapter 5. The question raised here is whether this leadership in SD has been extended to the institutional level, and if so, whether this has been done in a way that advances environmental integration in a coherent and consistent manner across nonenvironmental policies, practices, and institutions. This is important, as environmental integration efforts within government and society are not necessarily complementary and as their effectiveness may be constrained or even negated by the lack or incompatibility of integration efforts in some sectors of government and society. There is a need to design, adapt, and adopt institutions (rules and organizations) that promote and support internal integration.

The Netherlands, as discussed in chapter 5, has been a leader in green planning or policy-internal integration. The strength of Dutch green planning lies not only in its cognitive sophistication, rigor and comprehensiveness, but also in the fact that it has been institutionalized and been made a legal requirement upon governments. This has prevented green planning from being a one-shot exercise, as it has been in many other countries. The way green planning has been operationalized and institutionalized (target groups, target group coordinators, threat of sanctions, covenants with industries) also promotes the integration (internalization) of environmental responsibilities by those who contribute most to environmental problems. Also, the interpretation of sustainability underlying Dutch green planning has been quite specific; it is more in line with the three dimensions of environmental policy described in chapter 1 than with the broader notion advanced by the Brundtland report. The Dutch interpretation is more akin to the notion of environmental space, recognizing natural, biophysical limits at the national and international level and the need to bring production and consumption in line with these constraints. Thus, in the Netherlands, sustainability, as the overarching aim of green planning, appears to function indeed as an (institutionalized) overarching principle for environmental integration.

However, as noted in chapter 5, Dutch green planning seems to have encountered its own limits. Although relatively successful in reducing environmental problems in a range of areas, the scale, structural aspects, and systemic factors that stand in the way of further and more fundamental improvements have also become apparent. This was acknowledged as such in the fourth National Environmental Policy Plan, released in June 2001, in which the need for systemic change (notably of production and consumption) was a central theme, but this recognition has thus far not been followed by concrete action toward institutional change. On the contrary, in the early part of the new millennium, the environment has taken a backseat in government priorities, while economic and social issues have moved into front seats. In the Netherlands, therefore, the notion of sustainability, although operationalized in quite specific terms in green planning, has not (yet) become the cognitive basis for more fundamental political, bureaucratic, economic, or social institutional or systemic change. Recent government decisions on spatial planning and infrastructure show that "sustainability is still not used as a guiding principle when important decisions are being made."[38]

One of Norway's prime ministers gave her name to the Brundtland report, and arguably Norway has been the torchbearer of the principle of sustainable development. The Norwegian government made a formal commitment to institutionalize the principle in the political structures, and to integrate sustainable development into all sectors of society. Sustainable development was declared "the overriding objective for the government's future policy," including foreign policy.[39] The principle was translated into specific objectives and targets for a wide range of sectors, including energy, transport, agriculture, consumer policy, and local administration. Sustainable production and consumption, linked with the notion of ecological space became central themes in the Norwegian interpretation of sustainable development. Several institutional mechanisms, including a National Committee for Sustainable Development, were put in place to coordinate environmental integration.

However, the Norwegian approach also has its weak spots: first, sectoral objectives and targets have not been pulled together into a coherent national plan and linked to national goals and targets. Environmental integration into the core sectors, notably energy, has remained halfhearted (no specific medium- and long-term environmental objectives for the energy sector, continued subsidization of sectors); and much of the burden of implementing sustainable development has been devolved to the municipalities without coordination at the national level. Because of the absence of a green plan, and because many of the goals and targets at the sector and local level are in conflict with each other, the implementation of sustainable development lacks consistency, and there "has been a growing gap between rhetoric and action."[40] Many pollution trends are still pointing upward, and unsustainable use of renewable resources continues.[41]

Norway's tradition of corporatist decision-making, combined with the political-economic weight of the oil and gas industry and other major energy-intensive industries that rely on Norway's abundance of hydropower, may help explain this discrepancy.[42] While, in general, corporatist decision-making is conducive to the integration of environmental concerns into decision- and policy-making processes, it does not guarantee that those concerns are given greater weight than other interests. On the contrary, the greater the absorption (co-optation) of environmental interest groups into the formal political institutions, the bigger the risk that such groups lose their bite and ability to push for more fundamental institutional change.[43] Norway's highly inclusive corporatist political system has enabled environmental concerns to be integrated into the political institutions without fundamentally altering the political-economic system that harbors the driving forces behind many environmental problems. Although Norway has institutionalized sustainable development perhaps more than any other country, this has not been matched by an equally strong degree of integration at the policy level, with the result that in many areas environmental deterioration continues.

Sweden, as mentioned before, has been an early leader in taking a more comprehensive approach to pollution control and, from the late 1980s, in the greening of sector policies, as well as in ecological tax reform. In 1997, it also integrated a range of environmental laws and regulations into a new Environment Code, achieving a significant degree of environmental-institutional integration.[44] As a consequence of its environmental forerunner status, Sweden is also often thought of as a leader in SD. However, although Sweden has institutionalized SD, it has done so relatively recently, and as only one of the principles underlying its environmental policy rather than as an overarching principle. Sweden' s environmental policy is based on a wide range of principles including prevention, precaution, ecocycle, best available techniques, substitution, internalization, and sustainable development.[45] The creation of a "green welfare society," rather than sustainable development, has been declared as the overarching goal by the Swedish government.

The goal of a green welfare society harks back to Sweden's traditional strength as a social welfare state, extending it to include environmental elements as conditions for human well-being. The notion is largely anthropocentric, and does not necessarily include the consideration of the interests of nonhuman nature. Nature conservation and the protection of biodiversity have, until recently, not been given a high priority, and in 2004 the OECD noted that the statutory protection of forests was lagging behind targets.[46] And although the notion of the green welfare society includes a concern about human health and the creation of jobs, in practice government efforts have been largely focused on increasing resource efficiency and technical solutions that are compatible with economic growth.[47] Overall, the overarching goal of a green welfare society is more in the nature of a general policy commitment and has not been formally legislated and translated into organizational mandates.

While, in many ways, Sweden's efforts toward environmental integration, especially on the policy-external dimension, have been strong, the country has not been a forerunner in the adoption of sustainable development. The government adopted its first sustainable development strategy only in 2002, and established a small secretariat for sustainable development within the prime minister's office in 2003. From January 1, 2003, the promotion of sustainable development was also incorporated as a principle in the constitution. The sustainable development strategy identifies eight strategic core areas, and "is intended to be a living document, continuously monitored and evaluated."[48] Thus, at the national level, sustainable development has been institutionalized only very recently, and it remains to be seen how enduring and effective it will prove to be. Arguably, Sweden's hesitation to embrace the notion of sustainable development is understandable and not necessarily a bad thing, given that the adoption of the principle often appears to lead to a dilution of environmental policy—or worse, to the subordination of environmental values and interests to economic goals. That Sweden is not immune from such a risk is indicated by the OECD's observations that, according to some stakeholders, "environmental considerations are sometimes given short shrift in planning processes in some sectors" and that "some actors in society may see environmental objectives as being balanced against other dimensions of sustainable development (i.e. economic growth and social objectives), which leads to environmental quality standards being set more as pragmatic 'bottom lines.' "[49] Thus, sustainable development, as discussed before, is not necessarily interpreted as implying a need to change or green economic and social institutions and policies.

This very succinct overview shows that even in countries that are generally regarded as environmental leaders, the notion of sustainable development has not been institutionalized in such a way that it effectively guides environmental integration efforts into the same direction. While sustainable development has commonly been adopted as a general (policy) goal or principle, and sometimes, as in the Netherlands, translated into specific objectives and targets, it has not itself been instituted in the form of rules and organizations that guide, let alone ensure, that all policies and decisions that potentially affect the environment, within and outside government, are indeed sustainable, even in the "weak" version of sustainability. Thus far, the adoption of the principle has done or meant little for the greening of nonenvironmental institutions, notably in the economic sphere, and it seems far from displacing economic institutions as the predominant and overarching framework within which most policies and decisions within government, and large parts of society, are made. The creation, in many countries, of councils or committees for sustainable development, to be discussed in the following section, may constitute a modest beginning in the process of transformation. However, before looking into the significance of these institutions, we still need to consider if any of the other principles mentioned can provide the basis for an overarching institutional framework for environmental integration, and have been used as such by governments.

The polluter pays principle (PPP) and the precautionary principle (PP) both enjoy international standing as important principles that should underlie environmental policy. Since the early 1970s, the OECD has played an important role in promoting the PPP, which implies that those responsible for pollution should pay the price for addressing it, not so much for moral reasons as to avoid a distortion of competition by government support/subsidies to polluters. The PPP is therefore more a form of external integration (the integration of environmental concerns into economic policies, if not of economic concerns into environmental policies and rules) than an overarching or holistic principle for environmental integration. That does not mean that it is unimportant. Making polluters responsible for bearing the costs of pollution is morally important and can be quite effective in reducing or mitigating environmentally damaging behavior and practices. Formally instituted and consistently implemented, it may even assist the greening of production and consumption. However, the PPP does not itself provide any guidance about what "greening" means and what environmentally sustainable production and consumption look like. Nor does it imply recognition of environmental or resource limits—all it does is integrate the costs of environmental damage, assessed tentatively in monetary terms, into the price mechanism. As discussed in previous chapters, this represents quite a limited and narrow notion of greening and environmental integration. Even if applied consistently, the principle does not guide governments and societies toward an environmentally—or, for that matter, socially or economically—sustainable world.

Given the inherent limitations of the PPP as an overarching principle for environmental integration, it cannot logically be expected to have been institutionalized as such by any government. As discussed in previous chapters, some governments, notably in Sweden and Denmark, have gone further than others in introducing environmental taxes, which in practice have been used as the main mechanism to make polluters pay. The relatively modest degree to which the PPP has been applied and institutionalized by governments, and consequently of the positive effects on the environment, have already been pointed out, and do not need to be repeated here. Although fines and penalties, effectively criminalizing pollution, are other means of making polluters pay, these have been used and institutionalized to an even lesser extent by governments. As crimes against the environment and the collective good of present and future generations can be regarded as at least as serious as many of the other crimes for which people are punished, such means can be well justified. However, like the criminal justice system in general, they may do little if anything for preventing crimes and for guiding behavior and practices in a positive direction.

The precautionary principle (PP) is a future-oriented concept. As such, it can be seen as a basis for the development of anticipatory policies, directed at the prevention of problems. Originating from the German *Vorsorge* principle, the PP has been interpreted in a variety of ways. O'Riordan and Cameron identify six core elements of the principle: preventative anticipation, safeguarding ecological space, proportionality of response, duty of care or burden of proof on those who propose change; promoting the cause of intrinsic natural rights; and paying for past ecological debt. They note that the principle "absorbs notions of risk prevention, cost effectiveness but in a looser economic framework, ethical responsibilities toward maintaining the integrity of natural systems, and the fallibility of human understanding."[50] But some of these elements, especially the last two, are not commonly accepted as defining principles, and there is an ongoing debate about the meaning and merits of the principle. While the principle has become a cornerstone of German environmental policy, it has been argued that the Americans and Japanese see it as a threat to free markets and technological innovation.[51] Some refer to it as a "shambolic concept" that, as yet, is unable to provide practical guidance,[52] whereas others note that, in Germany, it has played a powerful role in the development of environmental policy.[53]

In Germany, the home of the concept, the PP initially was used by environmental advocates to counterbalance other principles on which environmental policy was based, notably the "economic feasibility" principle.[54] It is thus only one of five principles on which German environmental policy is based, the others being the polluter pays principle, the "common burden" principle, the cooperation principle, and the proportionality (or "economic feasibility') principle. In 1976, the PP was enshrined in legislation, but it has not been incorporated into the federal constitution (although it has been in the constitutions of some *Länder*).[55] In Germany, the PP has been interpreted as requiring an active role of the government (as well as society) in the development of future-oriented policies that reconcile environmental, economic, and social interests. It thus fits in with the traditionally strong role of the government in Germany, acting on behalf of the collective interest: "*Vorsorge* means state influenced planning and is therefore ideologically in conflict with free market doctrines."[56] In its implementation, the Germans assign considerable discretion to the bureaucracy and rely on a traditional preference for a regulatory and "top-down" approach.[57]

The German interpretation of the PP suggests that the principle can, and perhaps does, function as an integrative concept or framework that guides governments and society toward collectively determined goals that encompass, and reconcile, environmental, economic, and social interests. It has been argued that, in Germany, the PP is used as principle for good government, for looking at the future (long term), and as a basis for formulating ambitious economic and environmental goals that are mutually compatible (which is something else than "traded off").[58] However, it appears that, in practice, the German implementation of the PP relies primarily on technological, managerial, and economic means, and on engineers.[59] This matches the relatively strong support in Germany for the "weak" version of the notion of ecological modernization, which also assumes that environmental problems can be solved by such means. Thus, the institutionalization of the PP does not necessarily imply recognition of biophysical limits to economic growth or of a need for fundamental change (greening) of the political-economic and sociocultural systems.

It is often said that the PP is not liked in the United States, but several authors note that de facto the principle of precaution has been enshrined in a range of statutes.[60] According to Bodansky, the precautionary principle underlay the first wave of environmental statutes adopted in the 1970s. However, in his view, the initially strict application of the principle did not produce the expected results and led to a backlash.[61] Jasanof argues that precaution, with prudential and moral components, played an important role in decision-making on hazardous chemicals, but as a result of several Supreme Court decisions the principle is increasingly implemented in the form of science-based, quantitative risk analysis, with the result that the moral and potentially proactive role of the PP tends to get lost. Apparently, the prevailing view of the PP in the United States is that it is a threat to innovation and property rights.[62]

Although the United States and the European Union are often seen as being at loggerheads over the interpretation of the PP, there are some significant similarities in their handling of the principle. In both systems, science and the courts play a dominant role: science in the analysis of risks and the courts with regard to determining whether applications of the principle are acceptable. In the European Union, risk assessment is regarded as primarily a task of science, based on the principles of excellence, independence, and transparency," as in the United States.[63] Case law from the European Courts (the Court of First Instance and the European Court of Justice), like in the United States, largely determines whether applications of the PP are acceptable. Economic concerns also play a role in the European implementation of the principle, as the proportionality principle implies that the measures taken by authorities to head off risks must be proportional to the costs. In practice, this amounts to a requirement for undertaking cost-benefit analyses.[64] The main difference between the two systems in their treatment of the PP appears to be that the European Court grants a greater degree of discretion to political authorities to determine what level of risk is deemed acceptable than in the United States. The difference is crucial, however, as it implies that the political dimension of risk assessment, even if circumscribed by the requirement to use science as a basis for assessing the risks and by the proportionality principle, finds more recognition in the European Union than in the United States.

Much depends, then, on the how the PP is interpreted. Narrow definitions of the PP, which emphasize the need for "hard" facts and the role of science, imply an interpretation and application that is almost similar to risk assessment (RA), while other interpretations emphasize the importance and role of values and interests in issues and science, and consequently recognize a need for involving the public in decision-making.[65] But even when the role of science is emphasized, and that of values and politics downplayed or ignored, the implementation of the PP is circumscribed by politics, as is perhaps more obvious in poorer countries where the PP has been formally adopted.[66]

Overall, there are few if any indications that the PP, in practice, is implemented and used as a broader or overarching institutional framework for guiding environmental integration efforts. In many cases, applications of the PP are focused on "risks," and are therefore drawn into a contest with "scientific" risk assessment, with its focus on single technologies, products, and issues. As discussed earlier, the notion of risk provides a narrow and quite negative perspective on what the environmental challenge is about. Also, with very few exceptions, the PP is invoked *reactively*, notably after technologies have already been developed and are proposed to be applied in the "real world" or on a larger scale. Although the PP can be, and has been, used to address or head off risks, and as a guiding principle for policies,[67] nowhere does it appear to have been adopted as a general *obligation* for the *development* of science and technology based on environmental and social parameters set by societies. To function as a more overarching integrative principle, the PP would need to be coupled with a more positive, goal-based approach to environmental decision-making, moving away from the narrow focus on potential harm, as suggested by O'Brien.[68] Although, as noted above, in Germany the PP has been used as a principle for good government, this has not been interpreted and implemented in a way that amounts to anything more than the trading off between economic, social, and environmental interests on a case-by-case basis.

Apart from the advancement of environmental integration through the adoption of the principles discussed above, environmental integration has become a principle in itself (EIP). The European Union arguably has gone further than most political systems in institutionalizing this principle. In 1987, the European Union made the integration of environmental considerations into nonenvironmental policy areas a formal commitment with the adoption of the Single European Act, and it became a legal requirement under the Treaty of Amsterdam in 1999.[69] Environmental integration has also been laid down as a principle in Article 6 of the European Community Treaty, which states: "Environmental protection requirements must be integrated into the definition and implementation of the Community policies and activities [. . .], in particular with a view to promoting sustainable development." Article 2 now places sustainable development among the European Union's objectives.[70] Under the Cardiff agreement, concluded in 1998, all European Union councils of ministers have been requested to develop environmental integration strategies, and to produce progress reports on their implementation.[71]

Despite this apparently high level of support for the EIP and its formal institutionalization in the European Union, in practice the operationalization and implementation of the principle has been patchy and its effectiveness unclear. The European Environment Agency notes that there is little agreement on the meaning of the principle, which "may have made it more acceptable to policy-makers, but it also makes it more difficult to put into practice and to evaluate progress."[72] The institutional arrangements for both the European Union's sustainable development strategy and the Cardiff integration strategies are also said to lack clarity, and there is "no independent SD or environmental advisory council or similar body to follow and review progress on integration and sustainable development issues."[73] In practice, economic and social goals, as set forth in the ten-year Lisbon strategy adopted in 2000, "to make the Union the most dynamic, competitive knowledge-based economy, enjoying full employment and strengthened economic and social cohesion," receive political priority.[74] It has been noted that "sectoral environmental integration does not appear to be a high priority for the Commission,"[75] and Lenschow argues that there is little evidence that EPI has served as a "rule of reference" or was even accepted as an "autonomous normative principle" in council decisions.[76] This is also reflected in the limited extent to which environmental concerns have been integrated into nonenvironment policy sectors at the European Union level, as pointed out in various studies.[77]

The European Union experience demonstrates that institutionalizing the EIP is not sufficient to ensure its implementation. Although political-economic obstacles arguably present the biggest hurdles to the greening of nonenvironmental policies and practices, the way the EIP is interpreted, operationalized, and institutionalized also matter. In this respect, the label that is commonly used to refer to the principle, "the environmental *policy* integration (EPI) principle," is itself a limiting factor, as it focuses attention mostly or exclusively on integrating environmental concerns into policies, diverting attention from the need to also green institutions (including agencies and decision-making structures), or to create new institutions, as reflected in the poor institutional backing of the principle in the European Union, noted above. Interpreted only in terms of policy integration, the EIP cannot and does not function as broader framework for the (re)design of the institutional frameworks that constrain environmental integration in more fundamental ways.

In conclusion, the institutionalization of integrative principles has become a common phenomenon, albeit that the popularity of particular principles differs across governments and countries. SD, PPP, PP, and EIP have found different levels of support among governments, fluctuating also over time, for various, political, sociocultural and economic reasons. The way these principles have been institutionalized, interpreted, and operationalized also differs significantly between countries and governments. However, even in countries where these principles have found strong support and been formally adopted as overarching principles of government policy, their operationalization and implementation does not guarantee that environmental concerns are adequately integrated into nonenvironmental sectors, and much less so that they function as an overarching framework of environmental parameters that are built into the design of institutions, policies, and practices. Like all principles, integrative principles are subject to interpretation shaped by differences in ideologies, interests, and power. How they are operationalized and implemented depends also on the role and relative power of those who can be regarded, or who regard themselves, as advocates for and agents of environmental integration.

AGENTS OF INTEGRATION: NATIONAL COUNCILS FOR SUSTAINABLE DEVELOPMENT

Following the publication of the Brundtland report in 1987, and the adoption of *Agenda 21*, a program of action, at the UNCED conference in Rio in 1992, in some seventy countries new bodies were established with the express aim to promote sustainability or sustainable development.[78] Although such bodies come under a variety of labels, they are referred to here as National Councils for Sustainable Development (NCSDs).[79]

From the point of view taken in this book, the importance of such organizations lies, first, in their actual or potential role as agents or actors of environmental integration, and second, in that they are possibly the starting point of a process of political-institutional change toward greener government and/or governance. Such councils almost inevitably play a role in the "politics of environmental integration" and, one would expect, strengthen the camp of those who advocate environmental integration. Also, as noted in chapter 6, efforts toward the greening of government, such as those in Canada and the United Kingdom, continue to be limited and constrained by vested, institutionalized interests, notably within the bureaucracy. To the extent that NCSDs are (relatively) independent from these vested interests, and are seriously committed to environmental integration, they could provide a breeding ground for further institutional innovation and the greening of institutions.

What role NCSDs play depends, of course, foremost on their specific mandates, functions, powers, composition, resources, the motivations and capabilities of their members, and many contextual conditions and factors. Their actual significance can only be assessed by empirical study in the context that they are operating in. Unfortunately, few such studies of NCSDs have been undertaken, especially on an independent, critical, and comparative basis.[80] Nonetheless, based on the available literature, several observations can be made.

First, although there is not even clarity or agreement on how many and which countries have established a NCSD or similar body, it is clear that, in quite a few countries that often are the subject of environmental policy research, such organizations do not exist or have ceased to exist. In the United States, the Presidential Council on Sustainable Development, established by President Clinton in 1993, was discontinued in 1999, although the country still has the Council of Environmental Quality that was created under NEPA in 1969. Australia had a very limited version of such a body until 1997.[81] New Zealand, where the government, in the late 1980s, abolished an Environmental Council that had existed since 1970, also does not have an NCSD. The German Council for Sustainable Development was established only in 2001, although this country has had a Council of (Scientific) Environmental Advisers since 1971.[82] In Norway, a self-proclaimed leader in sustainable development, the Committee for Sustainable Development has been described as "essentially moribund."[83] Obviously, NCSDs are not alive and well in all countries, not even in some that pride themselves on their environmental performance. When such bodies are created, their survival is far from guaranteed. In general, the legal-institutional basis of many councils is, or was, not secure, and their survival has been subject to the whim of governments. Relatively few councils have been given a legal basis.[84]

Second, there is a wide variation in the mandates and functions of NCSDs. Analysts appear to agree that the specific design of such organizations depends, and should be based on, the differences in political, economic, and social contexts. There is not one format or design that suits all countries.[85] However, somewhat contradictorily, a range of characteristics have been put forward as elements of "best practice": broad, multistakeholder representation, a clear mandate and tasks, sufficient resources, a consensus approach, transparency and public participation, and a legal basis.[86] A common assumption underlying most if not all discussions and analyses of NCSDs seems to be the need for, and superiority of, a participatory approach, and that "multistakeholder decision-making bodies resolve conflicts among competing interest groups and promote development policies that integrate economic, environmental and social considerations."[87] Sustainable development, and the way integration is interpreted in that context, is often seen to require such an approach: "[P]ursuit of sustainable development can only be effectively done through active partnership between all stakeholder groups in society. There is no other way."[88]

Third, most councils do not seem to live up to these standards of "best practice." Some fall short with regard to the criterion of broad representation, consisting only of government officials; others have no clear mandates or tasks and seem to be little more than "talk shops"; and many are insufficiently resourced, do not invite broad public participation, are unable to practice the consensus principle, and lack a legal basis. Perhaps not surprisingly, councils in low-income countries face greater obstacles in these respects than those in high-income countries, while the more exemplary or "interesting" councils are said to be found in rich countries—Belgium, Canada, Finland, Ireland, and the United Kingdom—even though most of the seventy councils established after 1992 reside in poorer countries.[89]

Fourth, although some councils are said to be performing better than others, there is very little evidence of their effectiveness in advancing sustainable development or, for that matter, of environmental integration. Considerable information is available on the organizational aspects of councils, and on what issues they have addressed and put on the agenda, but there is a dearth of independent analyses of their influence and what they have achieved. In the United States, the influence of the Council of Environmental Quality has fluctuated from president to president,[90] and the Council on Sustainable Development, which was dissolved in 1999, does not appear to have had much of an impact with regard to environmental policy integration at the national level.[91] Canada's Roundtable on Environment and Economy, one the few legally entrenched and most long-lived NCSDs, has been noted for having produced some good programs and reports, but not for its role in the development of Canada's Green Plan, while its influence on subsequent environmental or sustainable development policy remains unclear.[92] The lack of independent research on NCSDs, however, precludes drawing any firm conclusions about their effectiveness.

Much of the literature and discussion of NCSDs remains cast in normative terms, and appears to consider such entities as inherently good or positive. The main significance of such advisory bodies is often seen to lie in their encouragement of the involvement of societal actors in the policy process, and in providing a basis for policy learning and innovation as well as in the development of a (more) cooperative or consensual policy style, which has been found to be positively related to environmental policy performance.[93] Sometimes this evaluation is interwoven with an equally positive view of a development from government to governance, interpreted as the involvement of societal actors, often through "partnerships" in decision-making and management, notably in environmental matters.[94]

Such a view of the role of NCSDs has merits, but this does not make a critical analysis of their role and performance redundant. Though deliberative, discursive, and cooperative forms of policy development and environmental management may contribute to environmental integration, they also pose considerable risks. First, political reality, notably the inequalities of power in society, are often ignored or downplayed. Simply inviting a range of "representatives" from a variety of so-called stakeholders does not create a level playing field for resolving conflicts and creating consensus. Almost inevitably, representatives of strong economic interests will bring more weight to the roundtable than most other council members. This is also likely to apply to government officials representing "economic" departments vis-á-vis those that represent environmental interests. Second, NCSDs, whether their members are chosen by interest groups or appointed by governments, are not elected bodies and not necessarily representative of the wider population. Delegating decision-making to such bodies risks compromising fundamental democratic principles (of representation and accountability), as does the delegation of management responsibilities to "partnerships." Third, there is the obvious risk of the co-optation of environmental advocates, especially if mechanisms for holding them accountable to their environmental constituencies are weak or nonexistent. Fourth, as already discussed in earlier chapters, the idea that the promotion of sustainable development implies environmental integration cannot simply be assumed. In fact, for the aforementioned reasons, it is quite conceivable that NCSDs serve to subordinate environmental interests (even if interpreted as having human-environmental and resource components, as explained in chapter 1) to nonenvironmental interests, bringing about minimal environmental integration at most.

These reservations about NCSDs should not be taken as a case *against* the establishment of such councils, but rather as warnings that their role, functions, and outcomes do not necessarily contribute to environmental integration. Although there is a risk that they divert attention and efforts from the "hard" issues posed by the environmental *problématique*, they may also play a significant role in putting these issues on the agenda and in developing innovative proposals for institutional and policy change that bring about more meaningful and effective forms of environmental integration. However, much depends on their mandate, composition, their position vis-á-vis government, and their political support basis in the wider society. Contrary to what is often claimed, councils or agencies that have a "narrow" environmental mandate and that have the power to demand input in the (re)design of policies and institutions that affect the environment may well be more effective in advancing environmental integration than NCSDs with mandates based on very broad and general notions of sustainable development that open up the risk of making environmental concerns subservient to economic interests in particular.

CONCLUSION

This chapter has surveyed a range of reforms and innovations that arguably or potentially provide overarching institutional frameworks for environmental integration. The creation of such frameworks is important for promoting if not ensuring that environmental integration efforts, within and outside government, are, at the very least, compatible or, at best, mutually supportive. Given the diversity of forms of environmental integration and their capacity to serve a range of different and often conflicting interests and purposes, they may well cancel each other out. More fundamentally, most political, economic, and social institutions that have evolved in societies (and internationally) serve primarily nonenvironmental values and interests, often to the extent that they cause or contribute to environmental problems. A new, overarching institutional framework is required to guide the process of the greening of nonenvironmental institutions, policies, and practices. If environmental problems are to be effectively addressed at their roots and, ultimately, prevented rather than mitigated in the reactive and fragmented way that has been prevalent until now, all institutions will need to be (re)designed in line with the fundamental parameters set forth by such an overarching framework.

Not surprisingly, there are competing and conflicting ideas about what such a framework must or should entail. At the highest legal-constitutional level, the integration of environmental principles, duties, and/or rights in constitutions, a practice now common in many countries (although of considerable normative and symbolic value), has yet to demonstrate its effectiveness in terms in the greening of government policies and other institutions. In large part this can be attributed to the fact that, although constitutions lay down fundamental rules, they are rarely if ever used as a basis for proactive and positive action and change. Although in some countries, citizens and organizations can use constitutional rules and rights as a basis for protecting them if and when they are trampled upon, such rules and rights are rarely used as a basis for changing policies and institutions. Also, as environmental rights may conflict with other rights, and as the meaning and relative importance of rights depends on interpretation by courts (and political-ideological influence), they do not necessarily guarantee that environmental concerns are protected in practice. As discussed above, there are indications that countries with the loftiest constitutions do not seem to have a better record than others in upholding human or environmental rights.

As environmental institutions (rules and organizations) have evolved in a reactive, ad hoc and fragmented way, they have not, and in most cases still cannot, provide an overarching framework for environmental integration efforts. The integration of environmental institutions themselves can therefore be seen as a positive and necessary move toward institutional-internal environmental integration. However, as explained above, integration within the environmental sphere itself is only a partial form of internal integration if it does not also provide a basis for the (re)design of policies and institutions, based on environmental parameters, in nonenvironmental areas. Often, as in the case of New Zealand, the integration of environmental institutions appears to have been driven foremost by a concern about costs and efficiency (economic reasons), and not only or even primarily about their effectiveness, let alone by a desire to design an institutional framework for the greening of nonenvironmental policies and institutions. New Zealand has arguably gone further than many other countries with regard to providing an integrated legal-institutional framework for environmental decision-making at the local and regional levels, but it has left most nonenvironmental policies and institutions at the national level untouched, with the result that most environmental pressures continue to rise. The capacity of (institutionalized) environmental advocates to advance, let alone ensure, external and internal integration, especially at the national level, remains relatively weak. The same, it appears, applies to other countries, even those where there has been considerable effort toward the greening of government, such as in Canada and the United Kingdom.

The institutionalization of principles that, implicitly or explicitly, promote or require environmental integration is probably the most common form by which governments have endorsed overarching institutional-internal integration. In particular, sustainability or sustainable development (SD), which is claimed to imply the integration of environmental, social, and economic values and interests, has been institutionalized as a norm or basic principle in countries around the world. The PPP, PP, and EIP also have been formally adopted by many governments, though more so in higher-income countries. However, as discussed above, the formal institutionalization of such principles does not ensure the greening of nonenvironmental policies and institutions, as economic and social interests often impinge on the way these principles are interpreted, operationalized, and implemented. Green planning (such as sustainable development strategies) can provide a good basis for doing so but varies in scope, rigor and political support, and is often itself not institutionalized. The practical meaning and application of these principles is therefore often determined on an ad hoc basis, subject to political expediency and influence.

The institutionalization of environmental integration through the creation of organizations that have this as their main task arguably is the most crucial form by which it can be advanced, especially if such agencies have the formal and practical means to develop programs that direct environmental integration across policy areas and/or if they initiate and advance the greening of nonenvironmental institutions. All forms of environmental integration assume, depend on, and require agency. As the demand and support for the development of comprehensive and integrated environmental policy and other forms of environmental integration in societies tend to be small and weak,[95] their advancement depends mostly on institutionalized advocates. Strengthening the capacity of such advocates within the political-institutional framework, at all levels of government, is perhaps the most significant factor for advancing environmental integration. Strengthening institutional agency for environmental integration is likely to affect the politics of integration associated with all the other forms discussed in this book, and to make a difference in their use.

The point, of course, is that the creation of institutionalized advocates for environmental integration, and their operation, also depends on and is subject to politics. As noted above, NCSDs can and have been established in many different forms and shapes, and their role and effectiveness depends in large part on their (legal) basis, composition, mandate, and power, and on the capacity of their members. There is no guarantee that such bodies will indeed advance environmental integration, even if that is their official role. Therefore, the creation of such agencies requires strategic thinking and political efficacy on the part of environmental advocates. Once established, they can play an invaluable role in strengthening environmental capacity, and creating positive feedback loops. Whether this is indeed occurring in those countries that have created a NCSD is, however, far from clear.

8

Improving Environmental Integration

INTRODUCTION

That environmental considerations need to be incorporated into human thinking and actions is now widely recognized, by individuals as well as governments. However, although in many parts of the world environmental awareness may have grown in the last four decades, and governments have promoted the integration of environmental knowledge and values by a wide range of different means and across many areas of human activity, there is still a long way to go, as the analysis in preceding chapters has shown.

In this chapter I will discuss how the forms and approaches to environmental integration that have been adopted by governments could be improved, strengthened, or supplemented by other forms. Although forms of environmental integration are not just technical or managerial tools, but are based on often implicit interpretations, assumptions, values, and interests, the "practical" side of environmental integration is also important. Some means are more environmentally inclusive than others, taking into account the indivisibility of the environment and the linkages between the environmental dimensions. Similarly, there is scope for improving approaches to environmental integration by linking the cognitive, policy, and institutional dimensions of environmental management. Although the means and approaches adopted by governments are influenced by the nature of the political systems and dominant policy styles under which they operate, this does not mean that these "paths toward integration" cannot be changed and improved. Decisions on these matters are not predetermined, but depend on choices based on what is considered (more) feasible, suitable, and desirable. The selection of forms can be contested or changed, and new ones can be developed. The relative emphasis on approaches, or the particular pathways followed by governments, is also open to challenge.

First, I will summarize and revisit the main limitations of the forms and approaches discussed in the previous chapters. This section will be short, to avoid unnecessary repetition, but it is needed to highlight the main limitations and shortcomings as a basis for thinking about improvements.

Second, I will present some ideas about how forms of, and approaches to, environmental integration could be strengthened or improved. I will argue that there is significant merit and promise in the notion of environmental space as a basis for "improving" the now widely adopted discourse and practices based on sustainable development, but that this needs to be complemented by the adoption and implementation of "environmental design" to give a more positive direction to environmental integration.

REVISITING EXISTING APPROACHES TO AND FORMS OF ENVIRONMENTAL INTEGRATION

The main argument advanced in chapter 1 was that, to achieve environmental integration effectively and durably, it needs to be pursued concurrently, and in mutually supportive ways, in the three main areas or realms associated with management (cognitive, policy, and institutional). Within each realm, integration efforts can be distinguished between external and internal forms: external integration forms set out to incorporate an environmental dimension into nonenvironmental information/knowledge (cognitive-external forms), nonenvironmental policies (policy-external forms), and nonenvironmental institutions (institutional-external forms). To ensure that integration efforts undertaken by governments between and across these three realms are consistent and complementary, they need to be guided by some overarching cognitive framework, policy, and institution(s): forms of internal integration. A broad cognitive framework of some kind (some form of cognitive-internal integration) guides cognitive-external forms of integration, but is also the basis for formulating and "translating" common (substantive) policy objectives across and into all policy areas (policy-internal integration). To enhance the status, effectiveness, and durability of these environmental integration efforts, they need to be institutionalized (backed up by rules and organizations) and supported by mechanisms directed at the greening of nonenvironmental (economic, political, social) institutions (institutional-external integration). For the latter to occur, in a complementary manner there is a need for some higher-order institutionalized principles and/or rules, and for an organization that has a mandate for advancing and/or ensuring environmental integration (institutional-internal integration).

In reality, governments have taken a much less systematic approach to environmental integration than the one suggested above. Influenced by different historical, political-institutional, and sociocultural contexts, governments have approached environmental integration with more or less emphasis on external or internal forms of cognitive, policy, or institutional integration, and with varying levels of commitment. As a consequence, while some forms of environmental integration have been relatively well developed in some countries, their effectiveness has been constrained by weak(er) integration efforts in other areas. Moreover, the forms of integration adopted by governments are themselves limited in what they (can) do, both inherently and by (political) choices in their design. Therefore, in most countries, the environmental integration efforts of governments have had very limited effect on stemming the sources or causes of environmental problems, which in many cases continue unabated.

For instance, cognitive-external forms of integration (notably EIA, CBA, RA), in whose development the United States took the lead, may mitigate or prevent environmental damage on a case-by-case basis, but do not and cannot, on their own, provide guidance toward an environmentally sustainable society or world. These mechanisms have been designed to kick in *after* some fundamental decisions have been made on specific options (projects or proposals). Although they can and often do generate important environmental information and knowledge that can be used to minimize or mitigate the effects of a proposal, or to chose the option with the least adverse (or "optimal") effect, they do not question the rationales or policies underlying proposals, and are inappropriate means for determining the collective goals and objectives of "development," and for translating these into specific proposals.

As we have seen, some forms of integration (such as SEA) have been invented to overcome the limitations associated with previously introduced forms (such as EIA). Integrated environmental assessment (IEA) also builds upon EIA and can incorporate CBA and RA as well. IEA may generate comprehensive, and environmentally inclusive, knowledge and information about environmental processes and limits (parameters), as a basis for *informing* decisions and policies. But both "improvements" do not and cannot prescribe the kind of environment that societies find acceptable or desirable, or may aspire to. These are value-based decisions involving human perceptions of (the value of) nature and the place of humans therein, criteria for resource use (appropriateness and ethics, precaution, equity, future generations), and about what makes for a healthy and pleasant human (modified) environment.

Decisions on such matters are, by their nature, political. They involve and affect different ideologies, values, and interests. In societies that claim to be democratic, one would expect such issues to be decided collectively. Although it is utopian to think that, even in fairly small political systems, people will ever fully agree on such matters, the reality is that decisions affecting these issues are taken on a daily basis, not only by governments, but also (perhaps even more so) in the business world and by groups and individuals in society. In practice, some views on these matters prevail and dominate over others, steering "development" in a particular direction.

Denying the possibility or desirability of society to decide on these issues collectively by some democratic process implies leaving such decisions to those who wield more power and influence than others, including experts and the practitioners of the forms of cognitive-external integration mentioned. As discussed in chapter 2, even though such forms of environmental integration may be presented as, or seem to be, "objective," they are in fact rooted in values-based assumptions, interpretations, and decisions that affect, and can be manipulated to affect, their outcomes. Depending on their specific terms, these mechanisms can be, and often have been, used to give development a green gloss and to legitimate it.

The cognitive framework needed to give direction to the nature and modalities of development, and to guide cognitive-external integration, is, of course, also subject to the politics of environmental integration. As discussed in chapter 3, the notion of sustainable development is also often interpreted by governments in a way that implies little more than "business as usual." Sustainable development is often implied to mean that environmental, social, and economic values and interests are compatible or, if not, can or need to be "traded off" against one another. The discourse can be used to legitimate development that, in practice, treats environmental values and interests as subservient to economic and social interests (the latter often interpreted much more broadly than the human environment dimension as defined in chapter 1). Similarly, the weak notion of ecological modernization offers the prospect of an infinite process of economic growth made possible by science and technology, avoiding the need for more fundamental or structural change to economic, political, and social systems. EM, where adopted by governments, does not fundamentally question the goals and objectives of development, and denies that there are limits to development that cannot be overcome: it just puts (mostly high-income) countries on an ultramodernist path.

Many governments have now adopted some form of green planning (policy-internal integration), often based on the notion of sustainable development, that translates this general goal or principle into more-specific policy objectives. Such overarching policies are also meant to guide the integration of environmental concerns and objectives across (notably nonenvironmental) policy areas to promote the complementarity and consistency of (policy-external) efforts with one another and with the overarching objectives that have been put forth. As policy can be defined as "what governments do (or not do) intentionally," policy integration affects the core of government activity and its underlying rationale(s). Assuming that governments can and do make a difference through their policies, the greening of policies guided by an overarching green plan that itself rests on a cognitively well-supported basis is an important element of environmental integration.

However, the policy integration efforts of most governments have been halfhearted, and often mainly rhetorical by nature. Although governments in most countries have, sooner or later, adopted some kind of green plan, many of these have proven to be "one-shot exercises" and statements of symbolic intent rather than policy frameworks that have been backed up by effective action. Plans and strategies often do not survive changes of government, and as in most countries green planning has not been formally institutionalized, they fail to function as the long-term policy frameworks that they are supposed to be. Everywhere, even in the countries where green planning has been taken most seriously, the role of green plans in guiding environmental integration in nonenvironmental policy areas (policy-external integration) has been limited. Policy areas most crucial to the environment (notably economic policy, agriculture, energy, transport, and urban or spatial planning) continue to be driven foremost by nonenvironmental interests and objectives. Despite official commitment to environmental policy integration, such as in the European Union, the greening of nonenvironmental policies is still in its early stages and remains highly problematic. Strategic environmental assessment, sustainability assessment, and so-called new policy instruments (including economic instruments and voluntary agreements) are hardly making an impact, let alone that they are putting policies and practices onto environmentally sustainable paths.

The recent global upsurge in concern about climate change, and the adoption by governments of more ambitious climate change policies, may signal stronger commitment and efforts toward the integration of environmental concerns into nonenvironmental policies, given the need to curb greenhouse gas emissions generated by the energy, transport, agriculture, and other "nonenvironmental" sectors. However, whether or to what degree these developments herald the greening of these sectors is debatable. Many governments appear to seek ways of containing or reducing greenhouse gas emissions foremost by technological and managerial means (often "end-of-pipe" solutions). Meanwhile, economic growth remains a top priority for governments, and there is little if any evidence that consumers, even in high-income countries, are adopting less material-intensive lifestyles, as reflected in the consumption of goods, increased travel, and growing waste streams.[1] While technical and managerial "solutions" may bring about a mitigation of emissions, they are unlikely to be sufficient in the long run, but there are, as yet, few signs that governments are willing and able to address these underlying forces.

Climate change is just one of the many manifestations of the unsustainable development path the world is on. There is much more to the environmental *problématique* than reducing greenhouse gas emissions, however crucial that may be. As discussed in this book, coming to terms with this *problématique* requires a broader and more fundamental challenge:

the integration of collectively determined environmental considerations or imperatives into the cognitive, policy, and institutional spheres, at all levels of government and governance. Climate change creates a significant opportunity for promoting environmental integration, and one that surely must be taken up. But focusing all attention on greenhouse gas emissions, may also distract from the broader, underlying *problématique* and need for change, in particular when "solutions" are sought in carbon capture and storage, the expansion of nuclear power, and growing crops for biofuels.[2]

One of the reasons why the policy integration efforts of governments are having such limited impact is that they fail to be accompanied and supported by institutional changes. This does not only apply to green planning, as noted above, but also to policy-external integration efforts. Although policy-external integration has been made a formal requirement by the European Union, the institutional architecture for implementing and enforcing it is largely missing. In most countries, the actual processes by which nonenvironmental policies are developed have hardly changed, keeping environmental advocates largely locked out, let alone assigning them a prominent place in the formal institutional hierarchy. Economic institutions continue to be based on limited and flawed notions of value and well-being, notwithstanding the introduction of some limited form of green accounting in many countries. The integration of environmental values and interests into the institutions governing the business sector, beyond the enforcement of environmental laws and regulations, is largely optional and left to the sector itself (for instance, via environmental management systems). Most governments appear unwilling or unable to take a strong stand, and to spend much money, on the greening of production systems.

Official environmental agencies (ministries or departments) are often relatively weak and powerless vis-á-vis other (development-oriented) departments, and do not have the means to demand or ensure environmental integration. Although some governments (notably in Canada and the United Kingdom) have introduced rules and new agencies to promote the greening of government (institutions), their impact, in practical terms rather than commitments on paper, remains to be seen. Sustainable development councils usually have only an advisory function, and are often not much more than "talk shops," kept away from the mainstream policy process. High-level expressions of commitment to environmental values, rights, and principles, such as in constitutional articles, bills of rights, and normal legislation, usually cannot be relied upon by environmental advocates to address cases where such provisions appear to have been clearly flouted.

This litany of limitations should not be taken to mean that the integration efforts of all governments have been meaningless and useless. Clearly, some governments have taken environmental integration more seriously than others. Most if not all of the forms of environmental integration discussed here are likely to have made a (significant) difference at some times and in some countries. The main point to be derived from the analysis of these forms is that, when used on their own, their effect is likely to be limited in scope and/or time. Cognitive, policy, and institutional forms of integration, external *and* internal, need to be introduced and used in mutually supportive ways to enhance their effectiveness and durability.

But neither does this imply that that all existing forms of environmental integration are equally useful or effective and that there is no scope for improving them and/or for inventing new forms. Some forms, I have pointed out, are inherently limited or biased in the way they interpret the environment and (potential) environmental effects. CBA and RA, for instance, rather than providing an environmentally rational context for decision-making, are used mainly to subject environmental values to a narrow notion of economic rationality. Tradable permit schemes, provided they are effectively monitored and enforced, offer greater certainty with regard to environmental outcomes than environmental taxes, but may have undesirable political and social consequences (concentrating de facto ownership of resources and increasing inequity). However, the effectiveness of particular forms depends also very much on their design and implementation, and their desirability on one's political-ideological views, disciplinary background, and position in society. Forms of (and tools for) integration are never politically neutral, as they impact differently on different (groups of) people. Their choice and design are therefore subject to politics, and not just managerial, scientific, or technical matters, however complex the tools may be.

Ideas and proposals for improving forms of integration should therefore be seen against this light. The invention and introduction of environmental management systems in the corporate sector has been triggered by the growing threat of more stringent environmental regulation, and shaped by the imperatives and needs of business. Similarly, the introduction of voluntary agreements has been influenced strongly by economic interests and the supporters, often in powerful positions, of neoliberal ideology who advocate a rolling back of the state and more self-regulation by industry. The concept of sustainable development arose out of the growing tension between developmental and environmental interests, and the need for reconciling those in the international context. Keeping the concept vague helps to serve that purpose.

In most countries, the approach to environmental integration has been skewed toward one or two dimensions (or even forms) of environmental management, in part for reasons to do with the nature of the political systems and the dominant policy style under which governments operate. If, to be effective and durable, environmental integration requires a concerted and mutually supportive approach involving the cognitive, policy, and institutional dimensions of environmental management, governments will have to boost their efforts in the weak(er) areas of their performance. Although governments may be constrained in this for the aforementioned reasons, they can at least try to push the boundaries. However, doing so requires commitment (political will), political authority (respect), and political skills (the power to persuade), qualities that are often in low supply in government circles. Nonetheless, there are times and situations where opportunities arise for pushing governments toward adopting (new) forms of integration in areas of environmental management in which the need for improving performance has become more apparent.

Although politics is often about conflicting interests, the role and power of ideas should not be disregarded or underestimated.[3] Ideas how to improve environmental integration, especially through forms and approaches that may have appeal to a large proportion of the population (of countries and the world as a whole), play a crucial role in changing views on what is desirable, necessary, and feasible. Advocates of environmental integration need to come up with and push ideas for new and better forms of integration that can be advanced as feasible "solutions" when the streams of problems, politics, and policies converge to create policy windows for change.[4] In the following section I will present some ideas that have the potential to be used as starting points to that end.

ENHANCING INTEGRATION: FORMS AND APPROACHES

The discussion above indicates that there is scope for improving existing forms of and approaches to environmental integration. Even in countries that are often seen as leaders in the use of particular forms, performance is often adversely affected by the particular modalities by which the form is implemented, by absent or weak linkages with other forms, and/or by weak institutionalization.

Perhaps the most fundamental requirement for improvement is to clarify the notion of environmental integration. As discussed at the beginning of this book, there is still considerable confusion about what environmental integration means and why it is important. This is not just a matter of creating conceptual clarity; these questions lie at the heart of what the environmental *problématique* is about. Most popular forms of cognitive integration (both external and internal) seem to be based on the assumption that integration means that "the environment" is something that can and should be "added" to the picture that is used to guide people in their decisions and actions. Adding the environment (information, values, and interests) to the picture implies that it can then be "considered" together with (many) other things that people find important. In practice, this means that environmental concerns are "weighed" against other concerns, which also implies that they are given more or less weight in decisions. As I have argued in chapter 1, this is, in my view, a distorted or false view of what environmental integration is about. If integration means to combine parts into a whole, then this has consequences for all individual parts as well as for the overall picture on which decisions and actions are based.

In more specific terms, this means that the cognitive frameworks underlying decision-making in all areas that potentially affect the environment need to be changed to incorporate environmental imperatives, to the extent that environmental harm is avoided or repaired. As long as agricultural practices, transport, production processes, and other human activities continue to degrade the environment, these policy areas cannot be said to have been properly integrated environmentally. Of course, human activities will always have *some* impact on the environment. The test lies in whether ecological systems are altered to the extent that their self-restoring capacity is adversely affected and the long-term availability of resources (renewable and nonrenewable) is threatened. Linked to these (ecological and resource) criteria, where human practices modify the physical environment in ways that adversely affect human well-being (the human environment criterion), these also need to be greened or environmentally integrated.

Environmental integration, based on these criteria, is not something that can be easily and readily achieved. On these terms, "modern" production, transport and other systems are still rather primitive, despite some advances booked in recent decades. Since the Industrial Revolution, the performance of human systems, given their enormously increased impact on the environment, has declined rather than improved, perhaps with the exception of the human environment criterion (although this is also open for interpretation and likely to be more of a mixed bag, especially if considered on the global scale and if the social and psychological effects of these changes are included). This does not imply condemning all scientific and technological innovation and change. But it does mean that there is a need to put science and technological development within an environmental framework, and to be much more discerning in the promotion of (areas of) innovation. One of the big myths of this era is that scientific and technological innovation "just happen" and cannot be controlled, whereas in fact most innovation is steered and controlled (based on financial clout) by governments and big corporations. Greening science and technology requires policy and institutional changes, but it begins with accepting a cognitive framework that incorporates environmental imperatives as fundamental parameters.

Given the diversity of (often conflicting) views on the environment, it could be argued, there is simply no hope of reaching agreement on any overarching cognitive framework, let alone one that takes environmental parameters and criteria as its main elements. This problem can be illustrated with the ongoing discussion on the meaning of the notion of sustainable development, which some see as a legitimating device for "business as usual" scenarios and therefore advocate abandoning. Others argue that the lack of agreement on a definition of sustainable development is actually not a problem and that it should be seen as a discourse rather than a concept that can or needs to be sharply defined. In my view, the important point is not so much that people disagree in their views (they always will be barring totalitarian brainwashing) and that the meaning of ideas continues to be debated and contested, as that, inevitably, some views and interpretations always dominate over others when governments make and implement decisions and policies. Implicitly or explicitly, government decisions and actions privilege some views and interests over the many that exist (even when supporting the status quo), often under the guise of support for broad principles or goals. Policies, decisions, and actions have specific consequences (also for the environment), even if promulgated under broad notions or discourses like "sustainable development." What is done about environmental problems depends to a large extent on the capacity of individuals and groups to influence and persuade governments to take (or not take) specific measures, and to build support for such measures among opinion leaders and power holders, if not a majority of people. Advancing more effective environmental integration, therefore, requires greater clarity and specificity on what needs to be done, and when and how, and (greater) political power and support behind such ideas.

The dominance of the concept or discourse of sustainability and sustainable development, and the fact that it has already been adopted by governments and institutionalized all over the world, in large part because of its vagueness, provides a starting point for environmental integration. Rather than rejecting sustainable development because it fails to provide specific guidance and is being abused by many parties to advance their own nonenvironmental interests, it seems more realistic and productive to use it as a basis for advocating clear and specific objectives, courses of action, timetables, and outcomes. As we have seen, this is already occurring, notably under the umbrella of green planning, though more so in some countries than others. Green planning, particularly when combined with the notion of environmental space, can be used, and needs to be used more, to make sustainable development concrete.

Tagging the notion of "environmental space" onto the discourse of sustainable development may assist in this respect, not only because it sets out to make sustainability concrete, but also because of its association with a strong principle of equity. It thus can help to "improve" prevailing, fuzzy, and symbolic uses of the notion of sustainable development that often legitimate "business as usual" scenarios and continued environmental abuse, and to generate support for specific measures that serve the interests of many rather than few. If environmental space is limited, it is difficult to justify why some people or countries should be allowed to use or claim much more space than others. Advocates of the concept commonly presume that, a priori, on ethical grounds, all humans have an equal claim to environmental space, thus implying a case for the redistribution of (access to) resources, or of the benefits derived from them. The adoption and implementation of the concept of environmental space should therefore hold considerable appeal to the underprivileged, especially in relatively poor countries.

Ironically, though, thus far the concept of environmental space has only been applied in a limited way by some governments of a few rich countries (notably the Netherlands, Denmark, and Norway). However, the upsurge in concern about climate change may change this. Addressing global warming effectively requires recognition of (limited) environmental space (a maximum allowable level of emissions of greenhouse gases). This is, though only in embryonic form, recognized in existing international policy toward reducing greenhouse gas emissions (the Kyoto Protocol), even if the limits presently adopted are widely regarded as inadequate and just a beginning of what is needed. Not surprisingly, getting agreement on how the burden of reducing emissions should be shared proves to be as difficult as agreeing on the overall limits. It seems likely that reaching agreement on overall limits and creating commitment toward their effective implementation will only be achieved by invoking the strong equity principle often associated with the concept of environmental space. In particular, it is unlikely that relatively poor countries with rapidly growing economies and emissions, like China and India, will be willing to adopt limits on their emissions if already rich countries, which historically have contributed most to the problem and are better capable of reducing emissions, are not willing to accept responsibility for bigger reductions.

In recent years, the concept of "ecological footprint," the mirror image of environmental space, appears to have gained considerable international currency. As a composite measure of the amount of environmental space used by individuals and countries, making explicit the significant differences, it has strong moral overtones. It also gives an indication of the total amount of environmental space that the world has available, and how much of that space is already used or exceeded (eroding the natural capital basis). As explained in chapter 3, while the concept of ecological footprint is useful as an educational or awareness-raising (and perhaps guilt-raising) tool, it is less useful than that of ecological space as a basis for policy development, although recent applications of the former also make linkages with specific activities and consumption patterns that will need to be addressed if resource use is to be brought within ecological and sustainable limits.[5] Using the growing popularity, in some countries, of the notion of ecological footprint as a stepping-stone for advancing specific courses of action directed at the implementation of sustainability, in combination with the environmental space concept, may be both practically and strategically attractive.

However, although the notion of environmental space may be of considerable use in providing guidance to environmental integration efforts aimed at the protection of (local and global) ecosystems (the ecological dimension), and for determining limits on resource use (the resource dimension), it is less useful for guiding environmental integration with regard to the human-environmental dimension of the environment. Although there are aspects of the human environment for which limits can be defined (for instance, related to pollution that affects human health), these are insufficient to *guide* human decisions and developments toward a more overarching goal or scenario that ensures that the human-made environment contributes to human and ecological well-being as well as acceptable resource use. To that end, a more positive (rather than limiting) cognitive framework is required. The notion of "environmental design" appears useful and attractive in that context.

Environmental design, as used here, involves the design of the biophysical environment inspired by human, culturally rooted ideas of what is a pleasant, beautiful, and healthy environment, but in a way that simultaneously respects ecological limits and needs and collectively determined resource constraints. The most obvious application of environmental design lies in the area of urban and rural development, sometimes referred to also as spatial planning. But it also applies (or should apply) to the workplace and the design of industrial facilities and processes (which also affect the three dimensions of the environment), and agricultural, energy and transport systems. Inevitably, environmental design also has implications for the kind of technology that is used, or needs to be developed, within the envisaged environment.

Environmental design, inspired by collective aspirations rooted in sociocultural, historical, and geographical contexts, is an integrative process that provides a positive framework for guiding environmental integration in all areas of human action and behavior that (potentially) affect the biophysical environment (including the environment modified by humans). Rather than guiding people by relative degrees of *fear* (for risks), or assessments of potential environmental and/or social *damage* (as in much of EIA), it invokes people to think about the kind of environment that they wish to live in, while recognizing ecological and resource limits and *opportunities*. In many places and cases, the human environment seems to come about as the result of quasi-autonomous processes with just the slightest veneer of "planning" (if any at all). "Development" (in all areas and respects) is guided foremost by (market-driven) financial and economic considerations, and proceeds in a fragmented, uncoordinated way (for instance, between urban planning, transport planning, and energy planning), with many adverse consequences for the biophysical (including human) environment. Human technology, often developed on the basis of a mechanistic worldview and with total disregard of natural processes, has hardly started to recognize the need and potential for environmental integration and design, and in that respect is often crude and primitive.[6] Environmental design represents a positive, constructive, sophisticated, and exciting approach to the development of science and technology, in harmony with environmental parameters.

In combination, the notions of environmental space and environmental design can be used as a basis for providing more specific substance to the notion of sustainable development, and for guiding government efforts (and those of others) toward developing more effective forms of environmental integration in the policy and institutional realms, and ultimately in all areas of human thinking, decisions, and actions that potentially impact on (all three dimensions of) the environment. Although the notion of environmental design may itself sound rather vague, and the processes and institutions for enabling it still need to be mostly determined, its focus on creating a vision or sketch of a human environment, defined in material, biophysical, and geographical terms, in which people wish to live is ultimately quite concrete.[7]

The adoption of environmental space and environmental design as intermediate cognitive frameworks to give substance to sustainable development (cognitive-internal integration) also offers the prospect of the development of more attractive, positive, and potentially effective forms of cognitive-external environmental integration than those that have been adopted by governments thus far. Environmental design, in particular, moves away from the reactive and often negative nature associated with prevalent cognitive-external forms. Some of these may become superfluous, while others could be reconfigured to generate information and knowledge that contribute to positive objectives and designs. Such an approach also raises the prospect of enabling and mobilizing citizens to participate in the design of their own human environment, on a local but also national and international basis. While scientists and experts have an important role to play, notably in the assessment of environmental space, environmental design is a process and activity that is less likely to be able to be captured by any one discipline or group of experts, as it requires the involvement of a wide variety of disciplines and expertise (including urban planners, resource planners, transport and energy specialists, architects, design experts, physical and social geographers, psychologists, and ecologists), as well as citizens who are affected by the design.

Developments toward environmental design can already be found in phenomena like green architecture, the design of ecovillages, ecocities, industrial ecology, and permaculture.[8] However, many of the advocates of the various forms of environmental design appear to think or assume that the move toward sustainable societies will or can occur solely or mainly by the work and example of individuals, companies, or communities, and within the existing political and economic order. They tend to underestimate or even ignore the political-economic and sociocultural obstacles to change, and the importance of politics, power and governments in bringing about change. The means, policies, and institutions by which environmental design can be extended and become a basis for environmental integration within and across all sectors and levels of society still need to be designed and created. The (potential) advocates or agents for environmental design are neither a cohesive nor a powerful group, and they are often preoccupied with or locked into their own discipline or framework. National governments have an important role to play in environmental design, if only because many national policies and institutions presently constrain individuals, communities, and subnational governments to adopt and implement decisions based on environmental (ecological and resource) space or environmental design. Governments also play, or need to play, an important role in strengthening the capacity for determining environmental space and for facilitating environmental design. They also hold the key to introducing these mechanisms for environmental integration systematically across all areas that (potentially) impact significantly on the environment.

Improving the cognitive basis for environmental integration through such means as proposed above is not just a precondition for more effective policy integration, but is also itself dependent on supportive policies and institutions. The demand for environmental knowledge and information, and the nature of that demand, is shaped by the extent and form(s) by which policy integration is pursued. Green planning based on the notion of environmental space requires knowledge and information about specific (resource) limits. Adding environmental design to green planning requires the input, views, and knowledge of the people living in the area to which the design will apply. The more serious governments are about integrating environmental parameters into particular policy areas (such as energy or transport), the greater the demand will be for ideas, theories, models, and other forms of knowledge by which integration can be implemented. The extent to which environmental information is generated, and the capacity for generating it is built, depends in large measure on whether and how environmental monitoring and reporting have been institutionalized. Making annual state-of-the-environment reporting mandatory upon national governments, for instance, will significantly boost environmental knowledge, information, and cognitive capacity requirements.

Efforts directed at improving forms of cognitive environmental integration, therefore, need to be linked to efforts aimed at strengthening or improving forms of policy and institutional integration. Given the importance of green planning for guiding and coordinating environmental integration across policy areas (policy-external integration) and its cognitively demanding nature (to translate general goals and aims into specific objectives, targets, and time frames), the strengthening of green planning can be seen as a significant step or requirement for strategically boosting environmental integration in several ways and directions. As discussed in chapter 5, in many countries green planning has been confined to a "one-shot exercise" because of changes in government and/or government support. The institutionalization of green planning (making it mandatory upon governments, as in the Netherlands) appears to be a crucial requirement for surviving the vagaries of politics and for giving it continuity, even if with variable levels of commitment. It is not coincidental that, in the Netherlands, where green planning has been made mandatory, annual environmental reporting (tied in with the budget cycle) has also been institutionalized, and that cognitive environmental capacity is impressive compared to many other countries. Making green planning mandatory will also require boosting green planning capacity, which may involve creating an institution (and agency), like a National Sustainable Development Council, that can guide and oversee the green planning process and that takes it beyond short political (electoral) horizons. Green planning could be strengthened further by linking it to institutionalized principles and rights like the precautionary principle and the right to a healthy environment. Institutionalizing rights and processes enabling people to participate in the formative stages of a form of green planning that incorporates environmental design, as discussed above, is also likely to broaden the public support basis for policy-internal integration, especially at the local level. Although green planning may, in first instance, be undertaken at the national level, it will need to be linked with similar efforts at lower levels of government (state, regional, local) and at the international level (regional, global) to ensure consistency and effectiveness. This also makes strengthening it a strategic move and requirement.

Environmental integration in different policy areas is likely to be boosted by strengthening and improving green planning, but the latter is also dependent on the quality and effectiveness of the forms used to promote policy-external integration. The objectives and targets set forth in green plans are linked to what the actors in a particular policy area or network (government departments and affected interest groups) define and accept as realistic, feasible, acceptable, and desirable. However, as environmental concerns are by definition of secondary importance in nonenvironmental policy areas, existing mechanisms of policy-external environmental integration (or greening), as discussed in chapter 4, are inadequate. Often, environmental concerns are tagged on rather than treated as parameters in the design of policies. Consequently, green planning objectives and targets are often not met, and gains are eroded and even canceled out in the longer term by the effects of the largely unchanged ("business as usual") policies and practices aimed at continuing growth and expansion of, for instance, private transport, production and consumption, and the built environment.

Although cognitive frameworks like sustainable development and ecological modernization maintain that economic and environmental interests can be reconciled, most governments have hardly begun to create or adopt forms of integration that aim to put this promise into practice, apart from the modest use of financial (dis)incentives and some support for the development of "environmentally friendly" science and technology. Such measures are commonly introduced on an ad hoc basis (for different environmental issues) and are not part of an integrated strategy for the greening of whole industries, let alone sectors or industries combined. As industries are unlikely to be sufficiently greened by their own initiative and efforts, and as the greening of production, consumption, construction, and transport requires the transformation not only of individual products and services, but also of systems, governments play a crucial role in making this happen. However, as yet, they have developed neither the policies nor the institutions to engender such fundamental change. The "greening of government" and "greening of economic institutions" efforts discussed in chapter 6 fall woefully short of what is required to incite systemic transformation.

As indicated above, the greening of policies and the greening of institutions (political, economic, and social) are closely intertwined. On the one hand, political, economic, and social institutions guide and channel policy development and human behavior and actions, and impose constraints on environmental policy integration efforts. On the other hand, government policy frequently involves institutional change, notably in the form of legislation and the (re)allocation of responsibilities to public and private agencies. Governments, therefore, play a significant role in the greening of institutions, although their ability and willingness to do so varies and may be to some extent outside of their control. As discussed in chapter 7, overarching institutions (like constitutions, environmental rights and principles, and sustainable development councils), provide only weak (sometimes merely symbolic) guidance to environmental integration within and across policies and in regard to nonenvironmental institutions. Arguably, in their present forms, the main value of these institutions lies in the support and legitimacy that they provide to efforts and demands for further policy and institutional change.

Bringing about the systemic transformation that is required to realize more effective forms of integration is a big challenge. Most likely, this will need to involve a significant boost and shift in government funding for science and research, but also the creation of (institutional) capacity to design and implement integrated systems. It is also likely to require the (re)introduction of some form of economic planning rather than leaving things to "the market." In the present political climate, such ideas do not receive much support. Consequently, the development of more effective forms of policy-external integration will have to wait, but thinking that this will happen is not utopian, and there are some signs that the time for this may be ripe, as reflected in the growing pressure to integrate climate change "imperatives" into economic, energy, transport, and agricultural policies. However, as noted above, there is no guarantee that enhanced political commitment toward abating climate change will be translated into policies and institutional changes that address the *sources* of the environmental *problématique* and that meet the challenge of environmental integration as described in this book. Dominant interests and views make it more likely that responses will be confined to the promotion of "technofixes" (which offer scope for more economic growth, investments, and profits) rather than political, economic, and social transformation. Also, even though climate change may be one of the most serious environmental issues, and combating it offers scope for strategically advancing environmental integration into nonenvironmental policy areas, concentrating all or most efforts on this issue is, again, a limited, *reactive* and largely *negative* (risk-based) response to the need for environmental integration. It does not, necessarily, bring about the more proactive and positive approach advocated here.

CONCLUSION

In this chapter, I have looked at how forms and approaches to environmental integration can be improved. Summarizing the main weaknesses and limitations of existing forms and approaches is a basis for identifying in what respects improvement is desirable or necessary. Arguably, the first and most important priority is to advance a better understanding of what environmental integration means and implies, not just in conceptual terms, but also with regard to the challenges or tasks involved. The notion of environmental integration is often used in ways that imply merely the "weighing" and "balancing" of conflicting interests, not making the different spheres of human thinking and action compatible with collectively determined environmental limits and imperatives. The vagueness of the notion of sustainable development, presently the dominant discourse guiding environmental integration, contributes to the lack of clarity and recognition of the challenge that environmental integration poses. Tagging on the notions of environmental space and ecological footprint to the discourse of sustainable development can help to make the latter concrete. The existence of diverse and conflicting views, imperfect knowledge, and uncertainty is no reason for not defining more clearly what needs to be done; not doing so just means that, de facto, decisions on environmental limits (or their absence) are determined implicitly by some opaque process, within and/or outside government. Clarity should not be confused with rigidity: the limits and objectives determined on the basis of environmental space assessments and deliberations can be amended regularly in the light of changing knowledge and insights.

However, the notion of environmental space itself is limited in two main ways: first, it is inclusive only of the ecological and resource dimensions, but not the human-environment dimension; second, although it is suitable for creating greater clarity on ecological and resource limits, it cannot provide positive guidance for steering environmental integration. Humans have many possibilities and choices with regard to how they modify and shape the (bio)physical environment to enhance their own well-being as well as that of other species with which they share the earth, even when recognizing resource limits and respecting ecological processes. The notion of environmental design holds promise as a more inclusive and positive form of cognitive-internal integration. Environmental design, incorporating the contributions of a broad range of disciplines, the recognition of environmental space, and collectively defined aspirations, involves the modification and (re)shaping of the physical aspects of the environment with the aim to create a "good life," "good society," and "good world." This may sound fuzzy or woolly, but it is ultimately concrete, as it implies determining the kind of biophysical reality in which humans wish to live. At the moment, choices in this respect are largely left to the market, despite the spatial planning efforts in many countries, as cities, transport, energy, production, and distribution systems continue to develop and expand in largely uncoordinated ways, with no less concrete environmental and social effects and costs.

Environmental design can also assist in providing a clearer and more environmentally inclusive direction to green planning as a form of policy-internal integration. Green planning, even in the countries that have been considered leaders in this field, is still often guided mainly by "negative" objectives and targets (reducing emissions and problems). Although, more recently, the notion of "quality of life" (defined very broadly) has also been introduced as a guiding principle for green planning, this could be complemented by provisions for environmental design to give it a more tangible form. By including environmental design, green planning also becomes a focal point for the range and variety of fields of environmental design that have already emerged, providing a common basis for their coordination or integration.

Apart from introducing and enhancing the forms of integration mentioned, there is considerable scope for further improving and strengthening environmental integration by creating stronger linkages between the various forms and approaches. Giving green planning a strong(er) institutional basis, both in law and in the form of dedicated organizations, arguably is one of the most strategic ways to strengthen and entrench advocacy and capacity for environmental integration. Using institutionally reinforced green planning as a more explicit basis for policy-external integration can provide greater consistency and coherence to the greening efforts within and across the policy areas that crucially impact on the environment. Similarly, green plans and the institutions supporting them can improve the guidance and direction of efforts toward the greening of government itself, and for the greening of the economic system, although the latter probably requires more than just policy guidance. Many other forms of environmental integration that at present often operate as "stand-alone" mechanisms, such as CBA, EIA, RA, SEA, IPC, economic instruments, and green accounting, can also be used more fruitfully when they are explicitly linked to and guided by the overarching forms of integration of environmental design, green planning, and National Councils for Sustainable Development. Such mechanisms and tools, in adapted forms, could assist in the building of green plans and environmental design, and/or function as some of their operative arms.

Offering ideas about how forms and approaches to environmental integration can be improved is one thing. Putting these ideas into practice is another. Designing "ideal" forms of integration is unlikely to have any practical effect if the political aspect is not also considered. However, trying to change the "politics of environmental integration" without any idea of how integration can be made more effective is also unlikely to lead to improvement. We need ideas as well as political action and support to bring about more effective environmental integration—or rather, we need ideas that have the capacity to inspire and generate political support, action, and change. At the same time, we also need to consider and acknowledge how existing conditions and developments may stand in the way of introducing more effective forms of integration and the changes that may be required to put these into practice. Strategically advancing environmental integration, however, requires considering the (diverse) political, economic, and social (national and international) contexts within which it is pursued, something that is beyond the scope of this book. Whether and how the ideas and suggestions offered here are feasible, or even desirable, is a question best left to the advocates of environmental integration operating in the variety of contexts within which it needs to be pursued.

Notes

INTRODUCTION

1. Lomborg 2001. For different assessments on environmental conditions in Europe and other parts of the world, see European Environment Agency, 2004; and the United Nations Environment Programme volumes published annually by Oxford University Press under the title *Global Environment Outlook*. It is beyond the scope of this book to discuss the merits of Lomborg's assessment. Suffice to say here that his claims have been strongly contested, and that other environmental assessments, like the Environmental Outlook reports published by the United Nations Environment Programme, paint a much less rosy picture. However, Lomborg admits that, even if things are getting better, "they are not necessarily good" (2001, 4). Moreover, it is important to acknowledge that things do not get better by themselves, and that the actions of environmental advocates and governments are crucial if gains are to be consolidated or improved. Politics plays a key role in environmental performance, a point that seems to be largely ignored, or even denied, by Lomborg.

2. "Form" is used here as the generic term for the variety of ways by which environmental integration is sought, encompassing cognitive frameworks, principles, rules, procedures, and mechanisms or tools. While some forms are quite broad, others are very specific.

CHAPTER 1

1. Dryzek 1997.
2. Lafferty and Hovden 2003; and Lenschow 2002b.
3. Carter and Dale 1955; and Diamond 2005.
4. *The Concise Oxford Dictionary of Current English*, 8th ed. (Oxford: Clarendon Press, 1990), 616.
5. Bartlett 1986; Dryzek 1987.
6. Beck 1992.
7. Although this view is more often held by scientists and policy-makers than by Beck, who interprets the issue foremost as one of control over science, he says: "[W]e must, as it were, install brakes and a steering wheel into the 'non-steering' of the racing techno-scientific development that is setting explosive powers free" (Beck 1992, 180).

8. Longino 1983.

9. Meadows and Club of Rome 1974.

10. Arguably, these policy areas or policy sectors (comprising a range of policies addressing aspects of the same or similar functions) are the "big five" in terms of environmental impact. As such, they have become a focus for environmental policy integration or 'greening', but also prove to be most challenging.

11. Lafferty and Hovden 2003; and Lenschow 2002c.

12. Lafferty 2004, 204; and Lafferty and Hovden 2003, 12–17.

13. Bührs 1991.

14. Jänicke 1997, 13.

15. Almond 1988; and March and Olsen 1989. Some authors argue that organizations are not institutions, but I disagree with this view, and not only because it goes against the common practice or referring to organizations as institutions. Organizations are fundamentally bundles of rules (specifying aims, principles, authority structures, decision processes, etc.) that are often more enduring than the holders of the organization's positions. They guide and channel actions and behavior, on a daily basis for most people—for instance, in the workplace—and are therefore vital institutions, including in the context of environmental integration. Organizations are institutions, but not all institutions are organizations. Connor and Dovers 2004, 10–14.

16. Bartlett 1997.

17. Toth and Hizsnyk 1998.

18. Sexton et al. 1999.

19. Christoff 1996.

20. Weizsäcker, Lovins, and Lovins 1997.

21. Sachs, Loske, and Linz 1998, x, 39–40.

22. Christoff 1996; Dryzek 1997, 137–52; Jänicke 1993.

23. Buitenkamp, Venner, and Wams 1993, 17–18.

24. Bührs, 2004; and Bührs 2007.

25. Cortner and Moote 1998, 7.

26. Bartlett 1990a.

27. Lenschow 2002c, 7.

28. Connor and Dovers 2004, 162.

29. Jordan, Wurzel, and Zito 2003b.

30. Bührs 1996b; Dalal-Clayton 1996; Falloux and Talbot 1993; Jänicke and Jörgens 1998; and Johnson 1995.

31. Almond 1988; and March and Olsen 1989.

32. De Jongh and Captain 1999; Weale 1992; Winsemius 1990.

33. Birkeland-Corro 1988; Knoepfel 1995; Paehlke and Torgerson 1990.

CHAPTER 2

1. Caldwell 1995c, 127.

2. Caldwell 1995c, 136.

3. Caldwell 1995b, 171.

4. Clark 1984, 6.
5. Clark 1984, 3, 6.
6. Taylor 1984, 4.
7. Canter 1984, 23.
8. Wood 1995, 2; and Glasson, Therivel, and Chadwick 1999, 4.
9. Bartlett 1990b, 91.
10. For a succinct summary of these two models, see Culhane, Friesema, and Beecher 1987, chap. 1.
11. Taylor 1984, chap. 12.
12. Wandesforde-Smith 1989; and Wandesforde-Smith and Kerbavaz 1988.
13. Paehlke 1990.
14. Hyman and Stiftel 1988; Jain, Urban, and Stacey 1981, chap. 8.
15. Munn 1979, 85–86.
16. Canter 1984, 22–23.
17. Fairfax 1978; and Tester 1987.
18. Offe and Ronge 1979; Vanderpool 1981; and Amy 1990, 62.
19. Amy 1990, 63.
20. Vanderpool 1981. It should be noted that the author uses the term "social impact assessments" to refer to "assessments . . . designed to determine the costs and benefits of proposed courses of action that may be taken in implementing an environmental policy" (164). Therefore, the term "social impact assessment" is used here in a broader sense than usual.
21. Bartlett 1990b, 89.
22. Ashby 1976, 8–9.
23. Clark 1984, 9.
24. Clark 1984, 9.
25. Canter 1984; Bartlett and Malone 1993, 1.
26. Wood 1995, 3.
27. Harrop and Nixon (1999, 2) state that around two hundred systems of environmental assessments have been introduced in countries, states, and international organizations since the enactment of NEPA in the United States in 1970, but they provide no source for this information.
28. Glasson, Therivel, and Chadwick 1999, 363–68.
29. Hironaka 2002, 70–71.
30. Glasson, Therivel, and Chadwick 1999, 42.
31. Harrop and Ashley Nixon 1999; Petts 1999; Wathern 1988; and Wood 1995.
32. Glasson, Therivel, and Chadwick 1999, 8–14.
33. Glasson, Therivel, and Chadwick 1999, 4–6; and Weston 1997b, 6–7.
34. Wood 1995, 9–11.
35. Glasson, Therivel, and Chadwick 1999, 18.
36. Gibson 1993, 14.
37. Wood 1995, 87.
38. European Commission 2001.
39. Schijf, 1997.
40. Canter and Clark 1996; Wood 1999, 26.

41. Gibson 1993, 14.
42. Tribe 1972–73.
43. Cornwell 2003; and Monbiot 2006b. Some universities now offer courses on how to commercialize scientific research. See UCL Graduate School 2006.
44. Amy 1990.
45. Amy 1990, 60.
46. Amy 1990, 63.
47. Weston 1997a, 189, 192–93, 198.
48. Holland 1996, 8, 10, 15.
49. Briffett 1999, 336.
50. Union of Concerned Scientists 2004a, 16; Union of Concerned Scientists 2004b, 7–11.
51. Weston 1997a, 194.
52. Nakayama and Fujikura 2001.
53. Frost 1997, 143.
54. Frost 1997, 146–47, 161.
55. Wood 1995, 12.
56. Weston 1997b, 181.
57. Wood 1995, 291.
58. Weston 1997b, 198.
59. Briffett 1999.
60. Parliamentary Commissioner for the Environment 1995, 40–41.
61. Taylor 1984; Wood 1995, 26.
62. Wood 1995, 297.
63. D. W. Pearce 2000, 49.
64. Van der Straaten 2002.
65. D. W. Pearce 2000, 59, 65.
66. Lumley 2002, 96–97.
67. Hanley and Spash 1993.
68. Hanley and Spash 1993, 262.
69. Hanley and Spash 1993, 263.
70. Kelman 1981.
71. D. W. Pearce 2000, 70.
72. Lekakis 2002, 151–52.
73. Lumley 2002, 100; D. W. Pearce 2000, 60.
74. Hanley and Spash 1993, 161.
75. D. W. Pearce 2000, 62; Van der Straaten 2002, 324.
76. Hanley and Spash 1993, 263.
77. Lumley 2002, 100.
78. Hanley and Spash 1993, 261–62.
79. Hanley and Spash 1993, 266; Lekakis 2002, 159–60; D. W. Pearce 2000, 56.
80. Lekakis 2002, 161.
81. Hanley and Spash 1993, 160–63.
82. Lekakis 2002, 158.
83. D. W. Pearce 2000, 62.

84. Christoforou 2004, 49; Hanley and Spash 1993, 160–63, 264.
85. Lumley 2002, 106.
86. D. W. Pearce 2000, 71.
87. D. W. Pearce, 2000, 74.
88. Lumley 2002, 108, 110–11.
89. Hanley and Spash 1993, 168.
90. D. W. Pearce 2000, 72.
91. Armour 1993, 179; Swaney 1996, 463.
92. Russell and Gruber 1987.
93. Jacobs and Worthley 1999.
94. Andrews 1994, 212.
95. Russell and Gruber 1987.
96. Armour 1997, 46.
97. Andrews 1994, 215.
98. O'Brien 2001, 23–25.
99. Swaney 1996, 467–68.
100. Davies 1995, 8.
101. Andrews 1994, 213; Russell and Gruber 1987, 287.
102. Armour 1983, 189.
103. Tesh 1999, 43.
104. Finkel and Golding 1994a, 330; Finkel and Golding 1994b, 336; Tesh 1999.
105. Hornstein 1994, 150–51.
106. Clayton and Krier 1990, 151.
107. O'Brien 2001, 27–29.
108. O'Brien 2001, 35.
109. Holland and Kellow 2001, 238.
110. Hornstein 1994, 154.
111. Andrews 1994, 209; Davies 1995.
112. Hornstein 1994, 149.
113. Andrews, 224.
114. Swaney 1996, 468.
115. Lash 1994, 77.
116. Lash 1994, 81.
117. Swaney 1996, 469.
118. Swaney 1996, 467.
119. Sampson 2001, 15.
120. Perhac 1998.
121. Holland and Kellow 2001.
122. Christoforou 2004, 18.
123. Andrews 1994, 218–19.
124. Andrews 1994, 211.
125. Armour 1993, 184.
126. Beck 1992, 45, 58–59, 70.
127. Andrews 1994, 229; O'Brien 1994; O'Brien 2001.
128. Tol and Vellinga 1998, 181.

129. Toth and Hizsnyk 1998, 193–94.
130. Schneider 1997, 230; Toth and Hizsnyk 1998, 199.
131. Tol and Vellinga 1998, 183; Toth and Hizsnyk 1998, 194.
132. Schneider 1997, 235; Tol and Vellinga 1998, 182.
133. Toth and Hizsnyk 1998, 198.
134. Schneider 1997, 230–31.
135. Toth and Hizsnyk 1998, 194.
136. Toth and Hizsnyk 1998, 201–4.
137. Toth and Hizsnyk 1998, 204.
138. Schneider 1997, 246.
139. Tol and Vellinga 1998, 186–89.
140. Toth and Hizsnyk 1998, 205.
141. Tol and Vellinga 1998, 185.

CHAPTER 3

1. Dryzek 1997.
2. Lafferty and Meadowcroft 2000b.
3. Dryzek 1997, 121–36; Torgerson 1995, 4–20.
4. Barbier 1987, 101–10.
5. World Commission on Environment and Development 1987, 29–32.
6. World Commision on Environment and Development 1987, 51.
7. Daly 1996, 97–115; Daly, Cobb, and Cobb 1989, 62–84.
8. Gardner and Assadourian 2004; Hamilton 2003; Hirsch 1976.
9. Daly 1996, 75–87.
10. Daly 1996, 75–87.
11. Shiva 2002; Speth 2003.
12. Beder 1994.
13. Athanasiou 1996, 255, 296; Lafferty 1996; Lafferty and Meadowcroft 2000b.
14. Torgerson 1995, 12, 16.
15. Huber 2000.
16. Jänicke 1993.
17. Christoff 1996; and Hajer 1995.
18. Dryzek 1997, 137–52.
19. Christoff 1996.
20. Milanez and Bührs 2007.
21. Kovel 2002; M. O'Connor 1994; and Ophuls 1977.
22. Weidner 2002, 193.
23. Dryzek 1997, 148–50; Hajer 1995.
24. An example of this is the inquiry on genetic modification conducted by a royal commission in New Zealand in 2000–2001, which, despite the fact that it allowed for widespread public input, relied on quasi-legal (cross-examination) and science-based decision rules to produce its recommendations. The main issues that carried weight in the commission's findings were whether, from a scientific point

of view, genetic modification was safe, and the importance of genetic modification for the economy as a whole. Who stood to gain or lose from genetic modification, political issues (increased control over production of food by a few companies), and social, moral and ethical issues, although they were raised, especially in public submissions, were not considered important enough reasons for advising against the technology.

25. Milanez 2006.

26. Milanez and Bührs 2008.

27. Weizsäcker, Lovins, and Lovins 1997, 248.

28. Buitenkamp, Venner, and Wams 1993, 17–18.

29. Davidson 1995.

30. Carley and Spapens 1998, 60.

31. Buitenkamp, Venner, and Wams, 1993, 9.

32. Carley and Spapens 1998, 65–66, 77, 104–6; Sachs, Loske, and Linz 1998, 17.

33. Buitenkamp, Venner, and Wams 1993, 18; Carley and Spapens 1998, 66–74; Friends of the Earth Europe 1995, 8, 11, 19; Sachs, Loske, and Linz 1998, 14–16.

34. Carley and Spapens 1998, 30–47, 75–106; Sachs and Santarius 2007, 35–80.

35. Wackernagel and Rees 1996, 31–33.

36. Global Footprint Network, Footprint for Nations.

37. Wackernagel and Rees 1996, 48–49.

38. Aitken 1980.

39. Wackernagel and Rees 1996, 51. It should be noted that in Ecological Footprint discourse sustainability is measured on the basis of the amount of (productive) land within a country relative to the ecological footprint of its population, which disadvantages smaller and densely populated countries. If such assessments are used as a basis for determining entitlements to resources, this also raises equity issues.

40. Bührs 2004; 2007.

41. Andersen 1997, 169; Dalal-Clayton 1996, 111–12; Ministerie van Volkshuisvesting Ruimtelijke Ordening en Milieubeheer and Tweede Kamer der Staten-Generaal 1989.

42. Carley and Spapens 1998, 187, 192–93.

43. Capra 1982, 66.

44. Capra 1982, 6, 285.

45. Capra 1997, 289–95.

46. Deutsch 1977a, 11.

47. Deutsch 1977b, 24.

48. Easton 1965; Parsons 1971; Stewart and Ayres 2001, 80.

49. Capra 1997, 289–95.

50. Clayton and Radcliffe 1996, 208–37.

51. Diebold Institute for Public Policy Studies and Information-Based Infrastructure Project 1995; Li 2001.

52. Christensen et al. 1996, 670.

53. Caldwell 1970; Morrissey, Zinn, and Corn 1994; Scheiber 1997.

54. Christensen et al. 1996, 670.

55. Scheiber 1997, 636–37.

56. Scheiber 1997, 643.

57. Caldwell 1970. Although the title of the article suggests that he confined the application of the ecosystem principle to public land, Caldwell advocated that public land policy should also apply to private land, as the public has an interest in all land.

58. Caldwell 1970, 205.

59. Caldwell 1970, 210.

60. Caldwell 1970, 209–11.

61. Caldwell 1970, 219.

62. Reichman and Pulliam 1996, 694.

63. Christensen et al. 1996, 668.

64. U.N. FAO report, quoted in Scheiber 1997, 649.

65. Fitzsimmons 1996.

66. Bocking 1994; Cooperrider 1996; Fitzsimmons 1996; Grumbine 1994.

67. Bocking 1994, 17–18.

68. Cortner and Moote 1998, 45.

69. If the ecosystem concept were to have no scientific status at all, the notion of ecosystem management would make no sense. However, even a sharp critic of ecosystem management like Fitzsimmons does not deny that the ecosystem concept is useful as a scientific concept, but argues that it is too vague and complex to serve as a basis for management (Fitzsimmons 1994; Fitzsimmons 1996).

70. Berkes, Folke, and Colding 1998; Peine et al. 1999, 77–78.

71. Cordell and Bergstrom 1999; Cortner and Moote 1998; Freemuth 1996; Weber 2000; Yaffee 1994.

72. Cortner and Moote 1998, xi; Weber 2000.

73. Blount 1999, 116.

74. Bell 1994; and Freemuth 1996.

75. Weber 2000.

76. Freemuth 1996, 411.

77. Weber 2000, 256. Folke, Berkes, and Colding appear to share a "vision of a smaller-scale, community-based, more environmentally sound, and more socially sound future," and argue that "the power of centralized management agencies should be redistributed and balanced" though not eliminated (Folke, Berkes, and Colding 1998, 431–32).

78. Cortner and Moote 1998, 51.

79. Cortner and Moote 1998, 126.

80. Born and Sonzogni 1995; Lee 1993; Margerum 1999; Savory and Butterfield 1999

81. Caldwell 1994; Lee 1993; Morrissey, Zinn, and Corn 1994; Yaffee et al. 1996.

CHAPTER 4

1. Caldwell 1995a, 171.

2. Denmark and the Netherlands are two exceptions (Dalal-Clayton and Sadler 2004).

3. Dalal-Clayton and Sadler 2004, 27.
4. Dalal-Clayton and Sadler 2004, 93.
5. Dalal-Clayton and Sadler 2004, 49.
6. Dalal-Clayton and Sadler 2004, 300.
7. Dalal-Clayton and Sadler 2004, 11.
8. Dalal-Clayton and Sadler 2004, 15.
9. Brown and Thérivel 2000, 183.
10. Buckley 2000; Nooteboom 2000.
11. Renton and Bailey 2000.
12. Elling 2000.
13. Kørnøv and Thissen 2000.
14. Sheate et al. 2003, 11.
15. Sheate et al. 2003, 11.
16. Dalal-Clayton and Sadler 2004, 13.
17. Dalal-Clayton and Sadler 2004, 42.
18. Sheate et al. 2003, 14.
19. Dalal-Clayton and Sadler 2004, 300.
20. Dalal-Clayton and Sadler 2004, 45–46.
21. Buckley 2000, 210.
22. Dalal-Clayton and Sadler 2004, 56.
23. Dalal-Clayton and Sadler 2004, 57.
24. Dalal-Clayton and Sadler 2004, 58.
25. Organization for Economic Co-operation and Development 1999a, 127.
26. Organization for Economic Co-operation and Development 1999a, 127–28.
27. Rodgers 2005.
28. Organization for Economic Co-operation and Development 1999a, 28–29.
29. Rodgers 2005.
30. Organization for Economic Co-operation and Development 1999a, 29.
31. Dalal-Clayton and Sadler 2004, 74–75.
32. Dalal-Clayton and Sadler 2004, 76–78.
33. Connor and Dovers 2004, 155, 162–63.
34. Dalal-Clayton and Sadler 2004, 79–84.
35. Sheate et al. 2003, 13.
36. Dalal-Clayton and Sadler 2004, 1.
37. Pope, Annandale, and Morrison-Saunders 2004, 600.
38. Dalal-Clayton and Sadler 2004, 75.
39. Pope, Annandale, and Morrison-Saunders 2004, 595.
40. Gallagher and Blanco 2003; United Nations Environment Programme 2001, 35–36.
41. United Nations Environment Programme 2005, 109–12; United Nations Environment Programme 1999.
42. Gallagher and Blanco 2003; Schalatek 2004.
43. Organization for Economic Co-operation and Development 1994b; Organization for Economic Co-operation and Development 1999b; Organization for Economic Co-operation and Development 2000.

44. United Nations Environment Programme 2005; United Nations Environment Programme 2001; WWF International 1988.

45. Jackson 2001.

46. The European Union's assessments of trade agreements are an exception is this respect. See Jackson 2001.

47. Jackson 2001.

48. Pope, Annandale, and Morrison-Saunders 2004, 602–3.

49. Pope, Annandale, and Morrison-Saunders 2004, 603–4.

50. Gallagher 2004; Gallagher and Blanco 2003.

51. Australian Conservation Foundation 2004; Luttrell 2005.

52. Zerbe and Dedeurwaerdere 2003.

53. Tarakofsky 2000, 16.

54. In the literature, economic instruments are also referred to as "market-based instruments." As not all economic instruments are used in a market context (such as taxes), I prefer to use the more generic label "economic instruments."

55. In the literature, a variety of classifications and labels can be found. The categories put forward here are broad enough to capture the most commonly used economic instruments, but are not meant to be exhaustive.

56. Majone 1989, 116–44.

57. Stavins 2000, 35–39.

58. Jordan, Wurzel, and Zito 2003b also include voluntary agreements and "informational devices" under the label of "new" instruments. These, too, it can be argued, are hardly new, since in a variety of forms and countries these have been around for at least as long as governments have been engaged in environmental policy and management. What may be new are some of the forms these instruments have taken (such as some labeling and certification schemes), and the extent to which the use of such instruments has spread across countries.

59. Stavins 2000, 60–61.

60. Organization for Economic Co-operation and Development 1994a, 7.

61. Hahn 1995; Matsuno and Ueta 2000; Sprenger 2000; Stavins 2000; Tietenberg 2002.

62. European Environment Agency 2000, 8–9; Roodman 1999, 173.

63. Hahn 1995, 146.

64. Bressers and Schuddeboom 1994.

65. Andersen 2000a.

66. Sprenger 2000, 18.

67. Rietbergen-McCracken 2000, 12; Sprenger 2000, 14.

68. Majone 1989, 140.

69. Roodman 1997.

70. Sawin 2003; Flavin 2008, 88–89.

71. This happened, for instance, in the Netherlands, after a rather environmentally "unfriendly" government came to power in 2002, and in New Zealand (Bührs and Bartlett 1993, 108).

72. D. W. Pearce 2003, 11.

73. New Zealand is one of the few countries where, in the the mid-1980s, most direct agricultural subsidies were abolished. The adverse effects on the farming

community have been temporary, as farmers shifted toward economically more profitable activities. The environmental effects of exposing farming more to market forces have been mixed, however. Although the abolition of subsidies reduced economic activity on "marginal" land, the expansion of the dairy industry, in the wake of rising world prices for dairy products, has led to a significant increase in environmental pressures and problems from that industry. Bührs and Bartlett 1993, 107; Roodman 1997, 147–50. Ministry for the Environment 2007, 232–33.

74. Daly 1996, 48–52.

75. Jacobs 1995b, 52–53.

76. Kinrade 1995, 98.

77. Tietenberg 2002, 205, 210.

78. Hahn 1995, 132–42.

79. Jacobs 1995a, 114–16.

80. Dunn and Flavin 2002; Euraktiv 2005, 37.

81. Similar schemes have been implemented also in Australia, Canada, Iceland, the Netherlands, and the United States (McGinn 1998, 72–73).

82. Christoff 1995, 178–80; Roodman 1996, 179.

83. Two French companies, Vivendi Générale des eaux and Suez Lyonnaise des eaux, manage water supplies in 100 and 130 countries, respectively, together controlling nearly 40 percent of the created world market for water. The expansion of that market is pushed strongly by the World Trade Organization in the context of its trade liberalization agenda. Poupeau 2002.

84. Hahn 1995, 147–48.

85. Christoff 1995, 181.

86. Tietenberg 2002, 216–22.

87. Matsuno and Ueta 2000

88. Bressers and Huitema 2000, 83.

89. Enevoldsen and Brendstrup 2000.

90. Jordan, Wurzel, and Zito 2003a, 203.

91. This is most pronounced in the publications of the OECD, which has been a consistent and vigorous advocate for the use of economic instruments. But this stance is also reflected in a recent environmental publication that conveniently ignores the question of the effectiveness of economic instruments "because of space limitations." See Jordan, Wurzel, and Zito 2003b, 22.

92. Jacobs 1995b, 55.

93. Andersen 2000b; Bressers and Huitema 2000; Enevoldsen and Brendstrup 2000; Vatn 2000.

94. Daugbjerg 2000.

95. Roodman 1996, 176, 181.

96. For instance, it has been noted that, within five years after the introduction of the fisheries' individually tradable quota system in New Zealand, only three companies held half of all quotas in the system, forcing many small vessel owners and fishers into a subcontracting role or forcing them out of business completely (McGinn 1998, 73). In Chile, where water auctions began in 1981, most tradable water permits also ended up in a few hands (Roodman 1996, 181).

97. Goodin 1994.

98. Goodin 1994.
99. Dryzek 1995, 294–308; Kelman 1981.
100. Jordan, Wurzel, and Zito 2003b, 9.
101. Finger 2005; Heynen and Robbins 2005; Watts 2002.
102. Dryzek 1995, 306.
103. European Environment Agency 2000, 9; Jänicke 1993, 159–75.
104. Ameels, Suck, and DeClercq 2000.
105. Organization for Economic Co-operation and Development 2003, 34.
106. Lycos Environmental News 2002.
107. Glasbergen 1998.
108. Gutman 2003; Speth 2003.
109. De Jongh and Captain 1999, 166–69.
110. Ministerie voor Volkshuisvesting and Ruimtelijke Ordening and Milieubeheer 2001, 79.
111. Ameels, Suck, and DeClercq 2000.
112. Organization for Economic Co-operation and Development 2003, 14, 62.
113. Organization for Economic Co-operation and Development 2003, 14, 42–43.

CHAPTER 5

1. Guruswamy 1989; Guruswamy 1991; Haigh and Irwin 1990; Lundqvist 1974; Royal Commission on Environmental Pollution 1984; Weale, O'Riordan, and Kramme 1991.
2. Guruswamy 1989; Guruswamy 1991; Haigh and Irwin 1990; Jordan 1993.
3. Swaney 1996.
4. Commoner 1994, 203, 210.
5. Johnson 1995, chap. 5.
6. Bührs 2002; Bührs 2006; Bührs and Bartlett 1997.
7. Falloux and Talbot 1993, 106–16; Jänicke and Jörgens 1998.
8. Braybrooke and Lindblom 1963; Cohen, March, and Olsen 1972; Wildavsky 1979.
9. Dalal-Clayton 1996, 17–18; Lopez Ornat and International Union for Conservation of Nature and Natural Resources 1997, 3.
10. Lafferty and Hovden 2003, 9–12.
11. Carew-Reid et al. 1994, 41.
12. Falloux and Talbot 1993, xiv–xv, 19, 22–23.
13. World Bank 1995, vii.
14. Falloux and Talbot 1993, 32–80.
15. Germany perhaps can claim pioneer status in green planning, as a comprehensive environmental policy statement was adopted in 1971; but it proved to be short-lived (Jänicke, Carius, and Jörgens 1997, 61).
16. Jörgens 2003, 14, 19–20.
17. Dalal-Clayton and Bass 2002, 8–9.

18. For studies encompassing a range of countries, see Jänicke and Jörgens 1998; Dalal-Clayton 1996; and Lafferty and Meadowcroft 2000b.

19. Second Chamber of the States General 1989, 7.

20. Second Chamber of the States General 1989, 92.

21. Tweede Kamer der Staten Generaal 2006. The "Toekomstagenda Milieu," in the government's own words, does not introduce new policy and is not a new national environmental policy plan (what would be the equivalent of NEPP5), but accepts NEPP4 and the goals and objectives contained therein.

22. Toner and Doern 1994, 396–97.

23. Toner 1994, 231.

24. Toner 1994, 231.

25. Johnson 1995, 99.

26. Toner 2000, 60.

27. Robert Slater, interview (Ottawa: Environment Canada), 26 August 1998.

28. Bührs 2000.

29. Lafferty and Meadowcroft 2000b, 411–20.

30. Commissioner of the Environment and Sustainable Development 2005, chap. 7, exhibit 7.5. Although Environment Canada has adopted a sustainable development strategy, this is a departmental strategy aimed at promoting sustainable development within the department "and with its partners," it is not a federal (national) government strategy.

31. Commonwealth of Australia 1990.

32. Commonwealth of Australia 1992.

33. Department of the Environment Sport and Territories 1997, 2. Diesendorf and Hamilton 1997, 293–95.

34. Bührs 2000.

35. Bennett 1997, 74; De Jongh and Captain 1999, 40–51.

36. De Jongh and Captain 1999, 43.

37. Winsemius 1990.

38. Doern and Conway 1994, 118; Gale 1997, 100; Toner 1994, 232–33; Toner and Doern 1994, 401.

39. Hawke 1989.

40. Beder 1993; and Crook and Pakulski 1995.

41. De Jongh and Captain 1999, 105–8; Toner and Doern 1994.

42. Diesendorf and Hamilton 1997, 293–95; Harris and Throsby 1998.

43. Maartje Nelemans, interview (The Hague: Ministerie van Volkshuisvesting en Ruimtelijke Ordening, DGM/SP), 8 May 1998.

44. Tom Conway, interview (Ottawa: Resource Futures International), 10 September 1998; Toner 1996.

45. Beder 1993, 287.

46. Johnson 1995, 91.

47. Falloux and Talbot 1993, 83; Jänicke and Jörgens, 1998.

48. Dalal-Clayton 1996, 38; De Jongh and Captain 1999, 100–3.

49. Vogelaar 1998, 14.

50. Scruggs 2003, 9, 74–75.

51. Langeweg 1988.

52. Jänicke 2002, 122–61; Jänicke and Jörgens 1998; Scruggs 2001; Wallace 1995.

53. Liefferink 1997, 223–24.

54. Tweede Kamer der Staten-Generaal 1999, 9, 13.

55. Gerard Keijzers, interview (The Hague: Ministerie van Volkshuisvesting en Ruimtelijke Ordening, DGM/SP), 29 May 1998; Pieter Winsemius, interview (Rotterdam: McKinsey & Company), 20 May 1998.

56. Keijzers, interview; Papadakis 1993, 85–92; Winsemius, interview.

57. De Jongh and Captain 1999; Glasbergen 1998.

58. Winsemius, interview.

59. Bührs 2000; Kellow 1996.

60. Harrison 1996.

61. Doern and Conway 1994, 83–99; Harrison 1996, 20–24; Kellow 1996, 137–39.

62. Responsibility for the environment was assigned by the government to a state secretary outside the cabinet, significantly reducing the voice of environmental interests at the highest level of decision-making.

63. Mulder, Verhue, and Adriaansen 2005.

64. Ministerie van Volkshuisvesting, Ruimtelijke Ordening en Milieubeheer and Tweede Kamer der Staten-Generaal 1989. Although initially the aim of NEPP1 was to make the Netherlands sustainable in one generation (by 2010), it was soon realized that this was unrealistic. Instead, the aim became "to make these [environmental] problems manageable within that period." (Van Muijen 2000, 147).

65. Milieu en Natuurplanbureau-RIVM 2005, 9–16.

66. Milieu en Natuurplanbureau-RIVM 2005, 12; Ministerie van Volkshuisvesting, Ruimtelijke Ordening en Milieubeheer 2005, 6.

67. Rijksinstituut voor Volksgezondheid en Milieu 2005, 24.

68. Milieu en Natuurplanbureau-RIVM 2005.

69. Milieu en Natuurplanbureau-RIVM 2005, 13.

70. Milieu en Natuurplanbureau-RIVM 2005, 113.

71. Ministerie van Volkshuisvesting, Ruimtelijke Ordening en Milieubeheer 2005.

72. De Jongh and Captain 1999, 76–90.

73. Bennett 1997, 81.

74. Dryzek 1997, 138–39; Hajer 1995, chap. 5.

75. Christoff 1996, 490.

76. Ministerie voor Volkshuisvesting, Ruimtelijke Ordening en Milieubeheer 2001.

77. Ministerie voor Volkshuisvesting, Ruimtelijke Ordening en Milieubeheer 2001.

78. Ministerie van Volkshuisvesting, Ruimtelijke Ordening en Milieubeheer, 2005; Tweede Kamer der Staten Generaal 2006.

79. Organization for Economic Co-operation and Development 1995, 121, 135.

80. Kees Bastmeijer, interview (The Hague: Ministerie van Volkshuisvesting en Ruimtelijke Ordening, Afdeling Bestuurszaken), 28 May 1998; Nelemans, interview.

CHAPTER 6

1. Although the literature contains a variety of definitions of, and distinctions between, institutions (Vatn 2005, 9–14), most share the common feature of guiding human behavior, in varying degrees of formality or informality, and variously backed up by sanctions. Given its flexibility, the term rule seems well suited to capture the essence of what institutions are about. Formal organizations, although sometimes distinguished from institutions (Connor and Dovers 2004), are in fact nothing but bundles of rules centered around particular goals, prescribing positions, roles, tasks, lines of accountability, and so on. Given their omnipresence in modern societies—for instance, in the form of corporations—they are among the most important institutions that guide human behavior, even if they manifest themselves as "actors." In this context, it should be noted that institutions, including organizations, do not *determine* human behavior and that individuals may choose not to follow rules (strictly), or seek to change them.

2. March and Olsen 1989.

3. Readers may note that this depiction of institutions represents a "social constructivist" rather than a "methodological individualist" interpretation of institutions. However, it does recognize the interaction between structures and agents, and that institutions can be deliberately changed as a result of collective action by individuals. For a similar view of institutions, see Vatn 2005.

4. March and Olsen 1989.

5. Cairns 1991; Guruswamy 1989; Haigh and Irwin 1990.

6. In this context, to what extent the integration of climate change abatement objectives in sectors such as energy, transport, and agriculture represents a "greening" of policies and the (governmental and nongovernmental) institutions involved is questionable. Adopting greenhouse gas reduction targets neither necessarily implies a greening of policies (if other objectives with adverse environmental impacts are maintained), nor a greening of institutions (rules and organizations taking environmental imperatives as a basis or framework for policies and practices). Climate change is, of course, also just one environmental issue (albeit an important one). Policies aimed at abating it may do nothing, or even have an adverse affect on other environmental problems, and they may not address the drivers or underlying (human) causes of any of these problems.

7. Juillet and Toner 1997, 192.

8. Government of Canada 1995.

9. Commissioner of the Environment and Sustainable Development 1998.

10. Brian Emmett, interview (Ottawa: Office of the Auditor-General of Canada), 26 August 1998.

11. Commissioner of the Environment and Sustainable Development 1998. The Commissioner's Observations, 15.

12. Slater, interview.

13. Gene Nyberg, interview (Ottawa: National Round Table on the Environment and the Economy), 3 September 1998; David Runnals, interview (Ottawa: International Institute for Sustainable Development), 15 September 1998.

14. Organization for Economic Co-operation and Development 2004a, 24.

15. Commissioner of the Environment and Sustainable Development 2005, chap 7:4.

16. Commissioner of the Environment and Sustainable Development 2005, chap. 7:2.

17. Commissioner of the Environment and Sustainable Development 2001, The Commisioner's Perspective—2001, section 15.

18. Commissioner of the Environment and Sustainable Development 2005, chap. 7:6.

19. Commissioner of the Environment and Sustainable Development 2005, chapter 7:12.

20. Commissioner of the Environment and Sustainable Development 2005, chapter 7:8–9.

21. Newman 2006.

22. Commissioner of the Environment and Sustainable Development 2005, 4.

23. Wilkinson 1997, 88.

24. Wilkinson 1997, 91–92.

25. Wilkinson 1997, 92.

26. Wilkinson 1997, 92–93.

27. Department of the Environment, Transport and the Regions 2000, 3.

28. Young 2000, 254–55.

29. Young 2000, 256–58, 272.

30. House of Commons, Environmental Audit Committee 1999.

31. Revell 2005, 354; SDU: Sustainable Development Unit; DETR: Department of Environment, Transport and the Regions.

32. Revell 2005, 354.

33. Wilkinson 1997, 93–95.

34. Ross 2000, 191–92.

35. Ross 2000, 192–93.

36. United Kingdom Environmental Audit Committee 2003.

37. Revell 2005, 355–56.

38. Revell 2005, 355.

39. Lindblom 1982.

40. Funtowicz and Ravetz 1994; Sagoff 2004.

41. Daly 1996.

42. Shi 2004.

43. Daly, Cobb, and Cobb 1989, 401–55.

44. Cobb, Goodman, and Kliejunas 2000; Cobb, Halstead, and Rowe 1995.

45. Abramovitz 1997, 112.

46. Atkinson and Hamilton 1996, 16–25.

47. Nese 1996.

48. Costantino 1996.

49. Bartelmus and Seifert 2003b, xxi.

50. Costantino 1996, 198.

51. De Haan and Keuning 2003.

52. Ahmad, El Serafy, and Lutz 1989.

53. Atkinson 1995.

54. United Nations 1993; United Nations, European Commission, International Monetary Fund, Organization for Economic Co-operation and Development, World Bank 2003

55. Atkinson and Hamilton 1996; Bartelmus and Seifert 2003a, xi.

56. Bartelmus and Seifert 2003a, xi.

57. Bartelmus and Seifert 2003a, xi.

58. Bartelmus and Seifert 2003a, xvi, xxxi.

59. Pearce Markandya and Barbier 1989, 116.

60. Pedersen and de Haan 2006.

61. Atkinson 1995.

62. Nese 1996, 210.

63. Nese 1996, 210.

64. Bartelmus and Seifert 2003b, xxvi–xxvii.

65. Gallhofer and Haslam 1997.

66. Neumayer 1999; D. W. Pearce, Markandya and Barbier 1989, 34–38.

67. Atkinson 1995.

68. Delmas 2002.

69. Delmas 2002; Freimann and Walther 2001, 93; Peglau 2006.

70. Netherwood 1996, 53.

71. Freimann and Walther 2001.

72. Freimann and Walther 2001, 99.

73. Andrews et al. 2003.

74. Andrews et al. 2003, 193–94.

75. Andrews et al. 2003, ES-20-21, 296.

76. Freimann and Walther 2001, 95.

77. Freimann and Walther 2001, 95, 101.

78. Freimann and Walther 2001, 95–96.

79. Freimann and Walther 2001, 97.

80. Freimann and Walther 2001, 96.

81. Andrews et al. 2003, 19–20; Beder 1997, 301.

82. Athanasiou 1996; Beder 1997.

83. Gardner 2001, 197–200; Suzuki and Dressel 2002.

84. Gardner puts BP's promotion of itself as a "green energy company" in perspective by pointing out that its investment in solar energy was 588 times less than what it paid for buying another oil and gas company (Gardner 2001, 200).

85. MacDonald 2003; Monbiot 2006a; Monbiot 2006b.

86. MacDonald 2003; Shiva 2002.

87. Andrews et al. 2003; Rotherham n.d., 301.

88. Rotherham n.d., 10.

89. Gardner 2001, 197–200; Suzuki and Dressel 2002.

90. Vatn 2005, 426.

91. Daly 1996, 7.

92. Torgerson 1990.

93. Friedman 1999, 112–42.

94. Cerny 1997; and Weiss 1998.

95. Buttel 1998, 282.
96. Porritt 2005, 105.
97. O'Connor 1994, 154.
98. Kovel 2002.
99. Pepper 1993, 95.

CHAPTER 7

1. Kronsell 1997, 46–47.
2. Bryner 2000, 302; Funke 1993.
3. Broadbent 2002, 118, 128; Schreurs 2002, 43.
4. Sumikura 1998; Government of Japan 1993.
5. Hordijk 1996.
6. Ministerie van Volkshuisvesting, Ruimtelijke Ordening en Milieubeheer 1998, 357–59.
7. Kronsell 1997, 46–47.
8. Organization for Economic Co-operation and Development 2004b, 30.
9. Boston 1991.
10. Bührs 1996a; Bührs and Bartlett 1993.
11. Ong 2000.
12. Organization for Economic Co-operation and Development 1996a; Organization for Economic Co-operation and Development 2007, 171–72.
13. Ministry for the Environment 2007.
14. Bührs 2002; Bührs and Bartlett 1997; Parliamentary Commissioner for the Environment 2002.
15. Ministry for the Environment 2007. For analyses and assessments of many aspects of New Zealand's environmental performance, see the reports published by the Parliamentary Commissioner for the Environment, http://www.pce.govt.nz/reports/allreports/.
16. Hayward 2005, 22–23, n. 4.
17. Earthjustice 2005.
18. Earthjustice 2005, 99.
19. Earthjustice 2005, 88–89.
20. Earthjustice 2005, 91.
21. Hayward 2005, 5.
22. Hayward 2005, 22, n. 1.
23. Eckersley 1998; and Hayward 2005.
24. Hayward 2005, 143.
25. Eckersley 1998, 373.
26. Eckersley 1998, 357.
27. Dias 2000, 21.
28. Nickel and Viola 1994.
29. Hayward 2005, 12–13.
30. Hayward 2005, 16.
31. Hayward 2005, 201–2, 213, n. 10.

32. Hayward 2005, 203–5.
33. Earthjustice 2005, 39–40; Hayward 2005, 206–9.
34. Earthjustice 2005, 46.
35. Northern Alliance for Sustainability ANPED n.d.
36. Kraft 1996, 42–44; Rabe 1999, 422; Stavins 2000, 54.
37. Lafferty and Meadowcroft 2000c, 412–15.
38. Van Muijen 2000, 175.
39. Langhelle 2000, 179.
40. Langhelle 2000, 208.
41. Organization for Economic Co-operation and Development 2001, 25–30.
42. Langhelle 2000, 191–94.
43. Dryzek et al. 2003, 23–27.
44. Ministry for the Environment Regeringskansliet 1998.
45. Organization for Economic Co-operation and Development 1996b, 32, 2004b, 34.
46. Organization for Economic Co-operation and Development 2004b, 20.
47. Eckerberg 2000, 210, 222–24.
48. Organization for Economic Co-operation and Development 2004b, 98.
49. Organization for Economic Co-operation and Development 2004b, 99, 101.
50. O'Riordan and Cameron 1994a, 16–18.
51. Boehmer-Christiansen 1994, 36; O'Riordan and Cameron 1994a, 21.
52. O'Riordan and Cameron 1994a, 12; O'Riordan and Cameron 1994b, 292.
53. Boehmer-Christiansen 1994, 55.
54. Boehmer-Christiansen 1994, 33.
55. Boehmer-Christiansen 1994, 32, 36.
56. Boehmer-Christiansen 1994, 35–36.
57. Beuermann 2000; Boehmer-Christiansen 1994, 53; Jänicke and Weidner 1997.
58. Boehmer-Christiansen 1994.
59. Boehmer-Christiansen 1994, 50–52.
60. Bodansky 1994; Jasanoff 2003.
61. Bodansky 1994, 204–5.
62. Jasanoff 2003.
63. Da Cruz Vilaça 2004, 406.
64. Da Cruz Vilaça 2004, 396–99.
65. Kaiser 2003.
66. Quijano 2003.
67. Myers 2004.
68. O'Brien 2003.
69. Lenschow 2002c, 7.
70. European Environment Agency 2005, 12, 29.
71. European Environment Agency 2005, 29.
72. European Environment Agency 2005, 12.

73. European Environment Agency 2005, 34–35.

74. European Environment Agency 2005, 32–36.

75. European Environment Agency 2005, 36.

76. Lenschow 2002a, 222.

77. Lenschow 1999; Lenschow 2002b.

78. D'Evie et al. 2000, 2.

79. This may include National Councils on Environmental Policy, or organizations with similar names, if these are equipped with the task to promote environmental integration. However, such councils may also have more limited roles and mandates, such as providing advice on environmental issues and policies. Implicitly or explicitly, this may mean that they are not expected to advise on how economic and other "nonenvironmental" policies and institutions, falling within the domain of other agencies, could or should be changed to integrate environmental concerns.

80. Connor and Dovers 2004, 134.

81. Connor and Dovers 2004, 134, 145.

82. German Council for Sustainable Development 2006; Jänicke and Weidner 1997, 137.

83. Lafferty and Meadowcroft 2000c, 356.

84. D'Evie et al. 2000, 9.

85. Connor and Dovers 2004, 150; D'Evie et al. 2000, 125, 140.

86. Connor and Dovers 2004, 133; D'Evie et al. 2000, 13, 22, 153–54; Maurer 1999.

87. D'Evie et al., 2000, 14.

88. Habito 2000, 127.

89. Connor and Dovers 2004, 138–46; Maurer 1999.

90. Rosenbaum 1985, 57–59.

91. Bryner 2000, 273–302.

92. Connor and Dovers 2004, 140–42; Gale 1997, 113; Rabe 1997.

93. Crepaz 1995; Jahn 1998; Jänicke 1997, 13; Lafferty and Meadowcrof 2000a, 424, 432.

94. Habito 2000, 127.

95. Bartlett 1990a.

CHAPTER 8

1. European Environment Agency 2007, 252–89.

2. F. Pearce 2006b; Holtz-Giménez 2007; Righelato and Spracklen 2007.

3. Stone 1998.

4. Kingdon 1984.

5. Simms, Moran, and Chowla 2006.

6. As Janine Benyus (1997) shows, humans have much to learn from nature, whether in agriculture, the harnessing of energy, or the manufacturing of goods.

7. And an activity or process in which the use of computer-based progams like geographic information systems and computer-aided design can greatly assist. Arguably, a virtual reality based on existing ecological and resource conditions

and parameters, combined with interactive processes that bring in human needs and creative talent, can provide a helpful and fun way to design, and work toward desirable future human environments. Implemented along such lines, environmental integration would become a much more positive and constructive experience than that associated with most prevalent forms of integration.

8. Ayres and Ayres 2002; Jackson and Svensson 2002; Mollison 1999; F. Pearce 2006a; McDonough and Braungart 2002; Benyus 1997.

References

Abramovitz, Janet N. 1997. "Valuing Nature's Services." In *State of the World 1997*, edited by Lester Brown, Janet N. Abramovitz, Chris Bright, Christopher Flavin, Hillary F. French, Gary Gardner, Anne Platt McGinn, Michael Renner, David Malin Roodman, and Linda Stark. London: Earthscan Publications.

Ahmad, Yusuf J., Salah El Serafy, and Ernst Lutz, eds. 1989. *Environmental Accounting for Sustainable Development: Selected Papers from Joint UNEP/World Bank Workshops*. Washington, DC: World Bank.

Aitken, William. 1980. "The 'Carrying Capacity' Equivocation." *Social Theory and Practice* 6:1–11.

Almond, Gabriel. 1988. "The Return to the State." *American Political Science Review* 82:853–74.

Ameels, B., A. Suck, and M. DeClercq. 2000. "The Diffusion of Voluntary Agreements in the European Union: Critical Conditions for Success." In *International Workshop on Diffusion of Environmental Policy Innovations*. Berlin: Wissenschaftszentrum Berlin für Sozialforschung, Arbeitskreis Umweltpolitik.

Amy, Douglas J. 1990. "Decision-Techniques for Environmental Policy: A Critique." In *Managing Leviathan—Environmental Politics and the Administrative State*, edited by Robert Paehlke and Douglas Torgerson, 59–79. Peterborough, ON: Broadview Press.

Andersen, Mikael Skou. 1997. "Denmark: The Shadow of the Green Majority," In *European Environmental Policy: The Pioneers*, edited by Mikael Skou Andersen and Duncan Liefferink, 251–86. Manchester: Manchester University Press.

———. 2000a. "The Danish Waste Tax: The Role of Institutions for the Implementation and Effectiveness of Economic Instruments." In *Market-Based Instruments for Environmental Management: Politics and Institutions*, edited by Mikael Skou Andersen and Rolf-Ulrich Sprenger, 231–59. Cheltenham, England: Edward Elgar.

———. 2000b. "Designing and Introducing Green Taxes: Institutional Dimensions." In *Market-Based Instruments for Environmental Management: Politics and Institutions*, edited by Mikael Skou Andersen and Rolf-Ulrich Sprenger, 27–48. Cheltenham, England: Edward Elgar.

Andrews, Richard N. L. 1994. "Risk-Based Decisionmaking." In *Environmental Policy in the 1990s, toward a New Agenda*, edited by Norman J. Vig and Michael E. Kraft, 208–30. Washington, DC: CQ Press.

Andrews, R. N. L., et al. 2003. "Environmental Management Systems: Do They Improve Performance?" *Final Report of the National Database on Environmental Management Systems Pilot Project*. Chapel Hill, NC: Department of Public Policy, UNC-Chapel Hill.

Armour, Audrey M. 1993. "Risk Assessment in Environmental Policymaking." *Policy Studies Review* 12, no. 3/4: 178–96.

———. 1997. "Rethinking the Role of Risk Assessment in Environmental Policymaking." In *Environmental Policy: Transnational Issues and National Trends*, edited by Lynton K Caldwell and Robert V Bartlett, 37–59. Westport, CT: Quorum Books.

Ashby, Lord. 1976. "Background to Environmental Impact Assessment." In *Environmental Impact Assessment (EIA): Cutting Edge for the Twenty-First Century*, edited by T. O'Riordan and R. D. Hey, 3–15. Westmead, England: Saxon House.

Athanasiou, Tom. 1996. *Divided Planet: The Ecology of Rich and Poor*. Boston: Little, Brown.

Atkinson, Giles. 1995. "Greening the National Accounts: U.S. Congressional Budget Office." *Environment* 37:25–28.

Atkinson, Giles, and Kirk Hamilton. 1996. "Accounting for Progress: Indicators of Sustainable Development." *Environment* 38, no. 7:16–25.

Australian Conservation Foundation, 2004. *ACF Analysis of Australia–United States Free Trade Agreement*. Australian Conservation Foundation, http://www.acfontline.org.au/uploads/uafta_submission.pdf

Ayres, Robert U., and Leslie Ayres. 2002. *A Handbook of Industrial Ecology*. Chelthem, England: Edward Elgar.

Barbier, E. B. 1987. "The Concept of Sustainable Economic Development." *Environmental Conservation* 14, no. 2:101–10.

Bartelmus, Peter, and Eberhard K. Seifert. 2003a. *Green Accounting*. Aldershot, England: Ashgate.

———. 2003b. "Introduction: Accounting for Sustainability." In *Green Accounting*, edited by Peter Bartelmus and Eberhard K. Seifert, xiv–xviii. Aldershot, England: Ashgate.

Bartlett, Robert V. 1986. "Ecological Rationality: Reason and Environmental Policy." *Environmental Ethics* 8:221–39.

———. 1990a. "Comprehensive Environmental Decision-making: Can It Work?" In *Environmental Policy in the 1990s: Toward a New Agenda*, edited by Norman Vig and Michael Kraft, 235–54. Washington, DC: Congressional Quarterly Press.

———. 1990b. "Ecological Reason in Administration: Environmental Impact Assessment and Administrative Theory." In *Environmental Politics and the Administrative State*, edited by Robert Paehlke and Douglas Torgerson, 81–96. London: Bellhaven Press.

———. 1997. "Integrated Impact Assessment: The New Zealand Experiment." In *Environmental Policy: Transnational Issues and National Trends*, edited by Lynton K Caldwell and Robert V. Bartlett, 157–71. Westport, CT: Quorum Books.

Bartlett, Robert V., and Malone, Charles R. 1993. "Guidance for Environmental Impact Assessment." *Environmental Professional* 15, no. 1:1–3.

Beck, Ulrich. 1992. *Risk Society: Toward a New Modernity*. London: Sage Publications.

Beder, Sharon. 1993. *The Nature of Sustainable Development*. Newham, Australia: Scribe Publications.

———. 1994. " 'Revoltin' Developments: The Politics of Sustainable Development." *Arena Magazine*, June–July, 37–39.

———. 1997. *Global Spin: The Corporate Assault on Environmentalism*. Melbourne: Scribe Publications.

Bell, Anne. 1994. "Non-Human Nature and the Ecosystem Approach: The Limits of Anthropocentrism in Great Lakes Management." *Alternatives* 20, no. 3:20–25.

Bennett, Graham. 1997. "The Dutch Environmental Policy Plan." In *Nationale Umweltpläne in Ausgewählten Industrieländern*, edited by Martin Jänicke, Alexander Carius, and Helge Jörgens, 73–85. Berlin: Springer.

Benyus, Janine M. 1997. *Biomimicry: Innovation Inspired by Nature*. New York: Morrow.

Berkes, Fikret, Carl Folke, and Johan Colding. 1998. "Linking Social and Ecological Systems for Resilience and Reliability." In *Linking Social and Ecological Systems: Management Practices and Social Mechanisms for Building Resilience*, edited by Berkes and Folke, 1–25. Cambridge: Cambridge University Press.

Beuermann, Christiane. 2000. "Germany: Regulation and the Precautionary Principle." In *Implementing Sustainable Development: Strategies and Initiatives in High Consumption Societies*, edited by William M. Lafferty and James Meadowcroft, 85–111. Oxford: Oxford University Press.

Birkeland-Corro, J. 1988. "Redefining the Environmental Problem: Some Impediments to Institutional Reform." *Environmental and Planning Law Journal*. 5, no. 2:109–33.

Blount, Benjamin G. 1999. "History and Application of the Ecosystem Concept in Anthropology." In *Integrating Social Sciences with Ecosystem Management: Human Dimensions in Assessment, Policy and Management*, edited by H. Ken Cordell and John C. Bergstrom, 102–27. Champaign, IL.: Sagamore.

Bocking, Stephen. 1994. "Visions of Nature and Society: A History of the Ecosystem Concept." *Alternatives* 20, no. 3:12–18.

Bodansky, Daniel. 1994. "The Precautionary Principle in US Environmental Law." In *Interpreting the Precautionary Principle*, edited by Timothy O'Riordan and James Cameron, 203–28. London: Earthscan.

Boehmer-Christiansen, Sonja. 1994. "The Precautionary Principle in Germany—Enabling Government." In *Interpreting the Precautionary Principle*, edited by Timothy O'Riordan and James Cameron, 31–60. London: Earthscan.

Born, Stephen M., and William C. Sonzogni. 1995. "Integrated Environmental Management: Strengthening the Conceptualization." *Environmental Management* 19, no. 2:167–81.

Boston, Jonathan. 1991. "The Theoretical Underpinnings of Public Sector Restructuring in New Zealand." In *Reshaping the State: New Zealand's Bureaucratic*

Revolution, edited by Jonathan Boston, John Martin, June Pallot, and Pat Walsh, 1–26. Auckland: Oxford University Press.

Braybrooke, D. and Charles E. Lindblom. 1963. *A Strategy of Decision*. New York: Free Press.

Bressers, Hans Th. A., and Dave Huitema. 2000. "What the Doctor Should Know: Politicians Are Special Patients: The Impact of the Policy-Making Process on the Design of Economic Instruments." In *Market-Based Instruments for Environmental Management: Politics and Institutions*, edited by Mikael Skou Andersen and Rolf-Ulrich Sprenger, 67–86. Cheltenham, England: Edward Elgar.

Bressers, Hans Th. A., and Jeannette Schuddeboom. 1994. "A Survey of Effluent Charges and Other Economic Instruments in Dutch Environmental Policy." In *Applying Economic Instruments to Environmental Policies in OECD and Dynamic Non-Member Economies*, edited by Organization for Economic Co-operation and Development, 153–72. Paris: OECD.

Briffett, C. 1999. "Environmental Impact Assessment in Southeast Asia: Fact and Fiction?" *Geo-Journal* 49:333–38.

Broadbent, Jeffrey. 2002. "Japan's Environmental Regime: The Political Dynamics of Change." In *Environmental Politics and Policy in Industrialized Countries*, edited by Uday Desai, 295–355. Cambridge, MA: MIT Press.

Brown, A. L. and Riki Thérivel. 2000. "Principles to Guide the Development of Strategic Environmental Assessment Methodology." *Impact Assessment and Project Appraisal* 18, no. 3:183–89.

Bryner, Gary C. 2000. "The United States: 'Sorry—Not Our Problem.' " In *Implementing Sustainable Development: Strategies and Initiatives in High Consumption Societies*, edited by William M. Lafferty and James Meadowcroft, 273–302. Oxford: Oxford University Press.

Buckley, Ralf. 2000. "Strategic Environmental Assessment of Policies and Plans: Legislation and Implementation." *Impact Assessment and Project Appraisal* 18, no. 3:209–15.

Bührs, Ton. 1991. "Strategies for Environmental Policy Co-Ordination: The New Zealand Experience." *Political Science* 43:1–29.

———. 1996a. "Barking Up Which Trees? The Role of New Zealand's Environmental Watchdog." *Political Science* 48, no. 1:1–28.

———. 1996b. "Green Plans: A New Generation of Symbolic Environmental Policies?" Paper presented at *ECOPOLITICS X Conference*, September 26–29. Canberra, Australian National University.

———. 2000. "Green Planning in Australia and Canada: Dead or Alive?" *Environmental Politics* 9, no. 2:102–25.

———. 2002. "New Zealand's Capacity for Green Planning: A Political-Institutional Assessment and Analysis." *Political Science* 54, no. 1:27–46.

———. 2004. "Sharing Environmental Space: The Role of Law, Economics and Politics." *Journal of Environmental Policy and Management* 47, no. 3:431–49.

———. 2006. "Environmental Policy." In *New Zealand Government and Politics*, edited by Raymond Miller, 628–38. Melbourne: Oxford University Press.

———. 2007. *Towards a Global Political-Economic Architecture of Environmental Space*. *CSGR Working Paper Series*. Coventry: Centre for the Study of Globalization and Regionalization, University of Warwick. http://www2.warwick.ac.uk/fac/soc/csgr/researchworkingpapers/2007/wp23607.pdf

Bührs, Ton, and Robert V. Bartlett. 1993. *Environmental Policy in New Zealand. The Politics of Clean and Green?* Auckland: Oxford University Press.

———. 1997. "Strategic Thinking and the Environment: Planning the Future in New Zealand?" *Environmental Politics*, 6:72–100.

Buitenkamp, M., H. Venner, and T. Wams, eds. 1993. *Actie Plan Duurzaam Nederland (Translated in English in 1993 under the Title "Action Plan Sustainable Netherlands")*. Amsterdam: Friends of the Earth Netherlands.

Buttel, F. H. 1998. "Some Observations on States, World Orders, and the Politics of Sustainability." *Organization and Environment* 11, no. 3:261–86.

Cairns, John, Jr. 1991. "The Need for Integrated Environmental Systems Management." In *Integrated Environmental Management*, edited by John Cairns Jr. and Todd V. Crawford, 5–20. Chelsea, MI: Lewis Publishers.

Caldwell, Lynton K. 1970. "The Ecosystem as a Criterion for Public Land Policy." *Natural Resources Journal* 10, no. 2:203–21.

———. 1994. "Disharmony in the Great Lakes Basin." *Alternatives* 20, no. 3:27–31.

———. 1995a. "A National Policy for the Environment." In *Environment as a Focus for Public Policy*, edited by Robert V. Bartlett and James N. Gladden, 139–66. College Station: Texas A&M University Press.

———. 1995b. "The National Environmental Policy Act." In *Environment as a Focus for Public Policy*, edited by Robert V. Bartlett and James N. Gladden, 167–79. College Station: Texas A&M University Press.

———. 1995c. "Problems of Applied Ecology." In *Environment as a Focus for Public Policy*, edited by Robert V. Bartlett and James N. Gladden, 127–38. College Station: Texas A&M University Press.

Canter, L. 1984. "Environmental Impact Studies in the United States." In *Perspectives on Environment Impact Assessment*, edited by B. D. Clark, A. Gilad, R. Bisset and & P. Tomlinson, 15–24. Dordrecht: D. Reidel.

Canter, L. W. and E. R. Clark. 1996. *Scoping in the EIA Process in the United States*. Report of the EIA Process Strengthening Workshop, Canberra April 4–7, 1995. Canberra: Environmental Protection Agency.

Capra., Fritjof. 1982. *The Turning Point: Science, Society, and the Rising Culture*. London: HarperCollins (Flamingo).

———. 1997. *The Web of Life. A New Synthesis of Mind and Matter*. London: Flamingo.

Carew-Reid, Jeremy, Robert Prescott-Allen, Stephen Bass, and Barry Dalal-Clayton. 1994. *Strategies for National Sustainable Development: A Handbook for Their Planning and Implementation*. London: Earthscan Publications in association with IUCN and IIED.

Carley, Michael, and Philippe Spapens. 1998. *Sharing the World: Sustainable Living and Global Equity in the 21st Century*. London: Earthscan.

Carter, Vernon Gill, and Tom Dale. 1955. *Topsoil and Civilization*. Norman: University of Oklahoma Press.

Cerny, P. 1997. "Paradoxes of the Competition State: The Dynamics of Political Globalisation." *Government and Opposition* 36, no. 2:251–74.

Christensen, Norman L., et al. 1996. "The Report of the Ecological Society of America Committee on the Scientific Basis for Ecosystem Management." *Ecological Applications* 6, no. 3:665–91.

Christoff, Peter. 1995. "Market-Based Instruments: The Australian Experience." In *Markets, the State and the Environment: Toward Integration*, edited by Robyn Eckersley, 157–93. Melbourne: Macmillan.

———. 1996. "Ecological Modernization, Ecological Modernities." *Environmental Politics* 5, no. 3:476–500.

Christoforou, Theofanis. 2004. "The Precautionary Principle, Risk Assessment, and the Comparative Role of Science in the European Community and the US Legal Systems." In *Green Giants? Environmental Policies of the United States and the European Union*, edited by Norman J. Vig and Michael G. Faure, 17–51. Cambridge, MA: MIT Press.

Clark, B. D. 1984. "Environmental Impact Assessment (EIA): Scope and Objectives." In *Perspectives on Environment Impact Assessment*, edited by B. D. Clark, A. Gilad, R. Bisset, and P. Tomlinson, 3–13. Dordrecht: D. Reidel.

Clayton, Anthony M. H. and Nicholas J. Radcliffe. 1996. *Sustainability: A Systems Approach*. London: Earthscan.

Clayton, Gilette P. and James E. Krier. 1990. "Risk, Courts, and Agencies." *Pennsylvania Law Review* 138, no. 4:1027–1109.

Cobb, Clifford, Gary Sue Goodman, and Joanne C. May Kliejunas. 2000. "Blazing Sun Overhead and Clouds on the Horizon: The Genuine Progress Report for 1999." Oakland, CA: Redefining Progress. http://www.rprogress.org/projects/gpi/gpi1999.pdf.

Cobb, Clifford, Ted Halstead, and Jonathan Rowe. 1995. *Redefining Progress: The Genuine Progress Indicator. Summary of Data and Methodology*. San Francisco, CA: Redefining Progress.

Cohen, Michael D., James G. March, and Johan P. Olsen. 1972. "A Garbage Can Model of Organizational Choice." *Administrative Science Quarterly* 17, no. 1:1–15.

Commissioner of the Environment and Sustainable Development. 1998. "Report of the Commissioner of the Environment and Sustainable Development to the House of Commons—1998." Ottawa: Commissioner of the Environment and Sustainable Development.

———. 2001. "Report of the Commissioner of the Environment and Sustainable Development to the House of Commons—2001." Ottawa: Commissioner of the Environment and Sustainable Development.

———. 2005. Report of the Commissioner of the Environment and Sustainable Development to the House of Commons—2005." Ottawa: Commissioner of the Environment and Sustainable Development.

Commoner, Barry. 1994. "Pollution Prevention: Putting Comparative Risk Assessment in Its Place." In *Worst Things First? The Debate over Risk-Based National Environmental Priorities*, edited by Adam M. Finkel and Dominic Golding, 203–28. Washington, DC: Resources for the Future.

Commonwealth of Australia. 1990. "Ecologically Sustainable Development." A Commonwealth Discussion Paper. Canberra: Australian Government Publishing Service Press.

———. 1992. "National Strategy for Ecologically Sustainable Development." Canberra: Australian Government Publishing Service Press.

Connor, Robin D., and Stephen Dovers. 2004. *Institutional Change for Sustainable Development*. Cheltenham, England: Edward Elgar.

Cooperrider, Allen Y. 1996. "Science as a Model for Ecosystem Management—Panacea or Problem?" *Ecological Applications*. 6, no. 3:736–37.

Cordell, H. Ken, and John C. Bergstrom. 1999. *Integrating Social Sciences with Ecosystem Management: Human Dimensions in Assessment, Policy, and Management*. Champaign, IL: Sagamore.

Cornwell, John. 2003. "Just Following Orders?" *New Scientist*, September 27, 25.

Cortner, H. Hanna and Margaret A. Moote. 1998. *The Politics of Ecosystem Management*. Washington, DC: Island Press.

Costantino, Cesare. 1996. "Elements of Environmental Accounting in Some European Countries—A Methodological and Operational Analysis: The Cases of France, Germany and the Netherlands." In *National Accounts and the Environment*, edited by Ignazio Musu and Domenico Siniscalco, 189–204. Dordrecht: Kluwer Academic Publishers.

Crepaz, Markus M. L. 1995. "Explaining National Variations of Air Pollution Levels: Political Institutions and Their Impact on Environmental Policy-Making." *Environmental Politics*. 4, no. 3:391–414.

Crook, Stephen, and Jan Pakulski. 1995. "Shades of Green: Public Opinion on Environmental Issues in Australia." *Australian Journal of Political Science* 30:39–55.

Culhane, Paul J., H. Paul Friesema, and Janice A. Beecher. 1987. *Forecasts and Environmental Decisionmaking: The Content and Predictive Accuracy of Environmental Impact Statements*. Boulder, CO: Westview Press.

da Cruz Vilaça, José Luís. 2004. "The Precautionary Principle in EC Law." *European Public Law* 10, no. 2:369–406.

Dalal-Clayton, Barry. 1996. *Getting to Grips with Green Plans: National-Level Experience in Industrial Countries*. London: Earthscan.

Dalal-Clayton, Barry, and Stephen Bass. 2002. *Taking a Systematic and Strategic Approach to Sustainability: A Resource Book for Sustainable Development Strategies*. London: Earthscan for Organization for Economic Co-operation and Development and United Nations Development Programme.

Dalal-Clayton, Barry, and Barry Sadler. 2004. *Strategic Environmental Assessment: A Sourcebook and Reference Guide to International Experience*. London: International Institute for Environment and Development.

Daly, Herman E. 1996. *Beyond Growth: The Economics of Sustainable Development*. Boston: Beacon Press.

Daly, Herman E., John B. Cobb, and Clifford W. Cobb. 1989. *For the Common Good: Redirecting the Economy toward Community, the Environment, and a Sustainable Future*. Boston: Beacon Press.

Daugbjerg, Carsten. 2000. "Explaining Why the Swedes but Not the Danes Tax Fertilizers: A Comparison of Policy Networks and Political Parties." In *Market-Based Instruments for Environmental Management: Politics and Institutions*, edited by Mikael Skou Andersen and Rolf-Ulrich Sprenger, 129–47. Cheltenham, England: Edward Elgar.

Davidson, Marc D. 1995. "Basic Liberal Rights and the Environment: The Right to Environmental Utilisation Space as the Foundation for a Basic Income." http://www.vivant.org/vivant/site/nl/links/varia/liberale_grondrechten_en_millieu.htm.

Davies, Terry. 1995. "Congress Discovers Risk Analysis." *Resources*, Winter:5–8.

De Haan, Mark, and Steven J. Keuning. 2003. "Taking the Environment into Account: The NAMEA Approach." In *Green Accounting*, edited by Peter Bartelmus and Eberhard K. Seifert, 131–48. Aldershot, England: Ashgate.

De Jongh, Paul, and Sean Captain. 1999. *Our Common Journey: A Pioneering Approach to Cooperative Environmental Management*. London: Zed Books.

Delmas, M. A. 2002. "The Diffusion of Environmental Management Standards in Europe and in the United States: An Institutional Perspective." *Policy Sciences* 35, no. 1:91–119.

Department of the Environment Sport and Territories. 1997. "Summary Report on the Implementation of the National Strategy for Ecologically Sustainable Development." Canberra: Department of the Environment, Sport and Territories.

Department of the Environment, Transport and the Regions. 2000. "Greening Government." First Annual Report of the Green Ministers Committee—1998/99, http://www.defra.gov.uk/sustainable_development.gov.uk.publications/report1999/index.htm.

Deutsch, Karl W. 1977a. "Introduction." In *Ecosocial Systems and Ecopolitics: A Reader on Human and Social Implications of Environmental Management in Developing Countries*, edited by Karl W. Deutch, 11–20. Paris: UNESCO.

———. 1977b. "On the Interaction of Ecological and Political Systems: Some Contributions of the Social Sciences to the Study of Man and His Environment." In *Ecosocial Systems and Ecopolitics: A Reader on Human and Social Implications of Environmental Management in Developing Countries*, edited by Karl W. Deutch, 23–31. Paris: UNESCO.

d'Evie, Fayen, Mary MacDonald, Francisco Mata, and Rocio Rodriguez eds. 2000. *NCSD Report 1999–2000: National Experiences of Integrative, Multistakeholder Processes for Sustainable Development*. San Jose, Costa Rica: Earth Council.

Diamond, Jared M. 2005. *Collapse: How Societies Choose to Fail or Succeed*. New York: Viking.

Dias, Ayesha. 2000. "Human Rights, Environment and Development: With Special Emphasis on Corporate Accountability." Human Development Report 2000. Background paper. http://hdr.undp.org/docs/publications/background_papers/Dias2000.html.

Diebold Institute for Public Policy Studies. and Information-Based Infrastructure Project. 1995. *Transportation Infostructures: The Development of Intelligent Transportation Systems*. Westport, CT: Praeger.

Diesendorf, Mark, and Clive Hamilton. 1997. *Human Ecology, Human Economy: Ideas for an Ecologically Sustainable Future*. St. Leonards, Australia: Allen & Unwin.

Doern, G. Bruce, and Thomas Conway. 1994. *The Greening of Canada: Federal Institutions and Decisions*. Toronto: University of Toronto Press.

Dryzek, John S. 1987. *Rational Ecology: Environment and Political Economy*. New York: B. Blackwell.

———. 1995. "Democracy and Environmental Policy Instruments." In *Markets, the State and the Environment: Toward Integration*, edited by Robyn Eckersley, 294–308. Melbourne: Macmillan.

———. 1997. *The Politics of the Earth: Environmental Discourses*. New York: Oxford University Press.

Dryzek, John S., David Downes, Christian Hunold, David Schlosberg, and Hans-Kristian Hernes. 2003. *Green States and Social Movements: Environmentalism in the United States, United Kingdom, Germany, and Norway*. New York: Oxford University Press.

Dunn, Seth, and Christopher Flavin. 2002. "Moving the Climate Change Agenda Forward." In *State of the World 2002*, edited by Christopher Flavin, Hilary French, and Gary Gardner, 24–50. New York: W. W. Norton.

Earthjustice. 2005. "Environmental Rights Report: Human Rights and the Environment; Materials for the 61st Session of the United Nations Commission on Human Rights, Geneva March 14–April 22, 2005." Oakland, CA: Earthjustice. http://www.earthjustice.org/library/references/2005_environmental_rights_reportrev.pdf

Easton, David. 1965. *A Systems Analysis of Political Life*. New York: Wiley.

Eckerberg, Katarina. 2000. "Sweden: Progression Despite Recession." In *Implementing Sustainable Development: Integrated Assessment and Participatory Decision-Making Processes*, edited by William M. Lafferty and James Meadowcroft, 209–44. Oxford: Oxford University Press.

Eckersley, Robyn. 1998. "Environmental Rights and Democracy." In *Political Ecology: Global and Local*, edited by Roger Keil, David Bell, Peter Penz, and Leesa Fawcett, 353–76. London: Routledge.

Elling, Bo. 2000. "Integration of Strategic Environmental Assessment into Regional Spatial Planning." *Impact Assessment and Project Appraisal* 18, no. 3:233–43.

Enevoldsen, Martin, and Stefan Brendstrup. 2000. "Considering Feasibility and Efficiency: The Danish Mix of CO_2 Taxes and Agreements." In *Market-Based Instruments for Environmental Management: Politics and Institutions*, edited by Mikael Skou Andersen and Rolf-Ulrich Sprenger, 148–71. Cheltenham, England: Edward Elgar.

Euractiv. 2005. "Climate Change—EU Emissions Trading Scheme (EU-ETS)." http://www.euractiv.com/Article?tcmuri=tem:29-133629_16&type=LinksDossier.

European Commission. 2001. *Guidance on EIA: Scoping*. Luxembourg: Office for Official Publications of the European Communities.

European Environment Agency. 2000. *Environmental Taxes: Recent Developments in Tools for Integration*. Copenhagen: European Environment Agency.

———. 2004. *EEA Signals 2004: A European Environment Agency Update on Selected Issues*. Copenhagen: European Environment Agency.

———. 2005. *Environmental Policy Integration in Europe: State of Play and an Evaluation Framework*. Copenhagen: European Environment Agency.

———. 2007. *Europe's Environment: The Fourth Assessment*. Luxembourg: Office for Official Publications of the European Communities.

Fairfax, S. K. 1978. "A Disaster in the Environment Movement." *Science* 199:743–48.

Falloux, Francois, and Lee M. Talbot. 1993. *Crisis and Opportunity: Environment and Development in Africa*. London: Earthscan.

Finger, Mathias. 2005. "The New Water Paradigm: The Privatization of Governance and the Instrumentalization of the State." In *The Business of Global Environmental Governance*, edited by David L. Levy and Peter J. Newell, 275–304. Cambridge, MA: MIT Press.

Finkel, Adam M., and Dominic Golding. 1994a. "Recurring Themes and Points of Contention." In *Worst Things First? The Debate Over Risk-Based National Environmental Priorities*, edited by Finkel and Golding. Washington, DC: Resources for the Future.

———. eds. 1994b. *Worst Things First? The Debate Over Risk-Based National Environmental Priorities*. Washington, DC: Resources for the Future.

Fitzsimmons, Allan K. 1994. "Federal Ecosystem Management: A 'Train Wreck' in the Making." *Policy Analysis* 217, October 26.

———. 1996. "Sound Policy or Smoke and Mirrors: Does Ecosystem Management Make Sense?" *Water Resources Bulletin* 32, no. 2:217–27.

Flavin, Christopher. 2008. "Building a Low-Carbon Economy." In *State of the World 2008. Innovations for a Sustainable Economy*, edited by Linda Starke, 75–90. New York: W. W. Norton.

Folke, Carl, Fikret Berkes, and Johan Colding. 1998. "Ecological Practices and Social Mechanisms for Building Resilience and Sustainability." In *Linking Social and Ecological Systems: Management Practices and Social Mechanisms for Building Resilience*. Edited by Berkes, Folke, and Colding. Cambridge: Cambridge University Press.

Freemuth, John. 1996. "The Emergence of Ecosystem Management: Reinterpreting the Gospel?" *Society and Natural Resources* 9, no. 4:411–17.

Freimann, Jürgen, and Michael Walther. 2001. "The Impacts of Corporate Environmental Management Systems: A Comparison of Emas and ISO 14001." GMI 36:91–103.

Friedman, Thomas. 1999. *The Lexus and the Olive Tree*. London: HarperCollins.

Friends of the Earth Europe. 1995. *Towards Sustainable Europe: The Study*. Brussels: Friends of the Earth.

Frost, Richard. 1997. "EIA Monitoring and Audit." In *Planning and Environmental Impact Assessment in Practice*, edited by Joe Weston, 141–64. Harlow, England: Addison, Wesley Longman.

Funke, Odelia. 1993. "Struggling with Integrated Environmental Policy: The EPA Experience." *Policy Studies Review* 12, no. 3–4:137–61.

Funtowicz, Silvio O., and Jerome R. Ravetz. 1994. "The Worth of a Songbird: Ecological Economics as a Post-Normal Science." *Ecological Economics* 10:197–207.

Gale, Robert J. P. 1997. "Canada's Green Plan." In *Nationale Umweltpläne* in *Ausgewählten Industrieländern*, edited by Martin Jänicke, Alexander Carius, and Helge Jörgens, 97–120. Berlin: Springer.

Gallagher, Kevin P. 2004. "Economic Integration and the Environment in Mexico: Lessons for Future Trade Agreements." Discussion Paper No. 6, Working Group on Development and Environment in the Americas. Heinrich Böll Foundation North America. http://ase.tufts.edu/gdae/Pubs/rp/DP06GallagherJuly04.pdf

Gallagher, Kevin P., and Hernán Blanco. 2003. "Sustainability Assessments: Tools for Effective Trade Policy in the Hemisphere." *Americas Program*. Silver City,

NM: Interhemispheric Resource Center. http://www.americaspolicy.org/briefs/2003/0304sa.html.

Gallhofer, Sonja, and Jim Haslam. 1997. "The Direction of Green Accounting Policy: Critical Reflections." *Accounting, Auditing, and Accountability Journal* 10, no. 2:148.

Gardner, Gary. 2001. "Accelerating the Shift to Sustainability." In *State of the World 2001*, edited by Lester Brown et al., 189–206. New York: W. W. Norton.

Gardner, Gary, and Erik Assadourian. 2004. "Rethinking the Good Life." In *State of the World 2004*, edited by Linda Starke, 164–79. New York: W. W. Norton.

German Council for Sustainable Development. 2006. "The German Council for Sustainable Development." http://www.nachhaltiakeitsrat.de/service/download/pdf/RNE-Factsheet_English.pdf.

Gibson, Robert B. 1993. "Environmental Assessment Design: Lessons from the Canadian Experience." *Environmental Professional* 15, no. 1:12–24.

Glasbergen, P. 1998. *Co-Operative Environmental Governance: Public-Private Agreements as a Policy Strategy*. Dordrecht: Kluwer Academic Publishers.

Glasson, John, Riki Therivel, and John Chadwick. 1999. *Introduction to Environmental Impact Assessment: Principles and Procedures, Process, Practice and Prospects*. 2nd ed. Philadelphia: Spon Press.

Global Footprint Network. Footprint for Nations. http://www.footprintnetwork.org/en/index.php/GFN/page/footprint_for_nations/

Goodin, Robert E. 1994. "Selling Environmental Indulgences." *Kyklos* 47, no. 4:573–96.

Government of Canada. 1995. *A Guide to Green Government*. Ottawa: Government of Canada.

Government of Japan. 1993. "Basic Law of the Environment." http://www.env.go.jp/en/laws/policy/basic/ch1.htm.

Grumbine, W. Edward. 1994. "What Is Ecosystem Management?" *Conservation Biology* 8, no. 1:27–38.

Guruswamy, Lakshman. 1989. "Integrating Thoughtways: Re-opening of the Environmental Mind?" *Wisconsin Law Review*, 463–537.

———. 1991. "Integrated Environmental Control: The Expanding Matrix." *Environmental Law* 22:77–118.

Gutman, Pablo. 2003. "What Did WSSD Accomplish?" *Environment* 45, no. 2:21–28.

Habito, Cielito F. 2000. "NCSDs and the UNCSD: The Need for Multistakeholder Partnerships for Sustainable Development." In *NCSD Report 1999–2000: National Experiences of Integrative, Multistakeholder Processes for Sustainable Development*, edited by Fayen d'Evie, Mary MacDonald, Francisco Mata, and Rocio Rodriguez, 127–32. San Jose, Costa Rica: Earth Council.

Hahn, Robert W. 1995. "Economic Prescriptions for Environmental Problems: Lessons for the United States and Continental Europe." In *Markets, the State and the Environment: Toward Integration*, edited by Robyn Eckersley, 129–56. Melbourne: Macmillan.

Haigh, Nigel, and Frances Irwin, eds. 1990. *Integrated Pollution Control in Europe and North America*. Washington, DC: Conservation Foundation; Bonn: Institute for European Environmental Policy.

Hajer, Maarten A. 1995. *The Politics of Environmental Discourse: Ecological Modernization and the Policy Process*. Oxford: Clarendon Press.

Hamilton, Clive. 2003. *Growth Fetish*. Crows Nest, Australia: Allen & Unwin.

Hanley, Nick, and Clive L. Spash. 1993. *Cost-Benefit Analysis and the Environment*. Aldershot, England; Edward Elgar.

Harris, Stuart, and David Throsby. 1998. "The ESD Process: Background, Implementation and Aftermath." In *The ESD Process: Evaluating a Policy Experiment*, edited by Clive Hamilton and David Throsby, 1–21. Canberra: Australian National University.

Harrison, Kathryn. 1996. *Passing the Buck: Federalism and Canadian Environmental Policy*. Vancouver, BC: UBC Press.

Harrop, D. Owen, and J. Ashley Nixon. 1999. *Environmental Assessment in Practice*. New York: Routledge.

Hawke, R. J. L. 1989. *Our Country, Our Future: Statement on the Environment*. Canberra: Australian Government Publishing Service.

Hayward, Tim. 2005. *Constitutional Environmental Rights*. Oxford: Oxford University Press.

Heynen, Nik, and Paul Robbins. 2005. "The Neoliberalization of Nature: Governance, Privatization, Enclosure and Valuation." *Capitalism, Nature, Socialism* 16, no. 1:5–8.

Hironaka, Ann. 2002. "The Globalization of Environmental Protection: The Case of Environmental Impact Assessment." *International Journal of Comparative Sociology* 43, no. 1:65–78.

Hirsch, Fred. 1976. *Social Limits to Growth*. Cambridge, MA: Harvard University Press.

Holland, Ian, and Aynsley J. Kellow. 2001. "Trade and Risk Management: Exploring the Issues." In *Globalization and the Environment: Risk Assessment and the WTO*, edited by David Robertson and Aynsley J. Kellow, 229–48. Cheltenham, England: Edward Elgar.

Holland, Kenneth M. 1996. "Introduction." In *Federalism and the Environment: Environmental Policymaking in Australia, Canada, and the United States*, edited by Kenneth M. Holland, F. L. Morton, and Brian Galligan, 1–13. Westport, CT: Greenwood Press.

Holtz-Giménez, Eric. 2007. "Exploding the Biofuel Myths: Displaced Peasants, Higher Food Prices—and a Crutch for the Petrol Economy." *Le Monde Diplomatique (English edition)*, July, 10–11.

Hordijk, Margreeth G. 1996. *Environmental Law in the Netherlands: The Dutch Environmental Management Act*. The Hague: VROM.

Hornstein, Donald T. 1994. "Paradigms, Process, and Politics: Risk and Regulatory Design." In *Worst Things First? The Debate over Risk-Based National Environmental Priorities*, edited by Adam M. Finkel and Dominic Golding, 147–65. Washington, DC: Resources for the Future.

House of Commons, Environmental Audit Committee. 1999. "Environmental Audit Committee Press Notice No. 21 of Session 1998–99." Publication of Sixth

Report, Session 1998–99, HC 426, the Greening Government Initiative 1999, http://www.parliament.uk/commons/selcomBg/eapnt28.htm.

Huber, J. 2000. "Toward Industrial Ecology: Sustainable Development as a Concept of Ecological Modernization." *Journal of Environmental Policy & Planning*. 2, no. 4:269–85.

Hyman, E. L., and B. Stiftel. 1988. *Combining Facts and Values in Environmental Impact Assessment: Theories and Techniques*. Boulder, CO: Westview Press.

Jackson, Hildur, and Karen Svensson. 2002. *Ecovillage Living: Restoring the Earth and Her People*. Tetnes, England: Green Books in association with Gaia Trust Denmark.

Jackson, Wendy. 2001. "Strategic Environmental Assessment, International Trade Agreements and Developing Countries." Master's thesis, York University (North York, ON).

Jacobs, Laurence, and Reginald Worthley. 1999. "A Comparative Study of Risk Appraisal: A New Look at Risk Assessment in Different Countries." *Environmental Monitoring and Assessment* 59:225–47.

Jacobs, Michael. 1995a. "Financial Incentives: The British Experience." In *Markets, the State and the Environment: Toward Integration*, edited by Robyn Eckersley, 113–28. Melbourne: Macmillan.

———. 1995b. "Sustainability and 'the Market': A Typology of Environmental Economics." In *Markets, the State and the Environment: Toward Integration*, edited by Robyn Eckersley, 46–70. Melbourne: Macmillan.

Jahn, D. 1998. "Environmental Performance and Policy Regimes: Explaining Variations in 18 OECD-Countries." *Policy Sciences* 31, no. 2:107–31.

Jain, R. K., L. V. Urban, and G. S. Stacey. 1981. *Environmental Impact Analysis*. New York: Van Nostrand Reinhold.

Jänicke, Martin. 1993. "Über Ökologische und Politische Modernisierungen." *Zeitschrift für Umweltpolitik und Umweltrecht*, 16, no. 2:159–75.

———. 1997. "The Political System's Capacity for Environmental Policy." In *National Environmental Policies: A Comparative Study of Capacity Building*, edited by Martin Jänicke and Helmut Weidner, 1–24. Berlin: Springer.

———. 2002. "The Political System's Capacity for Environmental Policy: The Framework for Comparison. In *Capacity Building in National Environmental Policy: A Comparative Study of 17 Countries*, edited by Helmut Weidner and Martin Jänicke, 1–18. Berlin: Springer.

Jänicke, Martin, Alexander Carius, and Helge Jörgens. 1997. *Nationale Umweltpläne in Ausgewählten Industrieländern*. Berlin: Springer Verlag.

Jänicke, Martin, and Helge Jörgens. 1998. "National Environmental Policy Planning: Preliminary Lessons from Cross-National Comparisons." *Environmental Politics* 7, no. 2:27–54.

Jänicke, Martin, and Helmut Weidner. 1997. "Germany." In *National Environmental Policies: A Comparative Study of Capacity Building*. Edited by Martin Jänicke and Helmut Weidner, 133–55. Berlin: Springer.

Jasanoff, Sheila. 2003. "A Living Legacy: The Precautionary Ideal in American Law." In *Environmental Science and Preventive Public Policy*, edited by Joel A. Tickner, 227–40. Washington, DC: Island Press.

Johnson, Huey D. 1995. *Green Plans: Greenprint for Sustainability*. Lincoln: University of Nebraska Press.

Jordan, Andrew. 1993. "Integrated Pollution Control and the Evolving Style and Structure of Environmental Regulation in the UK." *Environmental Politics* 2, no. 3:405–27.

Jordan, Andrew, Rüdiger K. W. Wurzel, and Anthony R. Zito. 2003a. " 'New' Environmental Policy Instruments: An Evolution or a Revolution in Environmental Policy?" *Environmental Politics* 12, no. 1:201–23.

———. 2003b. " 'New Instruments of Environmental Governance: Patterns and Pathways of Change." *Environmental Politics* 12, no. 1:3–24.

Jörgens, Helge. 2003. *Governance by Diffusion—Implementing Global Norms through Cross-National Imitation and Learning*. Berlin: Environmental Policy Research Centre—Freie Universität Berlin.

Juillet, Luc, and Glen Toner. 1997. "From Great Leaps to Baby Steps: Environment and Sustainable Development Policy under the Liberals." In *How Ottawa Spends: 1997–98; Seeing Red: A Liberal Report Card*, edited by Gene Swimmer, 179–209. Ottawa: Carleton University Press.

Kaiser, Matthias. 2003. "Ethics, Science and Precaution: A View from Norway." In *Environmental Science and Preventive Public Policy*, edited by Joel A. Tickner, 39–53. Washington, DC: Island Press.

Kellow, Aynsley. 1996. "Thinking Globally and Acting Federally: Intergovernmental Relations and Environmental Protection in Australia." In *Federalism and the Environment: Environmental Policymaking in Australia, Canada, and the United States*, edited by Kenneth M. Holland, F. L. Morton and Brian Galligan, 135–56. Westport, CT: Greenwood Press.

Kelman, Steven. 1981. *What Price Incentives? Economists and the Environment*. Boston: Auburn House.

Kingdon, John W. 1984. *Agendas, Alternatives, and Public Policies*. Boston: Little, Brown.

Kinrade, Peter. 1995. "Toward Ecologically Sustainable Development: The Role and Shortcomings of Markets." In *Markets, the State and the Environment: Toward Integration*, edited by Robyn Eckersley, 86–109. Melbourne: Macmillan.

Knoepfel, Peter. 1995. "New Institutional Arrangements for the Next Generation of Environmental Policy Instruments: Intra- and Interpolicy Cooperation. In *Environmental Policy in Search of New Instruments: With Special Reference to Germany*, edited by Bruno Dente, 197–223. Dordrecht: Kluwer Academic.

Kørnøv, Lone and Wil A. H. Thissen. 2000. "Rationality in Decision- and Policy-Making: Implications for Strategic Environmental Assessment." *Impact Assessment and Project Appraisal* 18, no. 3:191–200.

Kovel, Joel. 2002. *The Enemy of Nature: The End of Capitalism or the End of the World?* New York: Zed Books.

Kraft, Michael E. 1996. *Environmental Policy and Politics: Toward the Twenty-first Century*. New York: HarperCollins.

Kronsell, Annica. 1997. "Sweden: Setting a Good Example." In *European Environmental Policy: The Pioneers*, edited by Mikael Skou Anderson and Duncan Liefferink, 40–80. Manchester: Manchester University Press.

Lafferty, William M. 1996. "The Politics of Sustainable Development: Global Norms for National Implementation." *Environmental Politics* 5, no. 2:185–208.

———. 2004. "From Environmental Protection to Sustainable Development: The Challenge of Decoupling through Sectoral Integration. In *Governance for Sustainable Development: The Challenge of Adapting Form to Function*, edited by William M. Lafferty, 191–220. Cheltenham, England: Edward Elgar.

Lafferty, William M., and Eivind Hovden. 2003. "Environmental Policy Integration: Toward an Analytical Framework." *Environmental Politics* 12, no. 3:1–22.

Lafferty, William M., and James Meadowcraft. 2000a. "Concluding Perspectives." In *Implementing Sustainable Development*, edited by Lafferty and Meadowcraft, 422–59. New York: Oxford University Press.

———. 2000b. *Implementing Sustainable Development: Strategies and Initiatives in High Consumption Societies*. New York: Oxford University Press.

———. 2000c. "Patterns of Governmental Engagement." In *Implementing Sustainable Development. Strategies and Initiatives in High Consumption Societies*, edited by William M. Lafferty and James Meadowcroft, 337–421. New York: Oxford University Press.

Langeweg, F., ed. 1988. *Zorgen voor Morgen (Concern for Tomorrow)*. Bilthoven Netherlands: Rijksinstituut voor Volksgezondheid and Milieugygiene (RIVM).

Langhelle, Oluf. 2000. "Norway: Reluctantly Carrying the Torch." In *Implementing Sustainable Development: Strategies and Initiatives in High Consumption Societies*, edited by William M. Lafferty and James Meadowcroft, 174–208. New York: Oxford University Press.

Lash, Jonathan. 1994. "Integrating Science, Values, and Democracy through Comparative Risk Assessment." In *Worst Things First? The Debate over Risk-Based National Environmental Priorities*, edited by Adam M. Finkel and Dominic Golding, 69–86. Washington, DC: Resources for the Future.

Lee, Kai N. 1993. *Compass and Gyroscope: Integrating Science and Politics for the Environment*. Washington, DC: Island Press.

Lekakis, Joseph N. 2002. "Cost-Benefit Analysis and the Environment: A Critical Assessment." In *Cost-Benefit Analysis: Environmental and Ecological Perspectives*, edited by K. Puttasmamaiah, 151–80. New Brunswick, NJ: Transaction Publishers.

Lenschow, Andrea 1999. "The Greening of the EU: The Common Agricultural Policy and the Structural Funds." *Environment and Planning C-Government and Policy*, 17, no. 1:91–108.

———. 2002a. "Conclusion: What Are the Bottlenecks and Where Are Opprotunities for Greening the EU?" In *Environmental Policy Integration: Greening Sectoral Policies in Europe*, edited by Andrea Lenschow, 219–33. London: Earthscan.

———, ed. 2002b. *Environmental Policy Integration: Greening Sectoral Policies in Europe*. London: Earthscan.

———. 2002c. "Greening the European Union: An Introduction." In *Environmental Policy Integration: Greening Sectoral Policies in Europe*, edited by Andrea Lenschow, 1–21. London: Earthscan.

Li, Wenhua. 2001. *Agro-Ecological Farming Systems in China*. New York: UNESCO, Parthenon Pub. Group.

Liefferink, Duncan. 1997. "The Netherlands: A Net Exporter of Environmental Policy Concepts." In *European Environmental Policy: The Pioneers*, edited by Mikael Skou Andersen and Duncan Liefferink, 210–50. Manchester: Manchester University Press.

Lindblom, Charles E. 1982. "The Market as Prison." *Journal of Politics* 44:324–36.

Lomborg, Bjørn. 2001. *The Skeptical Environmentalist: Measuring the Real State of the World*. New York: Cambridge University Press.

Longino, Helen. 1983. "Beyond 'Bad Science': Skeptical Reflections on the Value-Freedom of Scientific Inquiry." *Science, Technology & Human Values* 8, no. 1:7–17.

Lopez Ornat, Arturo, and International Union for Conservation of Nature and Natural Resources. 1997. *Strategies for Sustainability: Latin America*. London: Earthscan.

Lumley, Sarah. 2002. "Cost-Benefit Analysis, Ethics and the Natural Environment." In *Cost-Benefit Analysis: Environmental and Ecological Perspectives*, edited by K. Puttasmamaiah, 95–114. New Brunswick, NJ: Transaction Publishers.

Lundqvist, L. J. 1974. *Environmental Policies in Canada, Sweden, and the United States: A Comparative Overview*. London: Sage Publications.

Luttrell, K. M. 2005. "The Politics of Integrating Environment and Trade: New Zealand's Practice?" Master's thesis, Lincoln University (Canterbury, New Zealand).

Lycos Environmental News. 2002. "Europe: Voluntary Agreements Supplant Legislation." http://ens-news.com/ens/jul2002/2002-07-17-03.asp.

MacDonald, David. 2003. "United Nations Falls from Grace." *Alternatives Journal* 29, no. 1:6–7.

Majone, Giandomenico. 1989. *Evidence, Argument, and Persuasion in the Policy Process*. New Haven, CT: Yale University Press.

March, James G., and Johan P. Olsen. 1989. *Rediscovering Institutions: The Organizational Basis of Politics*. New York: Free Press.

Margerum, R. D. 1999. "Integrated Environmental Management: The Foundations for Successful Practice." *Environmental Management* 24, no. 2:151–66.

Matsuno, Yu, and Kazuhiro Ueta. 2000. "A Socio-Economic Evaluation of the SO_2 Charge in Japan." In *Market-Based Instruments for Environmental Management: Politics and Institutions*, edited by Mikael Skou Andersen and Rolf-Ulrich Sprenger, 194–214. Cheltenham, England: Edward Elgar.

Maurer, Crescencia. 1999. *Rio+8: An Assessment of National Councils for Sustainable Development*. Washington, DC: World Resources Institute.

McDonough, William, and Michael Braungart. 2002. *Cradle to Cradle: Remaking the Way We Make Things*. New York: North Point Press.

McGinn, Anne Platt. 1998. "Promoting Sustainable Fisheries." In *State of the World 1998*, edited by Lester Brown et al., 59–78. London: Earthscan.

Meadows, Donella H., and Club of Rome. 1974. *The Limits to Growth: A Report for the Club of Rome's Project on the Predicament of Mankind*. London: Pan Books.

Milanez, Bruno. 2006. "Friend or Foe? Ecological Modernisation in Brazil." PhD diss., Lincoln University (Canterbury, New Zealand).

Milanez, Bruno, and Ton Bührs. 2007. "Marrying Strands of Ecological Modernisation: A Proposed Framework." *Environmental Politics* 16, no. 4:565–83.

———. 2008. "Ecological Modernisation Beyond Western Europe: The Case of Brazil." *Environmental Politics* 17, no. 5:784–803.

Milieu en Natuurplanbureau—RIVM. 2005. *Milieubalans 2005*. Bilthoven, Netherlands: Milieu en Natuurplanbureau—RIVM (Rijksinstituuut voor Volksgezondheid and Milieu).

Ministerie van Volkshuisvesting, Ruimtelijke Ordening en Milieubeheer (VROM). 1998. *Nationaal Milieubeleidsplan 3*. The Hague: VROM.

———. 2001. *Een Wereld En Een Wil: Nationaal Milieubeleidsplan 4*. The Hague: VROM.

———. 2005. *Hoofdlijnennotitie Toekomstagenda Milieu*. The Hague: VROM/DGM.

Ministerie van Volkshuisvesting, Ruimtelijke Ordening en Milieubeheer and Tweede Kamer der Staten-Generaal. 1989. *To Choose or to Lose: National Environmental Policy Plan*. The Hague: SDU Publishers.

Ministry for the Environment. 2007. *Environment New Zealand 2007*. Wellington: Ministry for the Environment.

Ministry for the Environment Regeringskansliet. 1998. *The Environmental Code*. Stockholm: Ministry of the Environment.

Mollison, B. C. 1999. *Permaculture Two: Practical Design for Town and Country in Permananent Agriculture*. Updated 1999 ed. Tyalgum, Australia: Tagari.

Monbiot, George. 2006a. "The Denial Industry." *Guardian Weekly*, September 29–October 5, 15–16.

———. 2006b. "Just Follow the Money; Academics and the Media Have Failed Dismally to Ask the Crucial Question of Scientists' Claims: Who Is Paying You?" *Guardian Weekly*, February 14.

Morgan, Richard K. 1984. *Environmental Impact Assessment: Current Status and Future Prospects*. Dunedin: University of Otago, Department of Geography.

Morrissey, Wayne A., Jeffrey A. Zinn, and M. Lynne Corn. 1994. *Ecosystem Management: Federal Agency Activities*. Washington, DC: Library of Congress Congressional Research Service.

Mulder, Sibolt, Verhue, Dieter and Adriaansen, Maud. 2005. *Wat Is Het Milieu Ons Waard? De Acceptatie Van Milieubeleid En Milieumaatregelen*. Amsterdam: TNS NIPO Consult en Veldkamp for Ministerie van VROM/DGM.

Munn, R. E. 1979. *Environmental Impact Assessment: Principles and Procedures*. Toronto: John Wiley.

Myers, Nancy. 2004. "The Rise of the Precautionary Principle. A Social Movement Gathers Strength." *Multinational Monitor*, September, 9–15.

Nakayama, Mikiyasu, and Ryo Fujikura. 2001. "Political Bias and Methodological Failure in Assessing Environmental Impacts of Development Projects: Comparative Analysis of the High Aswan Dam and Calaca Thermal Power Plant Development Projects." *Journal of Comparative Policy Analysis: Research and Practices* 3:291–310.

Nese, Annamaria. 1996. "Environmental Accounting and Environmental Policy: The Case of Norway." In *National Accounts and the Environment*, edited by Ignazio Musu and Domenico Siniscalco, 205–13. Dordrecht: Kluwer Academic Publishers.

Netherwood, Alan. 1996. "Environmental Management Systems." In *Corporate Environmental Management: Systems and Strategies*, edited by Richard Welford, 35–58. London: Earthscan.

Neumayer, Eric. 1999. *Weak versus Strong Sustainability: Exploring the Limits of Two Opposing Paradigms*. Cheltenham, UK: Edward Elgar.

Newman, David. 2006. "Breathing New Life into an Old Challenge." *Summit* 9, no. 1:14–15.

Nickel, James W., and Eduardo J. Viola. 1994. "Integrating Environmentalism and Human Rights." *Environmental Ethics* 16, no. 3:265–73.

Nooteboom, S. 2000. "Environmental Assessment of Strategic Decisions and Project Decisions: Interactions and Benefits." *Impact Assessment and Project Appraisal* 18, no. 2:151–60.

Northern Alliance for Sustainability ANPED. "Human Rights and Sustainable Development." http://www.anped.org/index.php?part=29.

O'Brien, Mary. 1994. "A Proposal to Address, Rather Than Rank, Environmental Problems." In *Worst Things First? the Debate over Risk-Based National Environmental Priorities*, edited by Adam M. Finkel and Dominic Golding, 87–105. Washington, DC: Resources for the Future.

———. 2001. *Making Better Environmental Decisions: An Alternative to Risk Assessment*. Cambridge, MA: MIT Press.

———. 2003. "Science in the Service of Good: The Precautionary Principle and Positive Goals." In *Environmental Science and Preventive Public Policy*, edited by Joel A. Tickner, 279–95. Washington, DC: Island Press.

O'Connor, James. 1994. "Is Sustainable Capitalism Possible?" In *Is Capitalism Sustainable? Political Economy and the Politics of Ecology*, edited by Martin O'Connor, 152–75. New York: Guilford Press.

O'Connor, Martin. 1994. *Is Capitalism Sustainable? Political Economy and the Politics of Ecology*. New York: Guilford Press.

Offe, Claus, and Volker Ronge. 1979. "Theses on the Theory of the State." In *Critical Sociology*, edited by J. W. Freiberg, 345–56. New York: Irvington.

Ong, Su-Wuen. 2000. "A Question of Fairness: The Influence of Experts at the Environment Court and the Difficulties Gaining Access to Them." Master's thesis, Victoria University of Wellington.

Ophuls, William. 1977. *Ecology and the Politics of Scarcity: Prologue to a Political Theory of the Steady State*. San Francisco: W. H. Freeman.

Organization for Economic Co-operation and Development. 1994a. *Applying Economic Instruments to Environmental Policies in OECD and Dynamic Non-Member Economies*. Paris: OECD.

———. 1994b. *Methodology for Environmental and Trade Reviews*. Paris: OECD.

———. 1995. *OECD Environmental Performance Reviews: The Netherlands*. Paris: OECD.

———. 1996a. *Environmental Performance Reviews: New Zealand*. Paris: OECD.

———. 1996b. *Environmental Performance Reviews: Sweden*. Paris: OECD.

———. 1999a. *Environmental Performance Reviews: Denmark*. Paris: OECD.

———. 1999b. *Methodologies for Environmental Assessment of Trade Liberalization Agreements*. Paris: OECD.

———. 2000. *Assessing the Environmental Effects of Trade Liberalization: Methodologies*. Paris: OECD.

———. 2001. *Environmental Performance Reviews: Norway*. Paris: OECD.

———. 2003. *Voluntary Approaches for Environmental Policy: Effectiveness, Efficiency, and Usage in Policy Mixes*. Paris: Organisation for Economic Co-operation and Development.

———. 2004a. *Environmental Performance Review: Canada*. Paris: OECD.

———. 2004b. *Environmental Performance Reviews: Sweden*. Paris: OECD.

———. 2007. *Environmental Performance Reviews: New Zealand*. Paris: OECD.

O'Riordan, Timothy, and James Cameron. 1994a. "The History and Contemporary Significance of the Precautionary Principle." In *Interpreting the Precautionary Principle*, edited by O'Riordan and Cameron, 12–30. London: Earthscan.

———. 1994b. "Seeping through the Pores." In *Interpreting the Precautionary Principle*, edited by O'Riordan and Cameron, 292–98. London: Earthscan.

Paehlke, Robert C. 1990. "Democracy and Environmentalism: Opening a Door to the Administrative State." In *Managing Leviathan—Environmental Politics and the Administrative State*, edited by Robert Paehlke and Douglas Torgerson, 35–55. Peterborough, ON: Broadview Press.

Paehlke, Robert C., and Douglas Torgerson, eds. 1990. *Managing Leviathan—Environmental Politics and the Administrative State*. Peterborough, ON: Broadview Press.

Papadakis, Elim. 1993. *Politics and the Environment: The Australian Experience*. St. Leonards, Australia: Allen & Unwin.

Parliamentary Commissioner for the Environment. 1995. *Assessment of Environmental Effects (AEE): Administration by Three Territorial Councils*. Wellington: Parliamentary Commissioner for the Environment.

———. 2002. *Creating Our Future: Sustainable Development for New Zealand*. Wellington: Office of the Parliamentary Commissioner for the Environment.

Parsons, Talcott. 1971. *System of Modern Societies*. Englewood Cliffs, NJ: Prentice Hall.

Pearce, David W. 2000. "Cost-Benefit Analysis and Environmental Policy." In *Environmental Policy: Objectives, Instruments, and Implementation*, edited by Dieter Helm, 48–74. Oxford: Oxford University Press.

———. 2003. "Environmentally Harmful Subsidies: Barriers to Sustainable Development." In *Environmentally Harmful Subsidies: Policy Issues and Challenges*, edited by Organization for Economic Co-operation and Development, 9–30. Paris: OECD.

Pearce, David W., Anil Markandya, and Edward Barbier. 1989. *Blueprint for a Green Economy*. London: Earthscan.

Pearce, Fred. 2006a. "Ecopolis Now." *New Scientist*, June 17, 36–45.

———. 2006b. "Fuels Gold: Are Biofuels Really the Greenhouse-Busting Answer to Our Energy Woes?" *New Scientist*, September, 23, 36–41.

Pedersen, Ole Gravgard, and Mark de Haan. 2006. "The System of Environmental and Economic Accounts—2003 and the Economic Relevance of Physical Flow Accounting." *Journal of Industrial Ecology* 10, no. 1–2:19–42.

Peglau, Reinhard. 2006. "Worldwide Number of ISO 14001." Corporate Risk Management. http://www.ecology.or.jp/isoworld/english/analy14k.htm.

Peine, John D., Jones, Robert E., English, Mary R., and Wallace, Samuel E. 1999. "Contributions of Sociology to Ecosystem Management." In *Integrating Social Sciences with Ecosystem Management: Human Dimensions in Assessment, Policy and Management*, 73–99. Edited by H. Ken Cordell and John C. Bergstrom. Champaign, IL: Sagamore.

Pepper, David. 1993. *Eco-Socialism. From Deep Ecology to Social Justice*. London: Routledge.

Perhac, Ralph M., Jr. 1998. "Comparative Risk Assessment: Where Does the Public Fit In?" *Science, Technology and Human Values* 23, no. 2:221–40.

Petts, Judith, ed. 1999. *Handbook of Environmental Impact Assessment. Vol. 2, Environmental Impact Assessment in Practice: Impact and Limitations*. Oxford: Blackwell Science.

Pope, J., D. Annandale, and A. Morrison-Saunders. 2004. "Conceptualising Sustainability Assessment." *Environmental Impact Assessment Review* 24, no. 6:595–616.

Porritt, Jonathon. 2005. *Capitalism as If the World Matters*. London: Earthscan.

Poupeau, Franck. 2002. "Commodifying Rain: Global Market in Water." *Le Monde Diplomatique (English edition)*, May, 13.

Quijano, Romeo F. 2003. "Elements of the Precautionary Principle." In *Environmental Science and Preventive Public Policy*, edited by Joel A. Tickner, 21–27. Washington, DC: Island Press.

Rabe, B. G. 1997. "The Politics of Sustainable Development: Impediments to Pollution Prevention and Policy Integration in Canada." *Canadian Public Administration—Administration Publique du Canada* 40, no. 3:415–35.

———. 1999. "Federalism and Entrepreneurship: Explaining American and Canadian Innovation in Pollution Prevention and Regulatory Integration." *Policy Studies Journal* 27, 288–306.

Regeringskansliet, Ministry for the Environment. 1998. *The Environmental Code: A Summary of the Government Bill on the Environmental Code (1997/98:45)*. Stockholm: Ministry of the Environment.

Reichman, O. J., and Ronald Pulliam. 1996. "The Scientific Basis for Ecosystem Management." *Ecological Applications* 6, no. 3:694–96.

Renton, Stephen, and John Bailey. 2000. "Policy Development and the Environment." *Impact Assessment and Project Appraisal*. 18, no. 3:245–51.

Revell, Andrea. 2005. "Ecological Modernization in the UK: Rhetoric or Reality?" *European Environment* 15:344–61.

Rietbergen-McCracken, Jennifer A. 2000. "Introduction." In *Economic Instruments for Environmental Management: A Worldwide Compendium of Case Studies*, edited by Jennifer Rietbergen-McCracken and Hussein Abaza, 1–16. London: Earthscan.

Righelato, Renton, and Dominick V. Spracklen. 2007. "Environment: Carbon Mitigation by Biofuels or by Saving and Restoring Forests?" *Science* 317:902.

Rijksinstituut voor Volksgezondheid en Milieu. 2005. *Quality and the Future: Sustainability Outlook*. Bilthoven, Netherlands: Rijksinstituut voor Volksgezondheid and Milieugygiene (RIVM).

Rodgers, Penny. 2005. "Strategic Environmental Assessment in Denmark, Evaluation." United Nations University. http://www.onlinelearning.unu.edu/seaversion1/Resources/Systems/DENMARK%20eval.html.

Roodman, David Malin. 1996. "Harnessing the Market for the Environment." In *State of the World 1996*, edited by Lester Brown et al., 168–87. London: Earthscan.

———. 1997. "Reforming Subsidies." In *State of the World 1997*, edited by Lester Brown, Janet N. Abramovitz, Chris Bright, Christopher Flavin, Hillary French, Gary Gardner, Anne Platt McGinn, Michael Renner, David Malin Roodman, and Linda Starke, 132–50. London: Earthscan.

———. 1999. "Building a Sustainable Society." In *State of the World 1999*, edited by Linda Starke, 169–88. London: Earthscan.

Rosenbaum, Walter A. 1985. *Environmental Politics and Policy*. Washington, DC: CQ Press.

Ross, A. 2000. "Greening Government—Tales from the New Sustainability Watchdog." *Journal of Environmental Law* 12, No. 2:175.

Rotherham, Tom. n.d. *The Trade and Environmental Effects of Ecolabels: Assessment and Response*. United Nations Environment Programme (UNEP). UNEP, http://www.unep.ch/etb/publications/ecolabelpap141005f.pdf.

Royal Commission on Environmental Pollution. 1984. *Tenth Report: Tackling Pollution; Experience and Prospects*. London: HMSO.

Russell, Milton, and Michael Gruber. 1987. "Risk Assessment in Environmental Policy Making." *Science* 236:286–90.

Sachs, Wolfgang, Reinhard, Loske, and Manfred Linz. 1998. *Greening the North: A Post-Industrial Blueprint for Ecology and Equity*. London: Zed Books.

Sachs, Wolfgang, and Tilman Santarius. 2007. *Fair Future: Resource Conflicts, Security and Global Justice*. London and New York: Zed Books.

Sagoff, Mark. 2004. *Price, Principle, and the Environment*. Cambridge: Cambridge University Press.

Sampson, Gary P. 2001. "Risk and the WTO." In *Globalization and the Environment. Risk Assessment and the WTO*, edited by David Robertson and Aynsley Kellow, 15–26. Cheltenham, England: Edward Elgar.

Savory, Allan, and Jody Butterfield. 1999. *Holistic Management: A New Framework for Decision Making*, 2d ed. Washington, DC: Island Press.

Sawin, Janet. 2003. "Chartering a New Energy Future." In *State of the World 2003*, edited by Linda Starke, 85–109. London: Earthscan.

Schalatek, Liane, ed. 2004. *Globalization and the Environment: Lessons from the Americas Working Group on Develpment and Environment in the Americas*. Washington, DC: Heinrich Bell Foundation North America.

Scheiber, Harry N. 1997. "From Science to Law to Politics: An Historical View of the Ecosystem Idea and Its Effect on Resource Management." *Ecology Law Quarterly* 24:631–51.

Schijf, Bobbi. 1997. "Environmental Impact Assessment: A Comparison of the Netherlands and New Zealand." *Geovoice* 1. http://geovoice.otago.ac.nz/issue001/bschijf.html.

Schneider, Stephen H. 1997. "Integrated Assessment Modeling of Global Climate Change: Transparent Rational Tool for Policy Making or Opaque Screen Hiding Value-Laden Assumptions?" *Environmental Modeling and Assessment* 2:229–49.

Schreurs, Miranda A. 2002. *Environmental Politics in Japan, Germany, and the United States*. Cambridge: Cambridge University Press.

Scruggs, Lyle. 2001. "Is there Really a Link between Neo-Corporatism and Environmental Performance? Updated Evidence and New Data for the 1980s and 1990s." *British Journal of Political Science* 31, no. 4:686–92.

———. 2003. *Sustaining Abundance: Environmental Performance in Western Democracies*. Cambridge: Cambridge University Press.

Second Chamber of the States General. 1989. *National Environmental Policy Plan (NEPP)*. The Hague: SDU Uitgeverij.

Sexton, Ken, Alfred A. Marcus, K. William Easter, and Timothy D. Burkhardt. 1999. *Better Environmental Decisions: Strategies for Governments, Businesses, and Communities*. Washington, DC: Island Press.

Sheate, William R., Suzan Dagg, Jeremy Richardson, Ralf Aschemann, Juan Palerm, and Ulla Steen. 2003. "Integrating the Environment into Strategic Decision-Making: Conceptualising Policy SEA." *European Environment* 13:1–18.

Shi, Tian. 2004. "Ecological Economics as a Policy Science: Rhetoric or Commitment Toward an Improved Decision-Making Process on Sustainability?" *Ecological Economics* 48:23–36.

Shiva, Vandana. 2002. "The Great Betrayal: Why Civil Society Walked Out and Withdrew Consent from W$$D." http://www.solidaritetshuset.org/rorg/aktuelt/2002/dok/shiva.htm.

Simms, Andrew, Dan Moran, and Peter Chowla. 2006. *The UK Interdependence Report. How the World Sustains the Nation's Lifestyles and the Price It Pays*. London: New Economics Foundation.

Speth, James Gustave. 2003. "Perspectives on the Johannesburg Summit." *Environment* 45, no. 1:25–29.

Sprenger, Rolf-Ulrich. 2000. "Market-Based Instruments in Environmental Policies: The Lessons of Experience." In *Market-Based Instruments for Environmental Management: Politics and Institutions*, edited by Mikael Skou Andersen and Rolf-Ulrich Sprenger, 3–24. Cheltenham, England: Edward Elgar.

Stavins, R. N. 2000. "Market-Based Environmental Policies." In *Public Policies for Environmental Protection*, eddited by Paul R. Portney and R. N. Stavins, 31–76. Washington, DC: Resource for the Future.

Stewart, Jenny, and Russell Ayres. 2001. "Systems Theory and Policy Practice: An Exploration." *Policy Sciences* 34:79–94.

Stone, Deborah. 1988. *Policy Paradox and Practical Reason*. Glenview, IL: Scott, Foresman, and Company.

Sumikura, Ichiro. 1998. "A Brief History of Japanese Environmental Administration: A Qualified Success Story?" *Journal of Environmental Law* 10, no. 2:241–56.

Suzuki, David, and Holly Dressel. 2002. *Good News for a Change: Hope for a Troubled Planet*. St Leonards, Australia: Allen & Unwin.

Swaney, James A. 1996. "Comparative Risk Analysis: Limitations and Opportunities." *Journal of Economic Issues* 30:463–73.

Tarakofsky, Richard. 2000. "Report on the Workshop Methodologies for Environmental Assessment of Trade Liberalisation Agreements." In *Assessing the Environmental Effects of Trade Liberalisation: Methodologies*, edited by OECD, 11–18. Paris: OECD.

Taylor, Serge. 1984. *Making Bureaucracies Think: The Environmental Impact Statement Strategy of Administrative Reform*. Stanford, CA: Stanford University Press.

Tesh, Sylvia N. 1999. "Citizen Experts in Environmental Risk." *Policy Sciences* 32:38–58.

Tester, Frank. 1987. "Losing Ground: A Neo-Existential Critique of New Zealand Environmentalism." PhD diss., University of Waikato (Hamilton, New Zealand).

Tietenberg, Tom. 2002. "The Tradable Permits Approach to Protecting the Commons: What Have We Learned?" In *The Drama of the Commons*, edited by Elinor Ostrom, Thomas Dietz, Nives Dolšak, Paul C. Stern, Susan Stonich, and Elke E. Weber, 197–232. Washington, DC: National Academy Press.

Tol, Richard S. J., and Pier Vellinga. 1998. "The European Forum on Integrated Environmental Assessment." *Environmental Modeling and Assessment* 3:181–91.

Toner, Glen. 1994. "The Green Plan: From Great Expectations to Eco-Backtracking . . . to Revitalization?" In *How Ottawa Spends, 1994–95: Making Change*, edited by Susan D. Phillips, 229–60. Ottawa: Carleton University Press.

———. 1996. "Environment Canada's Continuing Roller Coaster Ride." In *How Ottawa Spends, 1996–97: Life under the Knife*, edited by Gene Swimmer, 99–132. Ottawa: Carleton University Press.

———. 2000. "Canada: From Early Frontrunner to Plodding Anchorman." In *Implementing Sustainable Development: Strategies and Initiatives in High Consumption Societies*, edited by William M. Lafferty and James Meadowcroft, 53–84. Oxford: Oxford University Press.

Toner, Glen, and Bruce Doern. 1994. "Five Political and Policy Imperatives in Green Plan Formation: The Canadian Case." *Environmental Politics* 3, no. 3:395–420.

Torgerson, Douglas. 1990. "Limits of the Administrative Mind: The Problem of Defining Environmental Problems." In *Managing Leviathan: Environmental Politics and the Administrative State*, edited by Robert Paehlke and Douglas Torgerson, 115–61. Peterborough, ON: Broadview Press.

———. 1995. "The Uncertain Quest for Sustainability: Public Discourse and the Politics of Environmentalism." In *Greening Environmental Policy: The Politics of a Sustainable Future*, edited by Frank Fischer and Michael Black, 4–20. New York: St. Martin's Press.

Toth, Ferenc L., and Eva Hizsnyk. 1998. "Integrated Environmental Assessment Methods: Evolution and Applications." *Environmental Modeling and Assessment* 3:193–207.

Tribe, Laurence H. 1972–73. "Technology Assessment and the Fourth Discontinuity: The Limits of Instrumental Rationality." *Southern California Law Review* 46:617–60.

Tweede Kamer der Staten-Generaal. 1999. *Milieuprogramma 2000–2003*. The Hague: Tweede Kamer der Staten-Generaal.

———. 2006. *Toekomstagenda Milieu*. The Hague: Tweede Kamer der Staten-Generaal.

UCL Graduate School. 2006. *Commercialisation of Scientific Research—Turning Ideas into Products*. London: University College London. http://www.grad.ucl.ac.uk/courses/coursedetails.pht?course_ID=868.

Union of Concerned Scientists. 2004a. *Scientific Integrity in Policy Making: An Investigation into the Bush Administration's Misuse of Science*. Cambridge, MA:

Union of Concerned Scientists. http://www.ucsusa.org/scientific_integrity/interference/reports-scientific-integrity-in-policy-making.html.

———. 2004b. *Scientific Integrity in Policy Making: Further Investigation of the Bush Administration's Misuse of Science*. Cambridge, MA: Union of Concerned Scientists. http://www.ucsusa.org/scientific_integrity/interference/reports-scientific-integrity-in-policy-making.html.

United Kingdom Environmental Audit Committee. 2003. "Greening Government 2003." London: http://www.parliament.uk/parliamentary_committees/environmental_audit_committee/eac_13_11_03.cfm.

United Nations. 1993. *Integrated Environmental and Economic Accounting: Interim Version*. New York: United Nations, Department for Economic and Social Information and Policy Analysis, Statistical Division.

United Nations, European Commission, International Monetary Fund, Organization for Economic Co-operation and Development, World Bank. 2003. "Integrated Environmental and Economic Accounting." SEEA. http://unstats.un.org/unsd/envAccounting/seea2003.htm.

United Nations Environment Programme. 1999. *Trade Liberalisation and the Environment: Lessons Learned from Bangladesh, Chile, India, Philippines, Romania and Uganda; A Synthesis Report*. New York: United Nations.

———. 2001. *Reference Manual for the Integrated Assessment of Trade-Related Policies*. New York: United Nations.

———. 2005. *Handbook on Integrated Assessment of Trade Related Measures:The Agriculture Sector*. Geneva: UNEP.

Vanderpool, Christopher K. 1981. "Environmental Policy and Social-Impact-Assessment Ideology: Fishery Conservation and Management." In *Environmental Policy Formation: The Impact of Values, Ideology and Standards*, edited by Dean E. Mann, 161–76. Lexington: D. C. Heath.

Van der Straaten, Jan. 2002. "Challenges and Pitfalls of Cost-Benefit Analysis in Environmental Issues." In *Cost-Benefit Analysis: Environmental and Ecological Perspectives*, edited by K. Puttasmamaiah, 323–46. New Brunswick, NJ: Transaction Publishers.

Van Muijen, Marie-Louise. 2000. "The Netherlands: Ambitious on Goals—Ambivalent on Action." In *Implementing Sustainable Development: Integrated Assessment and Participatory Decision-Making Processes*, edited by William M. Lafferty and James Meadowcroft, 142–73. Oxford: Oxford University Press.

Vatn, Arild. 2000. "Efficiency and Fairness: The Norwegian Experience with Agri-Environmental Taxation." In *Market-Based Instruments for Environmental Management: Politics and Institutions*, edited by Mikael Skou Andersen and Rolf-Ulrich Sprenger, 111–28. Cheltenham, England: Edward Elgar.

———. 2005. *Institutions and the Environment*. Cheltenham, England: Edward Elgar.

Vogelaar, Mark. 1998. *Het NMP3: Een Open En Eerlijk Process*. The Hague, Netherlands: Ministerie van Volkshuisvesting and Ruimtelijke Ordening en Milieubeheer.

Wackernagel, Mathis, and William E. Rees. 1996. *Our Ecological Footprint: Reducing Human Impact on the Earth*. Gabriola Island, BC: New Society Publishers.

Wallace, David. 1995. *Environmental Policy and Industrial Innovation: Strategies in Europe, the USA and Japan*. London: Earthscan.

Wandesforde-Smith, G. 1989. "Environmental Impact Assessment, Entrepreneurship, and Policy Change." In *Policy through Impact Assessment: Institutional Analysis as a Policy Strategy*, edited by Robert V. Bartlett, 155–85. Westport, CT: Greenwood Press.

Wandesforde-Smith, G., and J. Kerbavaz. 1988. "The Co-Evolution of Politics and Policy: Elections, Entrepreneurship and EIA in the United States." In *Environmental Impact Assessment, Theory and Practice*, edited by Peter Wathern, 161–91. London: Unwin Hyman.

Wathem, Peter, ed. 1988. *Environmental Impact Assessment, Theory and Practice*. London: Unwin Hyman.

Watts, Michael. 2002. "Green Capitalism, Green Governmentality." *American Behavioral Scientist* 45, no. 9:1313–17.

Weale, Albert. 1992. *The New Politics of Pollution*. New York: Manchester University Press.

Weale, Albert, Timothy O'Riordan, and L. Kramme. 1991. *Controlling Pollution in the Round*. London: Anglo-American Foundation.

Weber, Edward P. 2000. "A New Vanguard for the Environment: Grass-Roots Ecosystem Management as a New Environmental Movement." *Society and Natural Resources* 13, no. 3:237–59.

Weidner, Helmut. 2002. "Environmental Policy and Politics in Germany." In *Environmental Politics and Policy in Industrialized Countries*, edited by Uday Desai, 149–201. Cambridge, MA: MIT Press.

Weiss, Linda. 1998. *The Myth of the Powerless State: Governing the Economy in a Global Era*. Cambridge: Polity Press.

Weizsäcker, Ernst von, Amory B. Lovins, and L. Hunter Lovins. 1997. *Factor Four: Doubling Wealth—Halving Resource Use*. St. Leonards, Australia: Allen & Unwin.

Weston, Joe. 1997a. "Lessons from EIA in Practice." In *Planning and Environmental Impact Assessment in Practice*, edited by Joe Weston, 180–200. Harlow, England: Addison Wesley Longman.

———, ed. 1997b. *Planning and Environmental Impact Assessment in Practice*. Harlow, England: Addison Wesley Longman.

Wildavsky, A. 1979. *The Art and Craft of Policy Analysis*. London: Macmillan.

Wilkinson, David. 1997. "The Drafting of National Environmental Plans: The UK Experience." In *Nationale Umweltpläne in Ausgewählten Industrieländern*, edited by Martin Jänicke, Alexander Carius, and Helge Jörgens, 87–96. Berlin: Springer.

Winsemius, Pieter. 1990. *Guests in Our Own Home: Thoughts on Environmental Management*. Rotterdam: McKinsey & Co.

Wood, Christopher. 1995. *Environmental Impact Assessment: A Comparative Review*. Harlow, England: Longman Scientific & Technical.

———. 1999. "Comparative Evaluation of Environmental Impact Assessment Systems." In *Handbook of Environmental Impact Assessment, vol. 2: Environmental Impact Assessment in Practice: Impact and Limitations*, edited by Judith Petts, 10–34. Oxford: Blackwell Science.

World Bank. 1995. *National Environmental Strategies: Learning from Experience*. Washington, DC: Land Water and Natural Habitats Division, Environment Department, World Bank.

World Commission on Environment and Development. 1987. *Our Common Future*. Oxford: Oxford University Press.

WWF International. 1998. *Developing a Methodology for Environmental Assessments of Trade Liberalization Agreements*. Gland, Switzerland. WWF, http://www.panda.org/resources/publications/sustainability/wto-papers/method.html.

Yaffee, Steven Lewis. 1994. *The Wisdom of the Spotted Owl: Policy Lessons for a New Century*. Washington, DC: Island Press.

Yaffee, Steven Lewis, Ali F. Phillips, Irence C. Frenz, Paul W. Hardy, Susanne M. Malek, and Barbara E. Thorpe. 1996. *Ecosystem Management in the United States: An Assessment of Current Experience*. Washington, DC: Island Press.

Young, Stephen C. 2000. "The United Kingdom: From Political Containment to Integrated Thinking?" In *Implementing Sustainable Development: Strategies and Initiatives in High Consumption Societies*, edited by William M. Lafferty and James Meadowcroft, 245–72. Oxford: Oxford University Press.

Zerbe, Noah, and Tom Dedeurwaerdere. 2003. "Trade, Societies and Sustainable Development." SUSTRA Network Sustainability Impact Assessment Policy Brief Paper. http://www.agro-montpellier.fr/sustra/publications/policy_briefs/policy-brief-sia-eng.pdf.

Index